Facts about Germany

Imprint

Published by:
German Federal Foreign Office
Communications section
Dep. K 03
Werderscher Markt 1
10117 Berlin
Germany
Internet: www.auswaertiges-amt.de
E-mail: k03-s@auswaertiges-amt.de

Production, copy and design:
MEDIA CONSULTA Deutschland GmbH
Wassergasse 3
10179 Berlin
Germany
Hildeboldplatz 15-17
50672 Cologne
Germany
Internet: www.media-consulta.com
E-mail: info@media-consulta.com

Editorial desk: Klaus Lantermann (editor in chief),
Dr. Heiko Fiedler-Rauer, Jens Specht
Project management and production: Jörg Kuhnke (head),
Diana Jungbluth
Translation: Dr. Jeremy Gaines
Design: Hans-Dieter Großjohann, Tobias Niering
Charts: Karl-Heinz Döring
Printers: GGP Media GmbH, Pößneck
Printed in Germany, 2003

Editorial deadline: May 31, 2003
ISBN: 3-936238-10-3

This book appears in Arabic, Chinese, English, Farsi,
French, German, Italian, Japanese Polish, Portuguese,
Russian, Spanish and Turkish

This book can also be viewed on the Internet in English,
French, German and Spanish by clicking:
www.tatsachen-ueber-deutschland.de.

Contents

Society and Culture

Alps nr. Berchtesgaden in Bavaria

The country
and the
people

The country

The Federal Republic of Germany is located in the heart of Europe, linking the west with the east, the north with the south. The most densely-populated country in Europe, Germany has been flanked by nine neighboring states since the unification of the two German states in 1990. An integral part of the European Union and NATO, Germany is a partner to the central and eastern European states that are en route to becoming part of a united Europe.

The Federal Republic of Germany covers an area of 357,022 square kilometers. The longest distance from north to south as the crow flies is 876 kilometers, and from west to east, 640 kilometers. There are some 82.6 million people living in Germany; the country boasts a great cultural diversity and special region-specific qualities, charming towns and attractive landscapes.

The countryside: The German landscapes are extraordinarily diverse. Low and high mountain ranges alternate with elevated plains, hilly and mountainous regions, lakelands and wide, open lowlands. From north to south, Germany is divided into five major landscape types:

The North German Plain boasts hilly landscapes with many lakes and is interspersed with heaths and moors as well as fertile land. It stretches down as far as the edge of the Central Upland Range. The lowland bays here comprise the Lower Rhenish Bight, the Westphalian Bight and the SaxonThuringian Bight. Located off the coast of this region in the North Sea are numerous islands such as Borkum, Norderney, Sylt and Helgoland. Situated in the Baltic Sea are Rügen, Hiddensee and Fehmarn. Some parts of the Baltic coast have flat, sandy shores, others steep cliffs. Between the North Sea and the Baltic lies an area of low hills known as Holsteinische Schweiz (Holstein Switzerland).

The Central Upland Range divides northern and southern Germany. The central Rhine valley and the Hessian depressions serve as natural north-south traffic arteries. The Central Uplands include the Hunsrück, Eifel, Taunus and Westerwald. Right in the heart of Germany are the Harz Mountains. The elevations in the east include the Bavarian Forest, the Fichtel Hills and the Ore Mountains.

On the edge of the upper Rhine lowlands lies the Black Forest, the Spessart and the Swabian Jura. In a narrow valley, the river Rhine, the main north-south axis, slices through the Rhenish Schist Massif.

Mountains, rivers, lakes, canals, islands

Mountains

Zugspitze (German Alps)	2,962 m
Watzmann (German Alps)	2,713 m
Feldberg (Black Forest)	1,493 m
Grosser Arber (Bavarian Forest)	1,456 m
Fichtelberg (Erzgebirge, Saxony)	1,215 m
Brocken (Harz, Thuringa)	1,142 m

Rivers

Rhine	865 km
Elbe	700 km
Danube	686 km
Main	524 km
Weser	440 km
Spree	382 km
Mosel	242 km

Shipping Canals

Mittellandkanal (Central Germany)	321 km
Dortmund-Ems-Canal	269 km
Main-Danube-Canal	171 km
North Sea-Baltic Sea Canal	99 km

Lakes

Lake Constance	305 km^2 *
Müritz	110.3 km^2
Chiemsee	82 km^2
Schweriner See	60.6 km^2
Starnberger See	57.2 km^2

*German part of 538 km^2

Dams

Bleiloch (Saale)	215 million m^3
Schwammenauel (Ruhr)	205 million m^3
Edersee (Eder)	202 million m^3

Islands

Rügen	930 km^2
Usedom	373 km^2 **
Fehmarn	185 km^2
Sylt	99 km^2
Föhr	83 km^2

**German part of 445 km^2

Hikers in the Zittau Mountains

The south German Alpine foothills boast hills and great lakes in the south, as well as broad gravel plains, the hilly landscape of lower Bavaria and the Danube valley. Characteristic features of this landscape are moors, dome-shaped hill ranges with lakes (Chiemsee, Starnberger See) and small villages.

The German part of the Alps between Lake Constance and Berchtesgaden represents only a narrow section of this mountain range. It is limited to the Allgäu Alps, the Bavarian Alps and the Berchtesgaden Alps. Within the mountainous Alpine landscape lie picturesque lakes such as Königssee (St. Bartholomew's Lake) near Berchtesgaden, and popular tourist resorts such as Garmisch-Partenkirchen and Mittenwald.

Climate: Germany is situated within the moderately cool west wind zone between the Atlantic Ocean and the continental climate to the east. Sharp temperature fluctuations are rare. There is precipitation in all seasons. In winter the average temperature fluctuates between 1.5 degrees Celcius in the lowland areas and minus six degrees Celcius in the mountains. In July, the average is around 18 degrees Celsius in the lowlands and 20 degrees Celsius in the sheltered valleys of the south. Exceptions are the Upper Rhine Trough with its very mild climate, Upper Bavaria with its intermittently occurring warm Alpine wind from the south (Föhn) and the Harz Mountains' special microclimate with its cold winds, cool summers and heavy winter snows.

Wintry atmosphere at the Elbsee, in the Allgäu region

The people

Some 82.6 million people live in Germany. Some 7.3 million of these citizens do not have their origins in Germany. This corresponds to 8.9 percent of the total population. And this means diversity, a diversity which is contributed to by the migrants living in Germany, the ethnic minorities, the regions and the different states with their traditions and dialects.

Population: The population in Germany is very unevenly distributed. Approx. one third of inhabitants, around 25 million people, live in 82 large towns. Some 50.5 million people live in communities and towns with between 2,000 and 100,000 inhabitants, around 6.4 million have their homes in villages with up to 2,000 inhabitants. Having experienced rapid growth since German unification, the catchment area in and around Berlin currently boasts more than 4.3 million inhabitants. The industrialized region on the Rhine and the Ruhr rivers, where the towns merge into one another without clear boundaries, is home to more than 11 million people. i.e., some 1,100 per square kilometer.

These densely populated regions contrast with very thinly populated areas such as large sections of the March of Brandenburg and Mecklenburg-Western Pomerania.

In a shopping street

With a population density of 230 persons per square kilometer, Germany is overall one of the most densely populated countries in Europe, although there are great differences between former West Germany and what was once the GDR. In the new federal states and east Berlin the population density stands at 140 persons per square kilometer and in the old west at 267.

With nine births per 1,000 inhabitants per year, Germany has one of the world's lowest birthrates. Too few children are being born too late. Most women are not having their first child until they are in their early thirties, and on average each woman only has 1.3 children. However, over the past years Germany's population has remained at a stable level. The deficit in births was compensated for by the immigration of some three million migrants. However, this low birthrate is coupled with an increasing life expectancy – currently 74.4 for a new-born boy and 80.6 for a new-born girl – which affects the age distribution of the population. It is projected that in 2030 the percentage of over-60-year-olds will have grown from today's figure of 23 to around 30 percent. The ratio between the proportion of the population in active employment and the percentage of pensioners is shifting in favor of those who have retired from the labor market.

Family on a North Sea beach

The family is still the preferred mode of coexistence. The lion's share of the population live as families, and almost half of them in a traditional family consisting of a married couple with children. The tendency is, however, towards smaller families, with the number of households on the increase. Every fourth inhabitant of a large town lives alone; in the countryside and in small towns the figure stands at every seventh person. Around 2.4 million people, mainly women, live alone with their children.

The German language: German is one of the large group of Indo-Germanic languages, and within this group is one of the Germanic languages, related to Danish, Norwegian and Swedish, Dutch and Flemish, as well as to English. At the end of the Middle Ages there were a large number of regional written languages. With the wide dissemination of Luther's Bible translation a uniform written language gradually became established, based largely on the official written language of Saxony (the written language of Meissen).

Germany has a wealth of dialects. Usually, a person's dialect or accent gives away where he or she comes from. If two people, one from Mecklenburg and one from Bavaria were to hold a conversation, each in their respective dialect, they would have great difficulties in understanding each other. Long ago, there were various different tribes living in what is now Germany – Franks, Saxons, Swabians and Bavarians, for instance. Today, these old tribes have not existed in their original form for a long time, but their traditions and dialects live on in regional groupings.

German is also the native tongue of Austria, Liechtenstein, the majority of Switzerland, South Tirol (northern Italy), northern Schleswig (Denmark) and in small areas of Belgium and Luxembourg along their borders with Germany. The German minorities in Poland, Romania and the countries of the former Soviet Union have also partly retained the German language. German is the native tongue of more than 100 million people. Around every tenth book that is published worldwide is written in German.

Ethnic minorities: There are four ethnic minorities traditionally resident in Germany: Sorbs (60,000), Frisians (10,000), Danes (50,000) and the German Romanies (70,000). The Lusatian Sorbs are descendents of Slavic tribes. They settled in the area to the east of the Elbe and Saale rivers in the course of the migration of peoples that

Sorbians in the Spreewald

took place in the sixth century. The first document in which they are mentioned dates from 631. In the 16th century a written Sorbian language evolved under the influence of the reformation. The Frisians are descendents of a Germanic tribe on the North Sea coast (between the lower Rhine and the Ems river) and have preserved many traditions, as well as their own language. A Danish minority lives in the Schleswig region of the state of Schleswig-Holstein, particularly around Flensburg.

The number of Romany people who are German citizens can only be estimated. The Central Council for German Romanies, which has received support from the German government since 1982, lobbies for compensation for Holocaust survivors, minority rights and the preservation of the Romany language as well as tackling discrimination and prejudice.

The immigrant population: There are currently just under 7.3 million immigrants living in Germany, which corresponds to 8.9 percent of the total population. At the beginning of the 1960s, many foreign workers started coming to West Germany. The expanding economy needed greater manpower and these people were called guest workers. The first to come were Italians, fol-

Foreigners in Germany

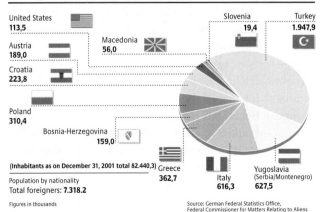

United States
113,5

Austria
189,0

Croatia
223,8

Poland
310,4

Bosnia-Herzegovina
159,0

Macedonia
56,0

Slovenia
19,4

Turkey
1.947,9

(Inhabitants as on December 31, 2001 total 82.440,3)

Population by nationality
Total foreigners: **7.318.2**

Figures in thousands

Greece
362,7

Italy
616,3

Yugoslavia
(Serbia/Montenegro)
627,5

Source: German Federal Statistics Office,
Federal Commissioner for Matters Relating to Aliens

Turkish football fans in Berlin

lowed by Spaniards and Portuguese, Yugoslavs and Turks. Many of them stayed in the country. At the end of 2002 around two thirds of these immigrants had been living in Germany for eight years or longer. One third had been resident in the Federal Republic for more than 20 years. More than two thirds of the children and young people descended from immigrants living in Germany were born here, too.

Immigration and right of asylum: Over the past decades, integration within the European Union, the dissolution of the Eastern Bloc and immigration from Asian and African countries have brought more people of diverse origins to the Federal Republic. Germany accepts a large number of asylum-seekers and war refugees and has always championed freedom of movement, freedom of occupation and freedom of establishment within the European Union.

Germany is at pains to integrate persons from other countries and other cultures. It is the federal government's policy to control and to limit immigration by foreigners by law. This policy is aimed at respecting both Germany's economic interests and the country's humanitarian obligations. At the same time, the government wishes to recruit a qualified workforce for the kind of jobs that cannot currently be filled from within the country despite high unemployment. This creates new jobs and improves the competitive position of the German economy and the German scientific community. There are also plans to simplify residence rights and to tighten the asylum procedure.

Germany grants asylum to many people who have been persecuted on political grounds. The German constitution, the Basic Law, guarantees protection against persecution on political grounds in the form of an individual basic right. In 1993, the right of asylum reverted to its original function, i.e., to protecting those who are actually suffering political persecution. Accordingly, foreigners entering the country via a safe third country can no longer invoke this basic right. Also, notwithstanding the Geneva convention relating to the status of refugees, Germany reserves the right to draw up a list of countries where, according to official sources, no-one is subject to persecution and thus, as a rule, there are no grounds for asylum. However, in Germany every asylum-seeker whose

Asylum seekers

application has been rejected is free to take legal action, if necessary, right through to the Federal Constitutional Court. Since 1992, and more especially since the new right of asylum came into force, the number of asylum-seekers has been falling constantly.

Whereas in 1992, 438,191 people applied, since 1998 the annual number of asylum-seekers has been under 100,000. In 2002, the figure stood at 71,127.

Nationality: In January 2000, important regulations came into force as part of the new law reforming citizenship. Accordingly, children of foreign parents born in Germany now acquire German citizenship at birth. The prerequisite is that one of their parents has been legally resident in Germany for eight years and is in possession of a residence authorization or has had an unlimited residence permit for three years. If, by virtue of their parentage, these children also acquire another nationality, they must choose between German and foreign citizenship when they come of age.

The law also grants children who were under ten on January 1, 2000 a special, limited right of citizenship under the same conditions. Additionally, foreigners may now claim citizenship after eight years (previously 15 years). This claim is dependent on an adequate command of the German language and an acceptance of the German constitution. A new "protective clause" prevents foreign political extremists from acquiring German citizenship. As a matter of principle, persons acquiring German citizenship are required to forfeit their previous nationality. Exceptions are determined according to law.

When an individual applies for and acquires foreign citizenship, he or she automatically forfeits German nationality, independent of whether or not he or she continues to reside in Germany. At the same time, the opportunity for receiving authorization to retain German citizenship has been extended. Emigrants of German origin from east Europe automatically become German citizens upon issuance of the relevant certificate confirming their status as persons of German origin seeking repatriation.

The interests of foreigners living in Germany are represented by the Federal Government's Commissioner for Matters Relating to Aliens. This official is responsible for formulating alien's policy and for individual issues relating to this. He conducts talks on the subject with German and foreign politicians, employer and employee representatives and other groups within society, is the person to contact for organizations actively involved in matters concerning foreigners, is in constant contact with the embassies of the countries from which Germany formerly recruited labor, and travels to the relevant countries to conduct talks with the representatives of their governments.

Information

www.bmi.bund.de
(Federal Ministry of the Interior)
www.statistik-bund.de
(German Federal Statistics Office)

The federal states

Germany is divided into 16 federal states (Länder), each responsible for the government of its own state, some of which look back over a long tradition. Germany has always been divided into states but over the course of the centuries the map has often changed its appearance. The states that exist today were established after 1945 but have in part retained their old ethnic traditions and characteristics as well as their historical boundaries.

Before German unification in 1990 the Federal Republic consisted initially of ten states, and later, after the reintegration of Saarland as of January 1, 1957, of 11 states, which were established in the zones occupied by the Western Powers (USA, Great Britain, France). In the Soviet-occupied zone, too, at the end of the War five states were formed in the territory which later became the GDR, but in 1952 these were transformed into a total of 14 districts (Bezirke). After the first free elections on March 18, 1990, it was decided to create five new states on GDR territory, very much along the lines of those that existed in the days before 1952. On October 3, 1990, the GDR and hence the states of Brandenburg, Mecklenburg-Western Pomerania, Saxony, Saxony-Anhalt and Thuringia acceded to the Federal Republic. At the same time, East Berlin was united with West Berlin.

Information
www.deutschland.de
www.bundesrat.de
www.bund.de

Heidelberg: historic town and castle

Population:	10.601 million
Area:	35,752 km²
Population per km²:	294
Capital:	Stuttgart

Baden-Württemberg

Baden-Württemberg boasts a large number of scenic regions. The Black Forest, Lake Constance, the river valleys of the Rhine, Danube and Neckar, the rugged Swabian Jura, the gentle Markgräfler Land and the striking hilly Kaiserstuhl region in the Upper Rhine plain are popular holiday destinations. Every year, more tourists come to Baden-Württemberg than the state has inhabitants.

At the same time, Baden-Württemberg is an important business location and Germany's top export state – not only because global companies such as Daimler-Chrysler, Bosch, Porsche, SAP and IBM are located here, but also thanks to the hundreds of small and medium-sized businesses that manufacture specialized products which are in demand all over the world.

In proportion to its gross domestic product, the state's expenditure on research ranks near the top worldwide, with the focus on information technology, energy and environmental technology, as well as biotechnology. The foundations for these future-oriented activities are laid at the state's nine universities, 39 institutes of higher education and approx. 130 research establishments.

But it is not only trade, industry and research that give the region its characteristic appearance. Almost 1,000 museums, two state theaters, 150 municipal, independent and private theaters, festivals, film festivals and rhe Schloss Solitude Academy near Stuttgart bear witness to the lively cultural life in the state.

The state capital Stuttgart (588,617 inhabitants) is the heart of one the strongest industrial regions in the Federal Republic. Tourists admire the city particularly because of its picturesque location in the basin of a valley.

Also worth seeing is Heidelberg (140,259 inhabitants), a university town on the Neckar. Its historic town boasts numerous renaissance buildings, over which the famous ruin of a 14th century castle looms. Freiburg im Breisgau (205,102 inhabitants) has attractive city gates and a Minster. Mannheim (306,729 inhabitants) enjoys distinctive architectural features with its chessboard-like layout dating from the 17h century, as does Karlsruhe (278,558 inhabitants), where 32 streets point towards the castle. Ulm (117,232 inhabitants) on the Danube has its Minster as its landmark with Germany's highest church tower. Other important towns are Heilbronn (119,304 inhabitants), Pforzheim (117,156 inhabitants), Tübingen (81,911 inhabitants), Reutlingen (110,650 inhabitants) and Konstanz (78,504 inhabitants) on Lake Constance.

Information

www.baden-wuerttemberg.de
www.tourismus-baden-wuerttemberg.de

Leopoldstrasse in Munich

Population:	12.330 million
Area:	70,549 km²
Population per km²:	173
Capital:	Munich

Free State of Bavaria

The historical term "Free State" indicates that Bavaria is a republican state and not a monarchy. The state and its inhabitants are proud of their history, which dates back as far as the 6th century. Bavaria owes its great appeal to tourists both to this rich cultural and historical heritage and to the charm of its natural beauty. The Alps, the Alpine foreland with its enchanting lakes, the Bavarian Forest with its national park, the Franconian Jura, the Fichtel Hills, the Steigerwald, the Spessart and many other scenic regions offer enticing opportunities for recreation and to enjoy nature.

What was originally an agrarian state has now become a modern industrial and service center with first-class scientific, economic and technical qualifications in all major future-oriented fields, home to such well-known operations as Siemens, BMW, Audi, Dasa-Aerospace and MAN. At the same time, Bavaria is a leading media location. Today, some 35 percent of the state's gross domestic product comes from industry and considerably more than half from the services sector. With 26 universities and institutes of higher education, three major research establishments, 11 Max Planck Institutes and seven Fraunhofer Gesellschaft establishments, Bavaria also has an outstanding research infrastructure.

Every year, Bavaria invests well over € 50 million in maintaining and extending its numerous museums, which now include the Pinakothek der Moderne, in its 33 permanent stages and 34 open-air stages, as well as in the internationally important Bayreuth Festival and the Oberammergau Passion Play which is only performed once every ten years.

The state capital Munich (1,260,597 inhabitants) has much to offer in the way of education and culture, boasts numerous listed buildings and the Oktoberfest, the world's largest public festival. One of the most popular tourist magnates in Bavaria alongside Munich and Nuremberg (488,400 inhabitants) is Rothenburg ob der Tauber (12,000 inhabitants). Inside the town walls, this old Franconian free town has remained practically unchanged since the Thirty Years' War. With its baroque buildings, the old bishopric Würzburg (127,966 inhabitants) not only attracts tourists, it is also a center for viti-culture and the wine trade in Franconia. Bamberg (69,430 inhabitants) is an old imperial Franconian city and bishopric with a historic town. Regensburg (125,676 inhabitants) is also a charming historic city. Bayreuth (73,661 inhabitants) is well-known because of the Richard Wagner Festival in the opera-house on the "Green Hill".

Information

www.bayern.de
www.bayern.by

Population:	3.388 million
Area:	892 km²
Population per km²:	3,793
Capital:	Berlin

Berlin

Since Berlin once again became Germany's capital the city has undergone an economic transformation, but not without some painful adjustments. Yet the prospects are good. As the political heart of the republic and the gateway to east Europe, endowed with a first-class infrastructure, both the city and the region can stand up to any comparison. Berlin's outstanding advantage as a business and industrial location is its network of close contacts between research and development, production and marketing.

During the Cold War, the city underwent a process of atrophy, leaving only a small number of large industrial companies such as the Schering pharmaceuticals group. Berlin's future as an industrial location lies in the modernization of traditional sectors; for example, electrical engineering, car construction, chemicals and pharmaceuticals, mechanical engineering, as well as in establishing and expanding new growth sectors in the field of intelligent technologies.

Three universities, four colleges of fine arts, the European School of Management, nine institutes of higher education, some 250 non-university research establishments and a multitude of small and medium-sized technology firms offer key potential for the kind of economic growth that the large number of businesses in the communications and media sector will also be able to share in.

With ten daily and four Sunday newspapers, 11 city and 12 advertising magazines, Berlin has the largest press selection in Europe. Numerous German and foreign news agencies and correspondents for national and international media here send their reports throughout the world. With 210 book publishers, Berlin is one of Germany's largest publishing cities. 25 regional radio stations can be heard here, an illustration of the city's cultural diversity.

Another aspect of this diversity is the museums and collections on Museum Island, in the Culture Forum and in the district of Dahlem. They are all world-class. The opera houses, theaters, concert halls and libraries, the Berlin Festival, the International Film Festival, the Berlin Theater Encounter and the Jazz Festival all contribute to making this European cultural metropolis so very attractive.

The government and parliament district acts like a magnet to tourists. The dome of the converted Reichstag building, now the seat of the German Bundestag, attracts many visitors, as do the chancellor's offices at the bend in the river Spree. Other popular tourist venues are the "East Center", from Pariser Platz to Alexander Platz, including the Brandenburg Gate, and the "West Center" from the Kurfürstendamm to Charlottenburg Castle, dating from the 17th and 18th centuries.

Information

www.berlin.de
www.btm.de

Reichstag building

The dome of the Reichstag building has become a
landmark of Berlin and attracts thousands of visitors
all year round.

Potsdam's Sanssouci Palace

Population:	2.593 million
Area:	29,476 km²
Population per km²:	88
Capital:	Potsdam

Brandenburg

In the 19th century, Theodor Fontane described Brandenburg's beauty and unspoilt charm. Much of this is still in evidence today: some 350 castles and manor houses are to be found here. Particularly noteworthy, alongside Sanssouci in Potsdam, are Rheinsberg and Branitz in Cottbus.

Compared to other states, Brandenburg is sparsely populated. The Havel and Spree rivers meander through its hilly landscapes. Nature conservation is practised in the numerous nature parks, natural reservations and biosphere reserves, in areas such as the Uckermark, the Elbtalaue, the Schorfheide, in the Spreewald and in the Lower Oder valley national park, which transcends the border to neighboring Poland and is jointly operated with the latter country.

Because of its poor sandy soil, in years past, Brandenburg was known as the "sandbox of the Holy Roman

Empire of the German nation". Today, the backbone of the state's economy is increasingly shifting from agriculture, with its traditional crops of rye and oilseed, to industries such as vehicle construction, mechanical engineering, electronics, the optical and energy industries, environmental technology, the food and chemical industries. The film industry has also taken a leap forwards in the traditional film city of Potsdam-Babelsberg with its film and television studios, its Academy of Films and Television, its High-Tech Center and numerous firms active in the media sector.

With its universities in Frankfurt/Oder, Cottbus and Potsdam, its five institutes of higher education and 15 technology centers, the state has developed into one of Germany's important research centers.

The Brandenburg capital, Potsdam (129,324 inhabitants), is famous for its castles and gardens dating back to the era of Frederick the Great dotted along the banks of the lakes on the Havel river and now part of UNESCO's World Heritage List. Cottbus too, (108,491 inhabitants) is a location of historical significance. The second largest town in Brandenburg, its Branitzer Park represents the last major German 19th century landscaped park, designed by Hermann, Prince of Pückler-Muskau. Located to the east of Berlin, Frankfurt/Oder (79,784 inhabitants) is an important hub for the countries of Eastern Europe. Reopened in 1991, its Viadrina European University has a long tradition.

Information

www.brandenburg.de
www.reiseland-brandenburg.de

Marktplatz and City Hall

Population:	0.66 million
Area:	404 km²
Population per km²:	1,633
Capital:	Bremen

Free Hanseatic City of Bremen

Together with Bavaria, Hamburg and Saxony, the Free Hanseatic City of Bremen is one of the political entities that existed before 1945 and consists of the city of Bremen itself, plus the city of Bremerhaven, located 65 kilometers further down the river Weser. The territory between the two cities belongs to the state of Lower Saxony.

Ports and shipping, international trade connections and products of the highest quality manufactured by state-of-the art industries are the foundations of Bremen's economic life. Every year, almost 10,000 ships link Bremen's ports with some 1,000 ports all over the world. Bremerhaven not only has the largest continuous container loading and unloading plant in Europe, it is also Europe's most important car loading point.

Bremen is also a center for the German food and luxury food and beverages industries: coffee, chocolate, flour, milk products, spices, fish products and beer are the best-known products. Key components for rockets, satellites and the Airbus are developed and built at the Bremen Aviation and Space Travel Center. The electrical and electronics industries and high-tech industries are also prominent.

Bremen's university specializes in engineering and natural sciences. The Institute of Applied Beam Technology and the Institute of Shipping Economics and Logistics are leaders in the field of basic research. The Center for Tropical Marine Ecology and the Max Planck Institute of Marine Microbiology devise modern concepts for marine research.

Bremen's major sights are: the marketplace with its Renaissance Town Hall, the Roland Statue and the Gothic Saint Peter's Cathedral, the famous Böttcherstrasse and the historic Schnoor Quarter. The Bremen Free Market, which has been held on the Bürgerweide for more than 960 years, is one of Germany's largest fairs.

The Art Gallery, the new Weserburg museum, the Gerhard Marcks House and the Paula Becker-Modersohn House display important works of art. The German Maritime Museum in Bremerhaven boasts impressive collections from all eras of seafaring. The Theater am Goetheplatz, the Bremer Shakespeare Company, the annual Bremen Music Festival and the International Fall Academy are household terms to music and theater aficionados.

Information

www.bremen.de
www.bremen-tourismus.de

Speicherstadt district

Population:	1.726 million
Area:	755 km²
Population per km²:	2,271
Capital:	Hamburg

Free and Hanseatic City of Hamburg

Hamburg is the second largest German city, and Germany's principal seaport and largest overseas trade center, with, for example, hundreds of companies from China, Japan and Taiwan maintaining offices here. All in all, there are over 3,000 firms engaged in the import and export businesses here. Traditional port-related industries include shipyards, refineries and processing plants for raw materials from abroad.

By means of a consistent policy of structural transformation, Hamburg has developed into a north European service metropolis. Future-oriented sectors such as the civil aviation, micro-electronics and communications industries are laying the foundations for the city's future as a modern location for business and industry.

Although Hamburg is Germany's second largest industrial center and the heart of a metropolitan area with a population of four million, it is considered one of Germany's greenest cities. 40 percent of its total area consists of arable land and garden plots, parks and public gardens, woodlands, moors and heaths. Landscape reserves and nature reserves cover 28 percent of the city area. In addition to the numerous parks there are more than 240,000 roadside trees. The Ohlsdorf Cemetery is the world's largest leafy cemetery.

The mercantile city of Hamburg is and always has been a place of freedom and tolerance and, at the same time, a seat of learning and culture. Ten institutes of higher education have made Hamburg a center of academic and scientific training, research and development. The opera, three state theaters and some 35 private theaters contribute to the city's cultural dimension, as does the extraordinary quality of the art collection at the Kunsthalle.

Sightseeing attractions in this town with its wonderful location on the Elbe and Alster rivers are the thronging crowds in the Sankt Pauli amusement district with the Reeperbahn, St. Michael's Church ("Michel") and its impressive port. And the latest vogues blossom continuously amongst the traditional office buildings and the renowned theaters, making the 1,200-year-old city equally attractive to the trendy and to culture-lovers.

Information

www.hamburg.de
www.hamburg-tourismus.de

Frankfurt Skyline

Population:	6.078 million
Area:	21,114 km²
Population per km²:	287
Capital:	Wiesbaden

Hesse

Today, Hesse is one of Germany's largest economic centers and ranks amongst the most dynamic regions in Europe. Four branches of industry – chemicals, vehicles, mechanical engineering and the electrical industry – have been instrumental in propelling Hesse to its position of economic strength, as has the service and banking metropolis of Frankfurt – the seat of the German Bundesbank, the European Central Bank and over 400 commercial banks and Germany's largest stock exchange.

Crucial to Hesse's economic success is its central location with its air, rail and waterway junctions. Frankfurt's Rhine-Main airport processes the largest amount of freight and the second largest number of passengers of all European airports and has thus become Germany's biggest local workplace.

Trade and industry, the academic world and the state government collaborate at the Hessian Technology

Foundation in the interests of innovation and competitiveness. Throughout the state there are five universities, five institutes of higher education and two academies of fine art catering to some 153,000 students.

Hesse, which only assumed its present-day dimensions in 1945 and was created out of what used to be Hesse-Darmstadt and Prussian territory, boasts a wealth of interesting museums and exhibitions. Two internationally outstanding cultural events are the world's largest book fair in Frankfurt and the "documenta" art exhibition in Kassel. Important festivals are held in Bad Hersfeld, Wetzlar, Wiesbaden and in the Rheingau.

The university towns of Marburg (77,083 inhabitants), Gießen (73,439 inhabitants) and Wetzlar (53,500 inhabitants) with their attractive historic towns enjoy picturesque settings. Fulda (61,728 inhabitants), an old bishopric with a baroque character, is located in east Hesse. Wiesbaden (270,109 inhabitants), the Hessian state capital, is a popular spa town and the home of the Federal Bureau of Criminal Investigation and the Federal Statistics Office. "Mainhattan", the nickname used for Frankfurt am Main (646,550 inhabitants), refers not only to the city's skyline, but also to its importance as a center of trade, industry and business, education and culture. Largely destroyed in the Second World War, Kassel (194,766 inhabitants) in north Hesse is a center of culture, business and industry with an international flair. Other important towns are Darmstadt (138,242 inhabitants), amongst other things home of the German Academy of Language and Literature and the German PEN center, Offenbach am Main (117,535 inhabitants) and Rüsselsheim (60,222 inhabitants) with its automobile industry (Opel).

Information

www.hessen.de
www.hessen-tourismus.de

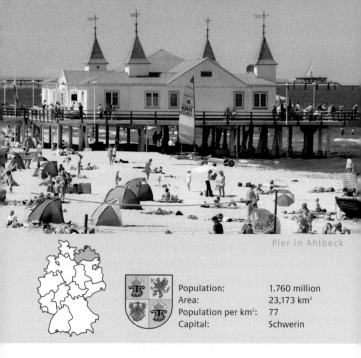

Population:	1.760 million
Area:	23,173 km²
Population per km²:	77
Capital:	Schwerin

Mecklenburg-Western Pomerania

The "state of a thousand lakes" is distinguished by its primarily agrarian character and its unspoilt nature. Its exceedingly varied coastline affords sweeping vistas, as do its manifold inland landscapes with their gently rolling hills, extensive forests, wide-open fields and pastures.

Consequently, here agriculture plays a more important role than in other states. Principal crops are grain, oilseed (rape) and potatoes. 80 percent of the total of 1.3 million hectares of land used for agriculture is worked by farms of more than 500 hectares in size.

But the restructuring of Mecklenburg-Western Pomerania's economy from a state-controlled economy to a market economy is well underway. The most important branches are the shipbuilding industry, the food, luxury food and beverages industry, the construction industry, mechanical engineering, the building materials industry and the wood industry. Mecklenburg-Western Pomerania's seaports continue to figure prominently in the state's economy.

Tourism is an important economic factor here. The best-known tourist magnet is Rügen, Germany's largest island. But Mecklenburg-Western Pomerania takes particular care to ensure that the growing tourist industry does not place too great a strain on the environment. 283 nature reserves, 110 landscape reserves, three national parks and two biosphere reserves attest to the importance which the state attaches to nature conservation and environmental protection. Mecklenburg-Western Pomerania also attracts tourists with its charming castles and manor houses and its summer music festivals.

The towns are also worth a visit. Stralsund (60,663 inhabitants) with its unique ensemble of buildings dating from the late Gothic to the Classical eras, is the ideal starting-point for a trip around the island of Rügen. Rostock (200,506 inhabitants) is a noteworthy harbor town with a university founded in 1419, the oldest in northern Europe, as well as being the center of the most important economic region in Mecklenburg-Western Pomerania. If Leipzig's bid for the 2012 Olympic Games is successful, the sailing competitions will be taking place in an area off Mecklenburg's Baltic coast. The state capital Schwerin (101,267 inhabitants) lies on the edge of the Mecklenburg lake plateau and attracts many visitors. It is the state's second largest city, has a charmingly renovated historic center and a castle, located on an island in Lake Schwerin and converted in the 19th century. Neubrandenburg (79,041 inhabitants) is a center of business, industry and culture in the east of Mecklenburg-Western Pomerania and boasts a completely preserved set of ring-like medieval fortifications and four town gates.

Information

www.mv-regierung.de
www.auf-nach-mv.de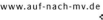

Population:	7.956 million
Area:	47,616 km²
Population per km²:	166
Capital:	Hanover

Lower Saxony

Lower Saxony is the second largest state in the Republic. It stretches from the North Sea island of Borkum with its maritime climate to the Harz Mountains with their winter sports regions and guaranteed snow. In between lie greater metropolitan Hanover and the Hildesheimer Börde with the most fertile arable soil in the Federal Republic.

But even if two thirds of the state's surface area is given over to agriculture, Lower Saxony cannot be classified as an agricultural state. Alongside the traditional industries such as shipbuilding, steel and chemicals, it is now a home to the electronics and computer industry, as well as the car industry, a particularly important sector, with Volkswagen AG, the state's largest employer, located in Wolfsburg (121,805 inhabitants) and the VW Foundation, the largest private German foundation that sponsors the sciences. There are 11 institutions of tertiary education in Lower Saxony, as well as two art academies and 13 institutes of higher education, plus 120 research establishments and technology transfer sites at all higher education institutions. The Hanover Fair and the CeBIT computer fair have made the Hanover area the most important exhibition center in the world.

Millions of guests go to relax on the seven East Friesian islands, in the Harz Mountains, in the Weser Hills, the Teutoburg Forest or the Lüneburg Heath. Also popular with tourists is the "Altes Land", Europe's largest fruit-growing region just outside Hamburg, especially when the apple orchards are in blossom. It is here that the "wet triangle" begins, the lowlands between the mouths of the Elbe and Weser rivers and the tidal mud flats known as the "Wattenmeer", Germany's largest national park.

Alongside Hanover (515,001 inhabitants) and Brunswick (245,816 inhabitants), the second largest city in the state, many towns with historical centers attract visitors from inside and outside Germany, including Celle (72,127 inhabitants), a former ducal residence on the southern edge of Lüneburg Heath with an intact historic town and a Renaissance castle. Another such town is Goslar (45,000 inhabitants), one of the few German towns that remained untouched by the Second World War. Goslar's historic town with its medieval Kaiserpfalz castle is on UNESCO's list of world heritage sites. The same is true of Hildesheim (103,990 inhabitants), with its Romanesque cathedral and St. Michael's Church. Clausthal-Zellerfeld (15,413 inhabitants), still bears witness to the fact that, in the 18th century, with its ore deposits, it was one of the world's principal industrial centers. Wolfenbüttel (53,602 inhabitants), the former residence of princes, with its restored historic town, houses the largest medieval library in the world.

Information

www.niedersachsen.de
www.reiseland-niedersachsen.de

Cologne cathedral

Population:	18.052 million
Area:	34,082 km²
Population per km²:	528
Capital:	Düsseldorf

North Rhine-Westphalia

This, the most heavily populated state, once dominated by factory smokestacks, winding towers and blast furnaces, has, over the past decades, undergone a profound structural change. The land of coal and steel has become a land with coal and steel and promising new industries.

The state long ago satisfied the 1960s call for "blue skies over the Ruhr". Almost 52 percent of North Rhine-Westphalia's land area is given over to agriculture, 25 percent is woodlands. Nevertheless, with some 4.8 million inhabitants, the Ruhr is Europe's largest industrial area. But today, around two thirds of the people in gainful employment in North Rhine-Westphalia work in the service industry.

This structural change was also always linked with ecological renewal. With its innovative companies in the field of environmental protection, the state has become one of Europe's foremost centers of environmental technology. North Rhine-Westphalia is also an important insurance, financial and trade fair location. Furthermore it is a media state with over 600 companies and 1,300 software houses.

Over the past three decades a dense and varied complex of higher education establishments has sprung up, with over 52 higher education institutions and technical colleges in more than 70 locations. A network of technology centers and transfer sites ensures that small and medium-sized businesses are able to profit from higher education know-how.

The cities of Düsseldorf (569,364 inhabitants) and the former federal capital Bonn (302,247 inhabitants) are worth a visit. Founded in Roman times, Cologne (962,884 inhabitants), has a particularly long history. Numerous cultural monuments to the past 2,000 years and notable museums stand in the shadow of the cathedral.

Aachen (243,825 inhabitants) is Germany's most western city and, as the location of medieval coronations, has an important place in the history of Europe. With its historic town center and numerous churches, bishopric and university town Münster (265,609 inhabitants) is at the center of the Münsterland region. The distinguishing feature of old Westphalian town Paderborn (139,084 inhabitants), an Imperial and Hanseatic city and a bishopric, is its impressive cathedral with its triple nave, dating from the late Middle Ages. With over 2,000 years of history behind it, Neuss (150,013 inhabitants) is one of the oldest towns in Germany. Many other towns in the Ruhr region also contribute to the diversity of North Rhine-Westphalia, including Dortmund (588,994 inhabitants), Essen (595,243 inhabitants) and Wuppertal (366,434 inhabitants), with the famed Pina Bausch dance company.

Information

www.nrw.de

www.nrw-tourismus.de

Burg Katz castle in the central Rhine area

Population:	4.049 million
Area:	19,847 km²
Population per km²:	203
Capital:	Mainz

Rhineland-Palatinate

Rhineland-Palatinate lies in the center of the Rhenish schist hills. One of Germany's most beautiful landscapes is the stretch of the Rhine valley between Bingen and Bonn. Dotted with castles, it is steeped in legend and it has been held up as a shining example by countless poets, painters and musicians. Here and in the valley of the Mosel river grow wines prized by connoisseurs throughout the world and in the other tributaries of the Rhine, Nahe, Lahn and Ahr rivers are wine-growing regions of great picturesque charm.

But the economy of this state is more varied than it would appear at first glance. Not only is Rhineland-Palatinate a wine-growing center, (two thirds of German wines come from here), it is also a major center of the chemical industry – Badische Anilin- und Soda-Fabrik (BASF) in Ludwigshafen is Europe's largest chemical factory complex and, at the same time, Rhineland-Palatinate's biggest manufacturing firm – as well as a leading wood producer and supplier of parts for the automotive industry. Other important facets of the economy are the gemstone industry in Idar-Oberstein, ceramic and glass products from the Westerwald and the leather industry in the Hunsrück and Palatinate regions.

Four universities and ten institutes of higher education offer more than 300 courses of studies. Special importance is attached to extending the institutes of higher education, a reaction to the growing demand for practice-oriented training.

The state's geographical situation is an advantageous one. Its network of autobahns and federal highways, its rapid rail links and two major waterways, the Rhine and the Mosel, coupled with its proximity to three economically strong centers – Rhine-Main, Rhine-Neckar and Rhine-Ruhr – have provided the framework for making Rhineland-Palatinate into what it is today – one of Germany's most dynamic regions.

In a charming location at the point where the Mosel flows into the Rhine lies Koblenz (107,950 inhabitants) with its intact historic town. Mainz (182,870 inhabitants), a real carnival bastion, attracts tourists from all over the world, year after year. The capital of Rhineland Palatinate, this city was once the cradle of German book printing, thanks to Gutenberg. Today it is a university town, a center for the German wine trade and the home of the Channel Two (ZDF) German broadcasting corporation. University town Trier (99,750 inhabitants) is a tourist magnate. Its history goes back to Roman times, as witnessed by the Porta Nigra, a mighty town gate which was once part of the Roman fortifications. Also of major significance is Speyer (49,850 inhabitants), a former imperial city with its imposing Romanesque cathedral at the heart of the town.

Information

www.rlp.de
www.rlp-info.de

Old steelworks in Völklingen

Population:	1.066 Million
Area:	2,569 km²
Population per km²:	416
Capital:	Saarbrücken

Saarland

Located between Lorraine, Luxembourg and Rhineland-Palatinate lies Saarland. At just under 2,600 square kilometers, Saarland is Germany's smallest state, but its appearance is shaped by three major areas: the Hunsrück hills, the stratified landscape of Lorraine-Palatinate, with the fertile landscapes on the Saar, Mosel and Blies rivers, and the Saar-Nahe hills.

The triangle of Saarland, Lorraine and Luxembourg is developing ever closer ties. Traditional branches of industry of supraregional importance are glass and ceramics as well as mechanical engineering, metal processing and chemicals. Saarland also furthers research projects of major significance. Future-oriented areas of focus include information and communications technology, materials research, electrical engineering, production technology and medical technology. These are investigated by a large number of university or university-affiliated institutes that form the interface between research and practice. These institutions include the Max Planck Institute of Computer Studies, the German Research Center for Artificial Intelligence and the world-famous Institute for New Materials. The Franco-German Institute of Higher Education is also based in Saarbrücken.

State capital Saarbrücken (183,257 inhabitants) is an industrial hub and a trade fair center on the Franco-German border. Many students from the neighboring countries attend the university and the academies of music and art. Saarlouis, today an important industrial city, is a reminder of the fact that around 300 years ago, French monarch King Louis XIV ordered a fortress to be erected here to defend his conquest in western Germany. Völklingen (42,435 inhabitants) was shaped by the ironworks founded here in 1873, which, by 1890, had already become one of the German empire's foremost iron producers. Shut down in 1986, the works were placed on UNESCO's World Heritage List in 1995 and today they are an industrial museum.

Information

www.saarland.de
www.tourismus.saarland.de

Dresden's baroque skyline

Population:	4.384 million
Area:	18,413 km²
Population per km²:	240
Capital:	Dresden

Free State of Saxony

Saxony is the most populous and densely populated of the east German states and boasts a long industrial tradition. Before the Second World War, the triangle of cities formed by Dresden, Leipzig and Chemnitz was the industrial heart of Germany. But the end of the GDR ushered in a massive structural transformation industrial sectors. A highly diversified and productive small and medium-sized business sector has emerged, comprising more than 132,000 companies.

The most impressive temples to the future are the universities in Leipzig, Freiberg, Dresden and Chemnitz, the 12 institutes of higher education and five colleges of art and the International Graduate School in Zittau, all of which give Saxony the most highly diversified network of higher education institutions in east Germany. The schools' clear focus on technology and the natural sciences makes Saxony a particularly attractive location for firms engaged in developing and distributing technical products and systems, especially in the field of nano- and micro-electronics. Companies in the high-technology sector located here include Infineon, AMD and Wacker Siltronic AG Freiberg.

Saxony also offers a wealth of magnificent castles and elaborately laid-out parks and gardens. As well as the Dresden Zwinger, attractive destinations include Moritzburg Palace, Rammenau Palace, the moated Klaffenbach Castle, Pillnitz Palace and Park and the gardens of Heidenau-Grosssedlitz. The "Silver Route" in the Ore Mountains and the "Saxon Wine Route" are also tourist magnets, as are the numerous festivals.

With its annual industrial and book fairs, Leipzig (439,208 inhabitants) is the home of numerous exhibitions. Its festival devoted to its most illustrious son, Johann Sebastian Bach, its Gewandhaus orchestra and its St. Thomas choir also attract visitors from all over the world. The Saxon metropolis is making a bid to host the 2012 Olympic Games. Located on the Neisse river, Görlitz (64,260 inhabitants) is also worth seeing. It is Germany's easternmost town, and boasts unique Gothic and Renaissance buildings. Meissen (29,500 inhabitants) is world-famous for its porcelain, produced by the State Porcelain Manufacturing Company. Dresden (477,807 inhabitants), the state capital, has regained much of its original charm, despite extensive War damage. A stroll through the center of this metropolis on the Elbe river is an inviting prospect, with its important architectural monuments to the Renaissance and Baroque eras, its Zwinger, the Semper Opera, the Brühl Terrace, the Residenz Palace and the Church of Our Lady, all currently in the process of renovation. Industrial center Chemnitz (259,246 inhabitants), by contrast, known, between 1953 and 1990 as Karl-Marx-Stadt, is characterized by the style of architecture used for the development of the GDR.

Information

www.sachsen.de

www.sachsen-tour.de

Quedlinburg's historic town center

Population:	2.581 million
Area:	20,447 km²
Population per km²:	128
Capital:	Magdeburg

Saxony-Anhalt

The Elbe river flows through Saxony-Anhalt over a distance of 300 kilometers, the vineyards along the Saale and Unstrut, the most northerly winegrowing region in Germany, past the industrial estates near Halle and Bitterfeld through to the Altmark in the North. The soil in the Magdeburger Börde and the forelands of the Harz Mountains is amongst the most fertile agricultural land in Germany. The main crops here are grain, sugar beet, potatoes and vegetables.

But in economic terms, since unification, Saxony-Anhalt has developed into a location attractive to many German and non-German firms alike. For example, Bayer produces its world-famous aspirin tablets in Bitterfeld, and the glass for the dome of the Reichstag building in Berlin came from US flat glass manufacturer Guardian Industries, which has now established itself in Wolfen. Saxony-Anhalt has attracted the most direct foreign investment of all the states in the eastern part of Germany. The main sources of economic growth in Saxony-Anhalt are the traditional chemicals industry, the food business and, increasingly, the ancillary industry for automobile manufacturers. The latter boasts some of the world's most modern production plants of their kind. In conjunction with the Free State of Saxony, the Halle-Leipzig region is also becoming a center for bio and gene technology. Modern information and communications technology are also increasing their presence in Saxony-Anhalt.

Founded in 1993, Magdeburg's Otto von Guericke University is the newest higher education institution in Germany. There is also the 300-year-old Martin Luther University in Halle-Wittenberg and the College of Art and Design at Giebichenstein Castle in Halle.

Magdeburg (231,450 inhabitants) is the political and industrial heart of the state, an important inland port and, as a former bishopric with a cathedral, a historical location. Naumburg (30,213 inhabitants) also offers a window on the past, with one of central Germany's most beautiful marketplaces and a late Romanesque cathedral featuring life-size figures of 12 of its benefactors. The same is true of Halberstadt (42,957 inhabitants). The historic town of Quedlinburg (25,478 inhabitants) with its castle, its collegiate church and its cathedral treasures has been placed on the UNESCO World Heritage List. Other noteworthy towns are Wernigerode (35,516 inhabitants) on the edge of the Harz Mountains, with its fine half-timbered houses, Halle/Saale (247,736 inhabitants), the largest town in Saxony-Anhalt, and Wittenberg (50,000 inhabitants), the home of Martin Luther. Dessau (80,965 inhabitants) is situated right in the middle of the Dessau-Wörlitz Garden Kingdom and boasts the famous Bauhaus that has been included on UNESCO's World Heritage List.

Information

www.sachsen-anhalt.de
www.lmg-sachsen-anhalt.de

Population:	2.804 million
Area:	15,761 km²
Population per km²:	177
Capital:	Kiel

Schleswig-Holstein

Schleswig-Holstein is the only German state bordered by two seas, the North Sea and the Baltic Sea. This sparsely populated state makes the most of its geographical location between Scandinavia and east Europe, aiming to be the hub for the countries along the Baltic coast, which, with more than 50 million inhabitants, constitute one of Europe's most promising up-and-coming regions.

Schleswig-Holstein is also the only German state in which three languages are spoken: not only German and Low German, but also Danish and Friesian. The Friesian ethnic group numbers 40,000 people, and is mainly to be found along the west coast, whereas the 50,000 Danes live in the north of the state.

Schleswig-Holstein has undergone a profound transformation from a region dedicated to agriculture and fishing to a modern location for business, industry and technology. Although large tracts of the state are still used for agricultural purposes, the future now belongs to modern technologies such as marine and medical technology, software production, energy and environmental technology. Schleswig-Holstein is Germany's number one wind power state; it also ranks near the top in terms of technology centers and boasts well in excess of 1,000 firms in the IT and communications sectors alone. The upcoming generation of academics and scientists can train at the state's three universities, four state and two private institutes of higher education.

Alongside Gottorf Palace outside Schleswig, which enjoys a high reputation nationwide as a regional museum, notable cultural attractions are the Molfsee open-air museum near Kiel, and the museum on the site of the old Viking town Haithabu. In the summer, the Schleswig-Holstein Music Festival transforms the state into a concert hall. Many prominent literary figures have also chosen to live in Schleswig-Holstein.

Schleswig (25,093 inhabitants), with its interesting Gothic cathedral, is one of the oldest towns in northern Europe. Kiel (232,612 inhabitants), the capital of Schleswig-Holstein, is a major seaport with the largest passenger port in Germany. Kiel Week is held here every year, and attracts visitors from all over the world. Lübeck (213,339 inhabitants), the "Queen of the Hanseatic Cities" is particularly charming. Its historic town center surrounded by water, is classed as a historical monument and has been placed on the UNESCO World Heritage List.

Information

www.schleswig-holstein.de
www.sh-tourismus.de

Population:	2.411 million
Area:	16,172 km²
Population per km²:	150
Capital:	Erfurt

Free State of Thuringia

Extensive forests and broad expanses of fields, romantic valleys and gorges make this state, which is at the geographic center of Germany and borders on five other federal states, the "green heart" of the Republic. Half of Thuringia's total area is given over to agriculture; some of its farmland is of the highest quality. Important crops are grain, rapeseed, potatoes and sugar beet.

But the industrialization of Germany in the 19th century began in Thuringia and Saxony; important sectors were mining (potash), porcelain, glass, toys, and, most important of all, machine tools and the optical industry. Thuringia has once again picked up the thread of these traditions. After the demise of the GDR, new structures in line with market conditions were developed, making it possible to attract future-oriented technologies to the Free State of Thuringia. Since the restructuring of

"Jenoptik" in Jena, for example, the company has risen to become a high-tech group with international operations.

Machinery is manufactured mainly in Gera und Erfurt. The state capital is also a center for microelectronics and the automobile industry traditionally predominates in Eisenach. With four universities, a number of institutes of higher education, some 50 research establishments and 20 technology centers, Thuringia has a strong academic and scientific base.

Culture and history are in evidence in a wealth of castles, palaces, museums, theaters and galleries. Architectural monuments from the Bauhaus era and places such as the Kyffhäuser attract thousands of visitors every year. And of course the names associated with Thuringia include Bach and Goethe, Schiller and Wieland, as well as locations such as the Wartburg and Weimar.

Weimar (62,452 inhabitants), a small town of great cultural and political significance, is the cradle of German Classicism, the first home of the Bauhaus movement, and the place where Germany's first republican constitution was signed in 1919. The Wartburg, with its long history, stands watch over the historic town of Eisenach (44,242 inhabitants) with its interesting market. According to legend, the bards held competitions here in the Middle Ages. Reformer Martin Luther translated the New Testament into German here in 1521-22. Gera (112,835 inhabitants) boasts an interesting, intact historical marketplace. Erfurt (200,564 inhabitants), both the capital of Thuringia and an administrative and service center, has numerous architectural monuments that are worth a visit. University town Jena (99,450 inhabitants), lies in the picturesque Saale valley, where the optical industry has its center.

Information

www.thueringen.de
www.thueringen-tourismus.de

Weimar

The Goethe-Schiller Monument in front of the German National Theater. Weimar is the cradle of German Classicism. After 1776, great literary figures such as Herder, Wieland, Goethe and Schiller worked here.

Berlin's museum isle

The historic town of Lübeck

Dessau-Wörlitz Garden Kingdom

The World Heritage

27 monuments in Germany are on UNESCO's World Heritage List. These are, in order of their inclusion on the list:

Aachen cathedral

Speyer cathedral

Würzburg Residence

Pilgrimage Church of Wies (Steingaden, Upper Bavaria)

Augustusburg and Falkenlust Castles in Brühl nr. Cologne

St. Mary's Cathedral and St. Michael's Church in Hildesheim

Roman monuments, Cathedral and Liebfrauen Church in Trier

Hanseatic City of Lübeck

Palaces and parks of Potsdam and Berlin

Abbey and Altenmünster of Lorsch

Mines of Rammelsberg and the Historic Town of Goslar

Historic town of Bamberg

Maulbronn Monastery complex (nr. Karlsruhe)

Historic town of Quedlinburg (Saxony-Anhalt)

Völklingen Ironworks (Saarland)

Grube Messel fossil deposits (nr. Darmstadt)

Cologne Cathedral

The "Bauhaus" in Weimar and Dessau

The "Bauhaus" in Dessau

Places of Luther's activities in Eisleben and Wittenberg (Saxony-Anhalt)

Classical Weimar

The Wartburg Castle (Eisenach, Thuringia)

Berlin's Museum Island

Dessau-Wörlitz Garden Kingdom

Monastic Island of Reichenau on Lake Constance

Zollverein coal pit in Essen

Historical towns of Stralsund and Wismar

Upper Middle Rhine valle

www.unesco-welterbe.de

Porta Nigra, Trier

Maulbronn Monastery

History

From the Middle Ages until 1945

For most of its history, Germany was not a unified state but a loose association of territorial states that together made up the "Holy Roman Empire of the German Nation". It was a long time until the founding of the German Reich in 1871.

The term "deutsch" first surfaced in the 8th century. It referred to the language spoken in the eastern part of the Franconian realm, and meant "as the people speak" – as opposed to Latin, the language of scholars. After Charlemagne's death in 814 the Franconian realm disintegrated, primarily along the linguistic divide between early Medieval French and Old High German. A feeling of belonging together emerged only gradually among the inhabitants of the eastern areas. "Germany" ought to be where "German" was spoken. Whereas the western border was established at an early date, settlement of the East did not come to a halt until the 14th century. The resulting contact between and intermingling of the German and Slavonic populations persisted until World War II.

The Middle Ages: In hindsight, the ascension to the throne of King Conrad I in 911 marked the transition from the East Franconian to a German empire. Yet due to Conrad's origins, his title was officially "King of Franconia", and later "Roman King". As of the 11th century, the German empire itself was called "Roman Empire", as of the 13th century "Holy Roman Empire" and in the 15th century the words "of the German Nation" were added. In this empire, the high nobility elected the King. With a few exceptions, the King was related to his predecessor. The Medieval empire had no capital city; the monarchy constantly moved from one city to the next. And there were no imperial taxes; the king drew his sustenance from "imperial estates" which he administered in trust. The King was perceived as a ruler bound by the laws of the people as handed down across time and subject to the approval of the great nobles of the realm, and yet he held the power to pass laws, decide on taxation, as well as over the courts and the army, added to which he was head of the Church. He was also the uppermost authority as regards the protection of peace. Otto I had himself crowned Kaiser in 962 in Rome.

This imperial status, which was likewise exercised by Otto's successors, amounted in theory to dominance over the entire Occident. There was, however, a very great divide between theory and practice. Because the Kings always had to make their way to Rome to be crowned Emperor, they also paid careful attention to ensuring they wielded some form of power in Italy as well. It was Henry IV who no longer allowed the clear supremacy of the Kaiser over the Papacy. A quarrel over the investiture of bishops ended with him doing penance to Pope Gregory VII in 1077 in Canossa, from which time onward the Pope and the Kaiser were equal-ranking powers. Despite an external show of power in the ensuing Staufen dynasty, territorial fragmentation ensued, and the ecclesiastical and temporal princes became semi-sovereign territorial rulers.

Whereas nation states were emerging in other western European countries, the forces in Germany tended to be disintegrative. Herein lies one of the reasons why down through the centuries Germany was considered a "belated nation".

Late Middle Ages to early modern times: The "Golden Bull" issued by Charles IV in 1356 was a form of Imperial constitution. It decreed that seven prominent princes, the Electors, were, amongst other thingsy awarded the exclusive right to elect the German king. Whereas the importance of the smaller counts, nobles and knights gradually declined, the economic power of the towns increased, even more so when they joined forces to form leagues: in the 14th century, the Hanseatic League became the leading Baltic power. In 1495, Maximilian I, the first Kaiser not to be crowned, created a new formal organization of the Empire with the Reichstag (Imperial Diet), Reichskreise (Imperial Counties) and Reichskammergericht (Imperial Court Chamber). But the reforms

In the harbor of a town belonging to the Hanseatic League

foundered, and instead a dualism of "Emperor and Reich" emerged: The King who headed the Reich was offset by the estates of the Reich, electors, princes and towns. Upon election, the emperors entered into "capitulations" and eroded their power more and more, whereas the princes, especially the powerful among them, increased their influence.

However, the Reich continued to hold together and within it the towns emerged as centers of economic power. In the textile and mining industries, forms of economic activity grew which outgrew the craftsmen's guilds system and, like the burgeoning long-distance trade, gradually bore early capitalist traits. A critical spirit, marked by the Renaissance and Humanism was also being kindled, and above all attacked church abuses. Following the emergence of Martin Luther, this dissatisfaction broke out with the Reformation, which began with the publication of Luther's 95 theses against abuses by the old Catholic church on October 31, 1517. It aimed to return the Christian religion to the truths of church doctrine as revealed in the Gospels. The consequences went far beyond the religious sphere. The social fabric started to come apart. Even the Knights of the Reich dared to rise up and attempts at political and social change led to the Peasants' Revolt in 1525, the first major revolutionary movement in Germany, which was crushed in a bloody manner.

Age of religious schisms: Politically, the Reformation enabled the territorial princes to increase their powers. After the changing fortunes of war, the 1555 Peace of Augsburg bestowed them with the right to dictate their subjects' religion ("cuius regio eius religio"). Henceforth Protestants enjoyed the same rights as Catholics, and Germany became four-fifths Protestant. Shortly thereafter, the era of Charles V came to an end. He had concentrated on international politics and had not shown much interest in the domestic position of the Kaiser. Thus the empire went in different directions, the

German territorial states, still integrated into the Holy Roman Empire of the German Nation, on the one hand, and the western European nation states, on the other. Such was the order of the new European system of states in the second half of the 16th century. Yet the struggle between the faiths continued, and during the Counter-Reformation the Catholic Church was able to recapture many areas. The differences between the faiths sharpened, leading to the formation of religious parties (the Protestant Union and the Catholic League), culminating in the Thirty Years' War. Between 1618 and 1648, this European conflict left a trail of blood behind it in many areas of Germany, which were left devastated and depopulated.

Age of Absolutism: During the following period the effects of French absolutism were felt strongly in court life in the individual German states. Almost unlimited power for the respective ruler of the state went hand in hand with tight administration, an organized fiscal policy and operational armies. Many princes aspired to create cultural centers and as representatives of enlightened absolutism encouraged science and to a certain extent critical thought. Austria repelled the approaching Turks, acquired Hungary as well as parts of the Balkans, and in doing so rose to become a great power. Under Frederic William I and Frederic the Great, Prussia also consistently grew into a strong military power, through which two outstanding powers arose in 18th century Germany, both of which lay claim to territories outside the Reich and both of which were pursuing growing and opposing interests on the European stage.

Age of the French Revolution: Prussia and Austria were in the same boat when they intervened by force in the revolutionary events in neighboring France in an attempt to save the crumbling feudal social order there. However, the vision of freedom and equality, of human rights and the division of powers began to run its own course. Instead of merely resisting the attempts at interference from the East, the French revolutionary armies went on the counter-attack. The Reich finally collapsed.

The left bank of the Rhine was occupied by the French and the remaining areas carved up anew, producing strengthened medium-sized states. Under French protection the Confederation of the Rhine (Rheinbund) emerged, and when in 1806 Emperor Franz II laid down the crown, the Holy Roman Empire of the German Nation formally ceased to exist.

Yet the revolutionary spark did not catch. What did become evident however was that a reform of the state was necessary. Feudal barriers were reduced, but not dismantled altogether and throughout the various German principalities the other objectives, such as freedom of trade, municipal self-administration, equality before the law and general conscription were pursued to varying degrees. Many of the reform moves were pulled up short, whereas others were adopted in the constitution.

The German Confederation and the 1848 revolution: The joint resistance to the push into German territory by the French and the victory over Napoleon served to nourish the longing of many Germans for their

The German Parliament convenes in the Paulskirche in Frankfurt/Main

The March Revolution

Encouraged by the successful February revolution in France, the citizens of the German states rose up against their rulers: as in the battles on the barricades in the Alexanderplatz in Berlin.

own national state. Yet the 1815 Congress of Vienna, which redrew the map of Europe, only produced the German Confederation, a loose association of individual sovereign states, with its sole organ the Federal Diet (Bundestag) in Frankfurt, which was not an elected but a delegated diet.

Indeed, the Confederation was also only in a position to act if the two great powers, Prussia and Austria, agreed. It saw its main task in suppressing all aspirations and efforts aimed at unity and freedom.

Although there was press censorship and close monitoring of the universities, not to forget that almost all political activity was suppressed, modern economic development had set in. Since a huge number of industrial jobs were created but there were no social welfare provisions, the pressure for a change in society increased. Much blood was shed when the weavers' uprising in Silesia was put down in 1844. In contrast to the revolution of 1789, however, the French revolution of 1848 triggered an immediate response in Germany. In March the princes were faced with uprisings in all the states and were forced to make concessions. The first genuine parliaments arose.

The greatest ray of light shone from the freely elected National Assembly, which convened in the Paulskirche in Frankfurt/Main. This combined free democratic wishes with the national wishes shared by a large majority of Germans. On paper it had an exemplary constitution, yet the ministry created by the National Assembly enjoyed no real powers of authority. In the tug of war between a solution for a smaller Germany (without Austria) and a larger Germany (with Austria), the transfer of executive power to Vienna came to nothing given Austria's demand that all nationalities, including non-German ones, be included in the new German Reich. Yet when King Frederick William IV of Prussia refused to don the crown of the smaller German Reich, the fate of the

Otto von Bismarck

National Assembly and of constitutional liberal principles was more or less sealed. Prussia was given an enforced constitution with three-tier voting rights. In many respects, 1850 witnessed the restoration of the former state of affairs.

The Bismarck Reich: The following were the important stages along the path to German unity:

- The German-Danish war of 1864, fought jointly by Prussia and Austria.
- Prussia's victory over Austria in the 1866 war, as a result of which Austria was excluded from the subsequent developments of the German state.
- The founding of the North German Confederation in 1867, with Bismarck as Federal Chancellor.

As Federal Chancellor, Bismarck worked towards achieving "smaller German" unity and, following a diplomatic conflict over succession to the Spanish throne, broke

France's resistance in the 1870-71 war. Patriotic enthusiasm for this use of arms was also strengthened in the southern German states, which then allied with the North German Confederation to form the German Reich. On January 18, 1871, King William I of Prussia was proclaimed German Emperor in a coronation ceremony in Versailles.

In other words, the German Reich had not been created by popular decision "from below" but by a treaty between princes "from above". The newly formed Imperial Diet (Reichstag) was elected by universal and equal suffrage. In addition, in Prussia and the other federal states there was a system of class suffrage dependent on income. Though economic success did strengthen the influence of the middle class, those that still called the tune in politics were the aristocrats, above all the army officer corps, where they dominated. In contrast to his far-sighted foreign policy, Bismarck, who was in office for 19 years, was at a loss to understand the democratic trends at home. He staged a bitter struggle against the left wing liberal middle class, political Catholicism and in particular the labor movement, which between 1878 and 1890 he effectively banned under the terms of the Socialists Act. Thus despite progressive, and for a long time even exemplary social legislation, large sections of the working class remained alienated from the state.

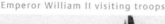

Emperor William II visiting troops

World War I: With regard to foreign affairs Germany under the young and inexperienced Emperor William II likewise got itself in deep water. He attempted to shorten the lead of the other imperialist great powers yet found himself increasingly isolated. At home the Social Democrats, the party with the most voters, continued to be more or less excluded from political power. It was not until the old establishment was defeated in World War I that they were given an opportunity.

It was a war that none of the powers involved consciously sought, even though tension had built up to such an extent in the Spring of 1914 that an armed solution to the various war aims of the European powers was considered a more or less welcome option. The Germans failed in their aim to quickly vanquish France. Yet after the Battle of the Marne both sides became embroiled in a gruesome war of attrition with an immense loss of human life and no clear military advantage, and which was no more than a senseless material battle. When the United States of America entered the war in 1917 this brought the turning point that had long been developing and which even the revolution in Russia and peace in the East could not halt. Political upheaval followed military defeat: as a result of the German revolution in November 1918 Emperor William II and the princes yielded their thrones. The

Euphoric volunteer soldiers

disaster abroad led to the failed monarchy ceding to an alternative at home that it had been combating for decades, namely a republic.

The Weimar Republic: Named after the National Assembly that convened in Weimar and drew up a new constitution, in the early years the young republic was formed and influenced by a parliamentary majority of Social Democrats, the German Democratic Party and the Catholic Center. Democracy was working. The Social Democrats had relinquished their revolutionary ideas of the early years and attempts to drive the revolution in a socialist direction were quelled. Private ownership of industry and agriculture remained untouched and the mostly anti-republican civil servants and judges retained their positions.

Yet as early as the 1920s it was becoming evident just how fragile support in the middle classes really was. Amidst general confusion in 1923, the economic crisis, inflation, the occupation of the Ruhr by the French and communist attempts to seize government all demonstrated that democrats were in a minority in Weimar. Ensuing economic recovery led to political pacification. In foreign affairs, Germany, having been defeated in the Great War, resumed its political place as an equal on the international stage among other things with the signing of the Treaty of Locarno in 1925 and accession to the League of Nations in 1926. With regard to the arts, science and culture some sections of the population were for a short time able to refer to the "golden Twenties". It was a period characterized by an intense but brief flowering, since the fall of the republic could already be foreseen in the next economic crisis in 1929.

The National Socialist dictatorship: At the end of the 1920s, left-wing and right-wing radicals were able to exploit the horrendous unemployment rate and widespread economic misery. No more majorities capable of government were to be formed in the Reichstag, and the cabinets depended on the emergency powers of the Reich President to issue decrees, meaning it was possible to govern without the support of parliament. As early as 1925 a candidate from the right, former Field Marshal Paul von Hindenburg succeeded Friedrich Ebert, a social democrat, as Reich President. Although he abided strictly by the constitution he never developed a personal commitment to the republic. At the beginning of 1933, when the worst periods of crisis were already abating, members of the right-wing camp reckoned on being able to use the extremely anti-democratic Adolf Hitler for their own ends by transferring the office of chancellor to him. As a result of the economic crisis, his National Socialist movement had become the strongest political force in Germany, without however enjoying majority support neither among the population nor in Parliament. Despite the greatest of misgivings, Hindenburg nonetheless appointed him head of government and agreed to his demand to dissolve the Reichstag. The Nationalist Socialists seizure of power had thus begun.

Even in the election campaign Hitler intimidated his opponents with violence and persecution. Despite opposition from the Social Democrats he exerted tremen-

An SS parade

dous pressure on those members of parliament who had not been arrested or had not fled to agree to an "Enabling Act", which accorded him almost unlimited political powers. Within just a few weeks the National Socialists had broken down all democratic barriers and replaced them with pseudo-legal structures. Hitler practically outlawed basic rights, banned trade unions and political parties (apart from his own), rescinded the freedom of the press and subjected those that disagreed to ruthless terror. Thousands disappeared without trial in concentration camps.

From the very beginning political persecution went hand in hand with racist mania. This was based on the myth of a "northern" race, and developed via thoughts about people being "unworthy of life", because they did not conform to ideal perceptions about life, leading to systematic euthanasia. Whereas the latter was conducted covertly for fear of protest, anti-Semitic excesses were carried out in public. Before the eyes of the general public, Jewish citizens were excluded from everyday life, humiliated, removed from public office, threatened with their lives and ultimately systematically persecuted. In 1938, synagogues and other Jewish buildings were destroyed in a pogrom. In many cases it was beyond people's imagination to imagine what the Nazi thugs did to the Jews who had been sent to concentration camps: "Extermination" by means of inhuman accommodation and exhaustion from work, medical experiments that showed no respect for human life, and ultimately in the final years the murder of all Jews, especially those in the conquered territories in the East, who fell into the hands of the regime. An estimated six million men, women and children were murdered in just a few years.

The German population's response to what was happening was conflicting. On the one hand, they experienced unbridled violence and, on the other, successful policies from which they benefited. From the point of view of the unemployed, Hitler increased the speed of economic recovery, which had already begun before he came to power and would have given a boost to any government, through widespread job creation programs that were used for propaganda purposes, not to mention an unprecedented policy of rearmament, which sooner or later would have driven the country to bankruptcy unless fresh funds were injected into the economy, for example through the exploitation of the conquered territories in the East. Success in foreign affairs, noticeably the return of the Saarland into the German Reich strengthened Hitler's position. Other significant foreign policy events included, in 1936, German troops reentering the Rhineland, which had been a demilitarized zone since 1919, the annexation of Austria in 1938 and in the same year the granting of the Sudetenland by the Western powers to Hitler.

World War II: Increasing the territories of the German Reich was not enough for Hitler. He wanted more. In March 1939, he ordered German troops to occupy Prague and on September 1 of the same year he unleashed World War II by invading Poland. It lasted five and a half years, killed 55 million people and devastated

The destroyed city of Cologne

much of Europe. In many countries the Germans were considered to be ruthless occupiers. The area conquered stretched from the Atlantic coast in France to just short of Moscow, from North Norway to North Africa. The attack on the Soviet Union on June 22, 1941 marked the beginning of a merciless campaign of destruction in the East.

The entry of the United States into the war and the defeat of the German army at Stalingrad marked a turning point. When liberating occupied territories, the Allied troops encountered resistance groups, some of which were better organized than others. Even in Germany there had been acts of resistance against the Nazis by individuals or resistance groups throughout the years. They came from all walks of life. A bomb attack initiated by Graf Stauffenberg and other resistance fighters on July 20, 1944 failed: Hitler survived and had more than 4,000 people executed in retaliation. The war continued, claiming huge casualties on both sides, until the Allies occupied the entire German Reich. Hitler committed suicide on April 30, 1945 and a week later the darkest chapter in the history of Germany was brought to an end with the country's unconditional capitulation.

The Brandenburg Gate

The Division of Germany and the Cold War

The zero hour: The zero hour for post-war Germany rang out with the capitulation of the country on May 8-9, 1945. The members of the last government of the German Reich, headed by Admiral of the Fleet Dönitz were arrested and together with other National Socialist leaders brought before the International Military Tribunal in Nuremberg and tried for crimes against peace and humanity. The four victorious powers, the United States, the United Kingdom, the Soviet Union and France assumed supreme authority and divided up the capital city into four sectors and the territory of the Reich into four occupation zones. The Eastern territories were placed under Polish or Russian administration.

At the Potsdam Conference in the summer of 1945 the four victorious powers were in agreement on the questions of denazification, demilitarization, economic decentralization and re-education of the German people along democratic lines. Admittedly not all those involved agreed on what these concepts actually entailed. In Potsdam the Western powers gave their consent to the expulsion of Germans from the German eastern territories, from Hungary and from Czechoslovakia. The West had insisted that the transfer be carried out in a "humane" fashion, but this demand was not observed and in the following years some 12 million Germans were brutally expelled by the new rulers.

A minimum consensus was at least reached in the form of an agreement to treat Germany as an economic entity and in the medium term to establish centralized administrations for Germany as a whole. This resolution had no effect as the different developments in the zones occupied by the Soviet Union and the Western Allies respectively, as well as the handling of the reparations issue, which was of particular importance for the Soviet Union, excluded any uniform arrangement for Germany from the very beginning.

Reparation payments: Moscow demanded that Germany be forced to make overall reparations of USD 20 billion to the victorious powers, above all by dismantling plant and by contributions from ongoing production, and

Removal of goods taken as reparations

claimed that USD 10 billion should go to the USSR. The solution that was finally devised entailed each of the victorious powers drawing the reparations due to it from the zone it respectively occupied, a process that contributed to the economic division of Germany. According to western calculations the Soviet occupation zone (it later formed the German Democratic Republic) made reparations payments to the Soviet Union of some USD 14 billion, more than it had initially demanded from the whole of Germany.

The Cold War: Germany was the country where the Cold War, which began shortly after the end of WW II, manifested itself most clearly. The Western and Soviet social systems could scarcely have been more different. With the assistance of the German Communist Party leadership, which had returned from exile in Moscow, the Soviet occupying power pushed ahead with political and social change. Termed an "anti-fascist democratic upheaval", this concentrated all political and social functions in the hands of the German communists and persons they trusted. Walter Ulbricht, the head of the communist group, set the tone when he said: "It has to look democratic, but everything must be in our hands." Parties were established at the zonal level as well as several central administrations. In the three Western zones, the development of a system of political administration was a bottom-up process. At first political parties were permitted only at local level, then at the state level after the federal states had been formed. Only much later were they allowed to form associations at the zonal level. Zonal administrative structures were materializing very slowly, and as the destroyed country's material needs could only be overcome by cooperation across state and zonal borders and as the Four Powers' administration was not functioning, the United States and the United Kingdom decided in 1947 to merge their zones economically into what was known as the "Bizone".

Allied airlift reaches Berlin

One particularly striking step towards the division of Germany was the April 1945 compulsory merger of the German Communist Party (KPD) and the Social Democratic Party (SPD) to form the Socialist Unity Party (SED). At the same time all other parties were grouped together in a communist-led block of parties. On the part of the Western powers, a change in attitude also gradually became apparent. In a speech on September 6, 1946 in Stuttgart, US Secretary of State James Byrnes presented the new approach. Poland's borders were now considered to be temporary, and the presence of the Western Allies in Germany was perceived less as an occupation and more as protection against the further advance of communism. Once the French had been convinced of the advantages of more intense cooperation, a unified Western economic area was established in the "Trizone".

The status of protective power was certainly put to the test when Soviet party leader and head of state Joseph Stalin took the occasion of the introduction of the Deutsche Mark (DM) to instigate a blockade of Berlin (West), aimed at annexing it to the Soviet occupied zone. During the night of June 23, 1948 all land routes between the Western zones and Berlin (West) were closed. Supplies of

The Parliamentary Council

energy and food from the surrounding zone of occupation were discontinued.

The response of the Allies was to organize an unprecedented airlift, which maintained supplies to the citizens of Berlin (West) until May 1949. Over 277,000 flights ferried a total of 2.3 million tons of food, medication, fuel and building material to the city, thus keeping it going. With this visible solidarity with Berlin (West) as an outpost of Western life and politics, America demonstrated its strength and determination.

Founding of the Federal Republic of Germany: In 1948, the minister presidents of the federal states convened as an assembly to draw up a constitution for the state that was emerging from the Trizone. From the very beginning this constitution was intended to be provisional until reunification of the country, and was thus known as the Basic Law. It included many of the intentions of the western occupying powers but above all reflected experiences with the fallen Weimar Republic.

The constitutional convention at Herrenchiemsee and the Parliamentary Council, which consisted of members of the state parliaments, decided in favor of a democratic and social federal state. It was these men and women of the republic's first hour who incorporated the spirit of the democratic traditions of 1848-49 and 1919 as well as the "revolt of the conscience" of July 20, 1944. They personified the "other Germany" and won the respect of the occupying powers. The formal proclamation of the Basic Law on May 23, 1949 marked the beginning of a new era. Following the elections to the first Bundestag on August 14, 1949 parliamentary life rounded out the constitution. The first federal government, led by Chancellor Konrad Adenauer, prepared for Germany's return to an "honorable position among the free and peace-loving nations of the world", a project that US Secretary of State Byrnes had announced three years earlier.

Adenauer, along with the first Federal President Theodor Heuss (FDP), Ludwig Erhard (CDU), the father of the "economic miracle", and the great opposition leaders of the SPD such as Kurt Schuhmacher and Erich Ollenhauer, gave the new party system in West Germany an unmistakable profile and created new confidence in the German state. Step by step they extended German say and its political influence on the occupying administration and committees. A consistent policy of reparation towards Israel and Jewish organizations helped to further the new respect Germany enjoyed throughout the world. As early as 1952 an act was signed in Luxembourg that regulated the payment of integration aid for Jewish refugees in Israel. Of the total of some DM 90 billion that has been paid for reparations over the course of time, around one third has been committed to Israel and Jewish organizations, in particular the Jewish Claims Conference, a hardship fund for Jewish refugees throughout the world.

The fact that Germans identified with their country, the young Federal Republic, was helped by a buoyant economy. At a time of immense personal hardship, millions of CARE packets from the USA had formed the basis for a feeling of solidarity between conquerors and conquered. American foreign aid had also laid further foundations. A decisive tool for the economic recovery was the European Aid and Reconstruction Program that US Secretary of State George C. Marshall had announced in June 1947, and from whose funds between 1948 and 1952 around USD 1.4 billion flowed into West Germany.

Founding of the GDR: Whereas in western Germany, a social market economy was set up, the Soviet occupation zone pressed ahead with a policy of nationalizing industry. On October 7, 1949 the proclamation of the constitution of the German Democratic Republic sealed the division between east and west in legal terms. Two states had arisen in Germany, both of which claimed to be the core and model for a single united Germany that was to be created in the future. With elections based on "Unity" lists of candidates, strict control and direction of government and society by the Socialist Unity Party, the GDR followed the pattern of the "people's democracies" set up as Soviet protectorates in eastern central and southeastern European states.

On the urgent advice of Adenauer, the Soviet proposal to reunite Germany as far as the Oder-Neisse line as a "democratic and freedom-loving country" with strictly

June 17, 1953 in East Berlin

neutral status was not pursued further by the Western forces. He did not want to risk the integration of the Federal Republic into the East and his suspicions seemed only too justified when, 12 months later, shortly after Stalin's death and changes in the leadership in Moscow, Soviet tanks bloodily put down a peoples' uprising in the GDR on June 17, 1953. In Hungary, Soviet troops also put down an uprising in November 1956. The Soviet Union sped up its program of nuclear armament and in October 1957 won the race into space, causing a "Sputnik shock" in the West.

It was against this backdrop that a status quo developed which lasted for many years. Whereas the Western powers guaranteed the freedom and safety of West Berlin with their presence in the city, the GDR increasingly isolated itself: on August 13, 1961 the Berlin Wall was built right through the city, and along the border between the two German states a death strip was set up. These aimed to bring the flow of refugees from the GDR to a halt.

Willy Brandt kneels before the monument to the Warsaw Ghetto

Overcoming the division

New "Ostpolitik": The atomic stalemate between the two
super powers initiated a period of détente, which despite
the quashing of the reform movement in Prague (the
"Prague Spring") in 1968 was pursued further and did produce some tangible results: the treaty signed on August 12,
1970 in Moscow between the Federal Republic of Germany
and the Soviet Union on the renunciation of force and the
permanent nature of European borders formed the center
piece of Willy Brandt's policy of détente and peace. In a
"Letter on German Unity" the Federal Government unilaterally confirmed its goal of German reunification. On December 7 of that year the Treaty of Warsaw was signed, which
normalized Germany's relationship with Poland and recognized the Oder-Neisse line as Poland's western border with
Germany. The Four Powers Agreement on Berlin (signed on
September 3, 1971) essentially affirmed the existing status
of the city. The Agreement envisaged that although the
western parts of the city were not a constituent part of the
Federal Republic, the "ties" between the two were to be
maintained and developed further.

"Practical improvements to the state of things" were made possible, making the division of the city more bearable and passing the Berlin Wall easier. On balance, the edge was taken out of the Berlin question, and the matter regulated. The relationship between the two German states was normalized in the Basic Treaty of December 21, 1971, and it was agreed that each would set up "Permanent Diplomatic Missions" in the other. This paved the way for a number of individual treaties. On September 18, 1973 both German states were admitted to the United Nations. On August 1, 1975 they both signed the Final Act of the CSCE in Helsinki on questions of security and cooperation in Europe.

In 1971, in honor of his "policy of reconciliation between old enemies", Willy Brandt became the first German post-War leader to be awarded the Nobel Peace Prize. At that point in time, the treaties had not yet been ratified. In parliament as well as throughout the country there were passionate discussions as to whether, in view of the facts, German reunification would be made more difficult, or whether in a Europe where people were united in friendship, access to the former German territories in the east would in fact be easier. The government's majority was crumbling, a situation which gave the leader of the opposition Rainer Barzel an opportunity to replace Brandt through a vote of no confidence. On April 27, 1972 the attempt failed. On May 17, 1972 the German Bundestag ratified the treaties with the Soviet Union and Poland, though most CDU/CSU members of parliament abstained. In an "interpretive resolution" the Bundestag declared that the treaties did not conflict with the aim of restoring German unity by peaceful means. A general election that had been brought forward early produced an increased majority for the coalition government of social democrats and liberals, a clear indication of the country's support for Willy Brandt's "Ostpolitik".

Willy Brandt visits Willi Stoph in Erfurt

Continuing the dialogue between the two Germanies: Following Willy Brandt's resignation in May 1974, when one of his aides was unmasked as being a GDR spy (it was called the "Guillaume affair"), Chancellor Helmut Schmidt continued the policy of developing a balanced relationship. The Final Act of the CSCE (Helsinki, 1975), which called for greater freedom of movement in cross-border traffic and more respect for human and civil rights, emerged as a platform to which internal oppositional groups, at loggerheads with the ossified authoritarian regimes of central and Eastern Europe, could appeal. For the sake of the people in the GDR, the Federal Government steadfastly pursued its policy of understanding and cooperation. To this end a motorway was built through the GDR from Hamburg to Berlin and the transit waterways to Berlin (West) repaired, with a considerable proportion of the financing for these projects being provided by the Federal Republic. Furthermore, the latter continued its policy of paying for the release of political prisoners from the GDR. Bonn ultimately paid some DM 3.4 billion to obtain the release of 33,755 people and to have 250,000 families reunited.

As of 1977, the German state and its population were subjected to spectacular challenges in the form of acts of terrorism perpetrated by the Red Army Faction, as it was known. Arson in department stores developed into assassination attempts, bomb attacks, hold ups and kidnappings. These acts of violence dominated political life for some time and resulted in several laws being tightened. Yet they did not succeed in calling into question the ability of the state to continue operating nor did they shake the population's support for the state.

NATO two-track resolution: Whereas the process of European integration proceeded steadily among West European nations, the transition from the 1970s, the decade of détente, to the 1980s was marked by fresh conflicts in East Europe. The Soviet invasion of Afghanistan, the imposition of martial law in Poland following the foundation of an independent workers' movement, and the deployment of new intermediate-range missiles in the Soviet Union threatened to cause a return to a policy of confrontation. As a form of protest against the invasion of Afghanistan, the United States, Canada, Norway and the Federal Republic of Germany all boycotted the 1980 Summer Olympic Games in Moscow. NATO responded to the renewed build-up of missiles by the Soviets with what was known as the two-track decision. This involved stationing new missiles in the West should the Soviet Union fail to dismantle its own new missiles.

As far as relationships between the two German states were concerned there were likewise efforts to minimize damage: The GDR drastically increased the minimum daily exchange requirement for those from the West visiting East Berlin and the GDR, and its leader Erich Honecker demanded recognition of a separate GDR citizenship as well as the upgrading of the "Permanent Diplomatic Missions" to the status of fully fledged embassies. Even a personal visit to the GDR by Chancellor Helmut Schmidt failed to achieve any substantial concessions. The GDR regime's hardening stance was not least a response to the growing protest movements in neighbor-

Chancellor Schmidt congratulates his successor Kohl

ing Poland, where people were ever more openly demanding economic reform, freedom and disarmament.

However it was not just in the East that the missile question led to a loss of authority. In Bonn, the FDP decided to change its outlook on economic policy and began to break away from the coalition. Grassroots SPD followers, largely owing to pressure from the peace movement and some trade union factions, withdrew their support of Schmidt in reaction to his adherence to the NATO two-track decision.

Following a vote of no confidence on October 1, 1982, Helmut Kohl became German Chancellor heading a CDU/CSU-FDP coalition government. He continued the Federal Government's security policy and close cooperation with Paris and Washington with a view to uniting Europe within a stable and secure framework. Despite massive and at times spectacular demonstrations for peace, Helmut Kohl's government stood its ground on rearmament and in November 1983, a Bundestag majority agreed. This also averted a crisis in NATO. A new dialogue on disarmament between the superpowers began as early as the mid-1980s and it was soon possible for the missiles that had just been deployed to be dismantled once again.

Decline of the GDR: Popular support for the leadership of the GDR was at all times dependent on what other alternatives were available. Despite the command economy, the secret police, the all-powerful Socialist Unity Party (SED) and strict censorship, a large majority of the citizens had come to terms with the system. Highly subsidized state-run basic amenities that were inexpensive for the man on the street played an important role here. The system possessed an intrinsic flexibility that enabled numerous lifestyles to be adopted in niches within it. Major successes by the GDR on the international sports stage provided compensation as well as satisfaction for the "working people" who, despite extremely high reparations payments to the Soviet Union, were soon able to boast the highest per capita production output and standard of living in the Eastern bloc.

Despite all the propaganda it became increasingly evident to the people that the GDR's intention of overtaking the Federal Republic economically would remain a dream. Depleted resources and a loss of productivity as a result of central planning forced the SED regime to water down its promises and raise large loans in the West again. Improvisation became the order of the day with regard to consumer goods. The younger generation in particular questioned a state in which it was permanently under observation and subjected to incessant propaganda. The people began to demand a say in the running of their own lives, more individual freedom as well as more and better consumer goods.

From the mid-1980s onwards, an increasing number of people flocked to the Permanent Diplomatic Mission of the Federal Republic in East Berlin and the German embassies in Prague and Warsaw, seeking new ways to leave the GDR for the Federal Republic. As of 1985, new Soviet leader Mikhail Gorbachev, who stood for a more relaxed approach, trust and transparency supported this desire for freedom. Yet the SED regime did not want to get caught up in the zest of Gorbachev's "perestroika" (conversion) and "glasnost" (openness).

As early as 1987 during a visit by Erich Honecker to Bonn, Helmut Kohl had seized on the new prospects for relations between the two German states that had resulted from the Soviet policies: "We respect the existing borders but we want to overcome the country's division by peaceful means through a process of mutual understanding."

Further successful disarmament negotiations between East and West led to increasing demands for greater freedom and reform in the GDR. During demonstrations in East Berlin in early 1988, 120 supporters of the church movement known as "the Church from Below" were arrested. The church held a prayer service for them that was attended by over 2,000 people. Two weeks later more than 4,000 assembled in the Church of Gethsemane. In Dresden, the police had to break up a demonstration for human rights, free speech and freedom of the press.

From the summer of 1989 onwards, the structures of the GDR became caught up in a vortex that was revolving ever more quickly. Hungary opened its borders for

GDR citizens scaling the wall to the German Embassy in Prague

Freedom to travel

On the evening of November 9, 1989 the GDR leadership announced new, less restrictive regulations
on travel. Happiness knew no bounds and the people
stormed the border crossings. To all intents and
purposes, the Wall had come down.

GDR citizens wishing to leave, enabling thousands of them to travel first to Austria and from there to the Federal Republic.

This breach of Warsaw Pact discipline encouraged ever more people in the GDR to take to the streets in protest. They were able to take their cue from the spreading opposition movement, which, after very modest beginnings, had formed at the beginning of the 1970s, primarily under the protection of churches. When with great pomp and circumstance the GDR leaders celebrated the 40th anniversary of the founding of the state at the beginning of October 1989, the first mass demonstrations began to take to the streets, primarily in Leipzig. "We are the people!" was the resounding cry. As opposed to 1953 in Hungary, 1968 in Prague and 1980 in Poland it very quickly became evident that this time the Soviet Union had no interest in suppressing the uprising by force, which increased pressure on the old administration still further. Even the resignation of Erich Honecker as head of state and as General Secretary of the SED and the

promise of "change" from his successor Egon Krenz were
unable to bring to a halt the process of disintegration,
and the Council of Ministers and the SED Politburo re-
signed en bloc.

The peaceful revolution: The "gentle revolution" in the GDR seemed to paralyze the state authorities.
On the evening of November 9, 1989 Günter Schabowski,
a member of the SED Politburo in Berlin announced new,
less restrictive travel regulations that kindled enormous
expectations on the part of GDR citizens and prompted
the opening of the border crossings in Berlin.

With the Berlin Wall to all intents and purposes
now down, the streets leading to the border and the Kurfürstendamm in West Berlin witnessed scenes of inde-
scribable joy during the night. The Lord Mayor of West
Berlin, Walter Momper, summed up the atmosphere
throughout Germany at the time when he said: "At the
moment, we Germans are the happiest people on earth."

The peaceful upheaval in the GDR now provided
an opportunity for what people had aspired to for

People on the Berlin Wall

1989: Helmut Kohl in Dresden.

decades, although many had given it up as a lost cause, namely the reunification of Germany. On November 28, 1989 Chancellor Kohl presented a ten-point program outlining a path to a confederation: a reunified Germany that included current economic aid, a fundamental change in the political and economic system, a contractual community and confederal structures. The opposition agreed with this point of view, but to the people in the GDR who had taken part in the demonstrations and protest actions it came across as too long-winded.

The chants on the streets of "We are the people" had long since become "We are one people". On January 15, 1990 a total of 150,000 people gathered in Leipzig chanting the slogan "Germany - A United Mother Country". The civil rights movement distrusted the new government headed by Hans Modrow. By the week, citizens became increasingly drawn to the West and the process of destabilization in the GDR accelerated rapidly.

Free elections in the GDR: On March 18, 1990 the citizens of the GDR were able to vote in free elections for the first time in 40 years. The CDU and Demokratisch-er Aufbruch (Democratic Renewal) pulled 41.7% of the votes, the SPD 21.9%, the Deutsche Soziale Union (German Social Union) 6.3% and the liberals 5.9%. The SED, which until then had been all-powerful and had renamed itself Partei des Demokratischen Sozialismus (Party of Democratic Socialism) received 16.45% of votes cast. It was essentially a vote in favor of speedier reunification. Lothar de Mazière headed a coalition of CDU, DSU, DA, SPD and FDP – and the Kohl government agreed a timetable with him for monetary, economic and social union with effect from July 1, 1990. There was no longer an economic basis for the GDR to continue on its own as an independent state. In August 1990, the Volkskammer of the GDR (the parliament) resolved to push for the fastest possible accession to the territory that came under the ambit of the Basic Law of the Federal Republic of Germany. The Unification Treaty of August 31 designated that the five newly formed federal states – Brandenburg, Mecklenburg-Western Pomerania, Saxony, Saxony-Anhalt and Thuringia – become states of the Federal Republic of Germany.

In Moscow, on September 12, 1990 the foreign ministers of the Federal Republic of Germany, the GDR, the Soviet Union, Great Britain and France signed the "Treaty on the final Provisions with respect to Germany" the "Two-plus-Four-Treaty" as it became known. On October 2-3, 1990 it was welcomed in a communiqué by the foreign ministers of the OSCE countries convening in New York. The GDR formally ceased to exist on October 3, 1990. The sovereign unity of Germany had been re-established.

The "Berlin Republic": Following the reunification of Germany, the German Bundestag resolved on June 20, 1991 by 337 to 320 votes to move the seat of government from Bonn to Berlin. The "core of government functions" was established in Berlin, and on January 31, 1994 President von Weizsäcker moved his primary seat of residence to that city. In 1996, the Bundesrat likewise decided to move there. Following extensive alterations to existing buildings and the construction of a host of new ones to accommodate the Bundestag, Bundesrat and governmental buildings, the final relocation took place in the summer of 1999. Six ministries remained in Bonn and at the same time several government authorities were moved there. On May 2, 2001 the Chancellor was presented with the keys to the newly constructed Federal Chancellor's Office on the Spreebogen opposite the Reichstag. All in all, the move to Berlin by parliament and government has injected new life into the German capital.

Berlin's Reichstag building

The State, the Legal System and the Citizens

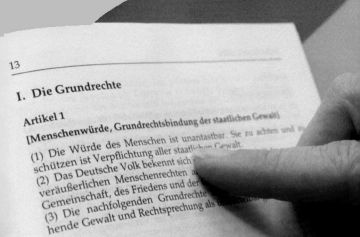

I. Die Grundrechte

Artikel 1
[Menschenwürde, Grundrechtsbindung der staatlichen Gewalt]

(1) Die Würde des Menschen ist unantastbar. Sie zu achten und zu schützen ist Verpflichtung aller staatlichen Gewalt.

(2) Das Deutsche Volk bekennt sich darum zu unverletzlichen und unveräußerlichen Menschenrechten als Grundlage jeder menschlichen Gemeinschaft, des Friedens und der Gerechtigkeit in der Welt.

(3) Die nachfolgenden Grundrechte binden Gesetzgebung, vollziehende Gewalt und Rechtsprechung als unmittelbar geltendes Recht.

Artikel 2 [Freiheit der Person]

Article 1 of the Basic Law

Structure of the state, the constitution and the legal system

The Federal Republic of Germany is a democratic and socially responsible federal country. The nationwide constitutional order of the Basic Law is expressed in the country's constitutional bodies, in the country's federalism, in the legal order and in the electoral system. These determine not only everyday political routine, but also the lives of the people in Germany.

German Coat of Arms

German Flag

The Basic Law

Post-War Germany has developed into the freest and most reliable state that has ever existed on German soil. The constitution, the Basic Law, has made a fundamental contribution to this. On the one hand, it provides stability while, on the other, it offers scope for adaptation. It guarantees the individual extensive personal liberties and rights of freedom as well as social security.

The Basic Law has been accepted by citizens of Germany to a far greater extent than any other German constitution before it. It bears remarking here that the constitution was originally designed as a provisional arrangement, which is why it was only called "Basic Law". Drawn up in 1949, its aim was to provide public life with a new, free and democratic order "for a transitional period". At the very outset, namely in the preamble, the German people were called on "to put the finishing touches to the unity and freedom of Germany in free self-determination." In other words, the intention was for the country, divided into a western and an eastern section, to again reunite as soon as possible and then give itself a joint free democratic constitution.

The Basic Law

Parliamentary Council: The constitution was drawn up by the Parliamentary Council, whose members had been delegated by the existing freely-elected parliaments of the individual federal states. There were 27 delegates each from the Social Democratic Party (SPD) and the Christian Democratic Union/Christian Socialist Union (CDU/CSU), five from the Free Democratic Party (FDP) and two from each of the following parties: the German Party, the Center Party and the Communists. All brought their direct experience of the totalitarian Nazi regime to bear, and took their cue from what they had learned. Accordingly, at many points in the constitution it is quite obvious that its authors were at pains to avoid the shortcomings of the Weimar Republic constitution, creating instead a state with clearly demarcated responsibilities. After extensive deliberations in committees and at general assemblies of all members, the Parliamentary Council, under the chairmanship of Konrad Adenauer, passed the Basic Law, which was then proclaimed on May 23, 1949 after being accepted by the local state governments (Landtage). At this point it came into effect. This is why May 23 is German Constitution Day.

The Basic Law's call for reunification was implemented in 1990. On the basis of the unification treaty of August 31, 1990, which regulated the German Democratic Republic's (GDR) accession to the territory of the Federal Republic of Germany governed by the Basic Law, the preamble to and the concluding article of the Basic Law were rewritten. The new text now documents that upon the GDR's accession, on October 3, 1990, Germany achieved unity.

Basic rights: The first item in the Basic Law is an enumeration of basic rights, expressing the state's commitment to respecting and protecting human dignity, along with the right of every single person to self-fulfillment. This affords comprehensive protection against unlawful interference in personal matters by the state. Both

Ei - nig - keit und Recht und Frei - heit
Da - nach lasst uns al - le stre - ben

für das deut - sche Va - ter - land!
brü - der - lich mit Herz und Hand!

Ei - nig - keit und Recht und Frei - heit

sind des Glü - ckes Un - ter - pfand.

Blüh im Glan - ze die - ses Glü - ckes,

blü - he, deut - sches Va - ter - land!

The German National Anthem

Germans and foreigners can rely in equal measures on the right to self-fulfillment. The classical freedoms listed in the Basic Law include freedom of belief and conscience, right of asylum, freedom of expression including freedom of art and scholarship, freedom of the press and the guarantee of property. Others are freedom of assembly, freedom of association, the right to form coalitions, the confidentiality of letters, the post and telecommunications, freedom of movement, freedom in the choice of profession, protection from forced labor, the inviolability of the home and the right of conscientious objection.

Alongside these civil liberties there are rights of equality. The Basic Law expresses the general principal that all persons are equal before the law by providing that no one may be discriminated against or given preferential treatment on the grounds of his or her sex, birth, race, language, national or social origins, faith, religious persuasion or political opinions. Nor may anybody be discriminated against because of disability. Equal rights for men and women are also expressly stipulated. Finally, the constitution guarantees all Germans equal eligibility for public office. As part of these basic rights, marriage and the family are placed under the especial protection of the national order.

The fundamental essence of all these basic rights is inviolable and they are directly applicable as law. This is one of the most important reforms represented by the Basic Law compared to earlier German constitutions. Today, all three pillars of the state, namely the legislative, the executive and the judiciary, are strictly bound to the basic rights. Every citizen has the right to lodge a constitutional complaint with the Federal Constitutional Court if he feels his basic rights have been impaired by decisions made by or actions performed by the state and has appealed to the appropriate courts without success.

By acceding to the European Convention for the Protection of Human Rights and Basic Freedoms and by ratifying the United Nations' international covenants on human rights, the Federal Republic of Germany is subject to international monitoring of human rights. Any individual may direct a complaint to the permanent European Court of Human Rights regarding the infringement of human rights.

System of government: In accordance with the Basic Law, the Federal Republic of Germany is a democratic and social federal state. It is also a constitutional state, and its role is to guarantee justice and security on the basis of law, as well as controlling the activities of the state by means of laws and rights. Germany consists of 16 federal states with their own sovereignty as regards legislation, administration and jurisprudence. This democratic state order is based on the principle of popular sovereignty. The constitution says that all public authority proceeds from the people. Here, the Basic Law assumes that the state is based on an indirect form of representative democracy with elements of direct democracy. For example, the Federal President and the Federal Chancellor are elected indirectly. Bundestag (Lower Chamber of Parliament) elections combine majority elections and proportional representation. Unlike the constitutions of some countries, the Basic Law uses forms of direct democracy such as plebiscites or referenda in the event of state boundaries requiring modification.

The Constitutional bodies

Federal President: Head of state of the Federal Republic
of Germany is the Federal President. He is elected by the
Federal Convention, a constitutional body which convenes for this purpose only. It consists of the members of
the Bundestag and an equal number of persons elected
by the state parliaments according to the principles of
proportional representation. Repeatedly, these latter
members include eminent personalities who are not
members of a state parliament. The Federal President is
elected by the Federal Convention by majority vote for a
five-year term of office. He may be re-elected for one period of office only.

The Federal President has largely representative
functions and acts as a mediator: as a neutral power and
defender of the constitution. He concludes treaties with
foreign states on behalf of the government; he accredits

and receives the ambassadors. The Federal President appoints and dismisses federal judges, federal civil servants, commissioned and non-commissioned officers of the armed forces. He can pardon convicted criminals on behalf of the government; he ensures laws have arisen in line with due constitutional process and arranges for them to be published in the Federal Law Gazette. The Federal President proposes a candidate for the office of Chancellor to the Bundestag (taking account of the majority situation in parliament) and appoints the latter after the relevant elections. In response to suggestions from the Federal Chancellor he appoints and dismisses the federal ministers.

The Federal President personifies the country's political unity in a special way. He possesses a neutral, mediating authority which extends beyond the confines of all party politics, and is expected to express his own personal opinions on central political and social questions. In this way, the Federal President can set standards for the public's political and moral guidance.

The Bundestag: The German Bundestag is the parliamentary assembly representing the German people. It is elected by the people every four years. It may only be dissolved prematurely under exceptional circumstance, the final decision lying with the President. The Bundestag's main functions are to pass laws, to elect the Federal Chancellor and to keep check on the government. The plenum of the Bundestag is the scene of great parliamentary debates, especially over crucial issues concerning domestic and foreign policy.

It is in the parliamentary committees, whose meetings are not usually open to the public, that the extensive preparatory work for all legislation is undertaken. Here it is a question of bringing political intentions into line with the detailed knowledge of experts – if necessary, after consulting competent specialists. It is likewise in the committees that parliament scrutinizes and controls govern-

The German Federal Presidents

Theodor Heuss (FDP)
1949–1959

Heinrich Lübke (CDU)
1959–1969

Gustav Heinemann
(SPD) 1969–1974

Walter Scheel (FDP)
1974–1979

Karl Carstens (CDU)
1979–1984

Richard v. Weizsäcker
(CDU) 1984–1994

Roman Herzog (CDU)
1994–1999

Johannes Rau (SPD)
since 1999

The German Federal Chancellors

Konrad Adenauer (CDU)
1949–1963

Ludwig Erhard (CDU)
1963–1966

Kurt Georg Kiesinger
(CDU) 1966–1969

Willy Brandt (SPD)
1969–1974

Helmut Schmidt (SPD)
1974–1982

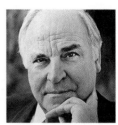

Helmut Kohl (CDU)
1982–1998

Gerhard Schröder (SPD)
since 1998

ment activities. The bodies in question range from the Committee on Foreign Affairs to the Budget Committee. The latter is particularly important because it represents parliament's authority over the budget. Anyone may directly address requests and complaints to the Petitions Committee of the German Bundestag.

Law enactment: From 1949 through 2002 more than 9,200 bills were brought before parliament and more than 5,640 enacted. Most of these were amendments to existing laws. Most bills are initiated by the Federal Government, a smaller proportion come from members of the Bundestag or from the Bundesrat (the Upper Chamber). The bills receive three readings and are generally referred to the appropriate committee for expert advice after the first reading. The final vote is taken after the third reading. With the exception of amendments to the constitution, a bill is passed if it receives a majority of the votes cast. The Basic Law distinguishes between simple laws and those requiring additional approval. However, the Bundesrat's scope for influencing even simple leg-

Allocation of seats in the Bundestag

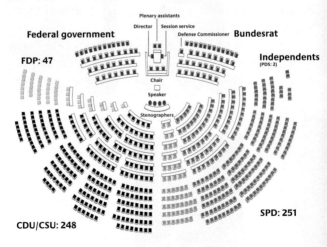

Plenary assistants
Director | Session service
Defense Commissioner
Federal government   **Bundesrat**

FDP: 47   **Independents** (PDS: 2)

Chair
Speaker
Stenographers

CDU/CSU: 248   **SPD: 251**

603 Members of Parliamant   **B'90/Die Grünen: 55**

The German Bundestag

islation is considerable. The Bundesrat has a right of initiative, it can appeal to the Mediation Committee and can veto any law passed by the Bundestag. In particular, approval is required for any laws that affect the fundamental interests of the states, for example, if they encroach upon the individual states' sovereignty or affect their finances. The Bundesrat's approval is also required in the case of amendments to the constitution and if the federal structure of government is affected. A two-thirds majority in both the Bundestag and the Bundesrat is required for any changes to the constitution.

Members of the German Bundestag: The members of the German Bundestag are elected in general, direct, free, equal and secret elections. They are representatives of the entire nation; they are not bound by any specific mandates and only by their consciences. Accordingly, if a member is expelled from his party or decides to resign from it, he retains his seat in the Bundestag. The relative strengths of parliamentary groups are determined in accordance with party membership, and are dependent on a particular party having won a minimum number of seats. The relative strengths of the parliamentary groups determine the numerical composition of the parliamentary committees.

Traditionally, the President of the Bundestag is elected from the ranks of the strongest parliamentary group. He chairs plenary sessions and ensures that parliamentary order is maintained.

The Bundesrat: The Bundesrat represents the 16 federal states and embodies the federal element of the federal state. It consists of members of the state parliaments. Each state has between three and six votes, depending on the size of the population. In the Bundesrat, the federal states are able to participate in legislation and governmental administration. The Bundesrat is not the organ of the individual states but a federal body that exercises exclusively federal powers.

If the political constellations in central and local state government should differ, the Bundesrat can act as a political counterweight and thus as the instrument of the opposition without inciting rebuke for obstructing the democratic process.

The Bundesrat elects its president from the various states for a one-year term following a fixed rotation schedule. The President of the Bundesrat exercises the

Seat allocation in the Bundesrat

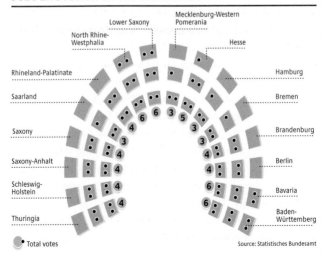

Lower Saxony

North Rhine-Westphalia

Mecklenburg-Western Pomerania

Hesse

Rhineland-Palatinate

Hamburg

Saarland

Bremen

Saxony

Brandenburg

Saxony-Anhalt

Berlin

Schleswig-Holstein

Bavaria

Thuringia

Baden-Württemberg

Total votes

Source: Statistisches Bundesamt

Bundesrat

powers of the Federal President in the event of the latter's indisposition.

The Federal Government: The Federal Chancellor and the federal ministers together form the Federal Government, the Federal Cabinet. The Federal Chancellor occupies an independent, elevated position within the Federal Government and vis-à-vis the federal ministers. He is head of the Federal Cabinet, he alone is entitled to choose the Cabinet. He selects his ministers and makes binding proposals to the Federal President regarding their appointment or dismissal. The Chancellor also decides upon the number of ministers and determines their responsibilities.

The main reason for the Chancellor's strong position is the fact that it is he who lays down the guidelines of government policy. The federal ministers run their departments independently, but within the framework of these guidelines. In political practice, in a coalition government the Chancellor must also take into account agreements reached with the other party in the coalition and he must convince the majority parties in parliament with regard to his policies.

The Federal Chancellor is the only member of the Cabinet elected by parliament and consequently it is he

The Federal President and the Cabinet

who is, in the first instance, accountable to the latter. However, so are the federal ministers, albeit indirectly.

The Bundestag can only express its lack of confidence in the Federal Chancellor by electing a successor by majority vote ("constructive vote of no confidence"). The Federal Chancellor can ask parliament to pass a vote of confidence. If this is refused him, he can ask the Federal President to dissolve parliament.

This procedure was introduced by the authors of the Basic Law in deliberate contrast to the Weimar constitution. Its purpose is to prevent opposition groups who agree only in their rejection of the government but not as regards an alternative program from overthrowing the government. Instead, if the Bundestag proclaims a vote of no confidence in the Chancellor it must, at the same time, elect a successor by majority vote. To date there have been two attempts to bring down the Chancellor with the help of the constructive vote of no confidence, but only one was successful. That was in October 1982 when, after a no confidence motion against Federal Chancellor Helmut Schmidt, Helmut Kohl was elected Federal Chancellor in his place.

The Federal Constitutional Court: The Federal Constitutional Court guards over adherence to the Basic

The Second Panel of the Federal Constitutional Court

Law. After the bitter experiences of the years between 1930 (the death throes of the Weimar Republic) and 1945, the authors of the Basic Law were determined to control the state's political powers. Accordingly, the Parliamentary Council embedded the Federal Constitutional Court, with its extensive scope of jurisdiction, in the Basic Law.

Only the Federal Constitutional Court is empowered to determine whether a particular party is a threat to the free and democratic constitutional order and is thus unconstitutional. In such cases, it orders the dissolution of the party. This indicates just how important the Federal Constitutional Court is in making certain the constitutional rules and regulations in force are adhered to and a stable situation maintained.

The Federal Constitutional Court only acts in response to petitions. Every citizen has the right to lodge a constitutional complaint if he feels that the state has infringed his basic rights. As a general rule, however, he must previously have appealed to the courts responsible and have been turned down by them.

The court also rules on disputes between central government and the states or between individual federal institutions. It checks whether federal and state laws can be reconciled with the Basic Law. If it declares a law to be null and void, the latter may no longer be applied. The Federal Constitutional Court can, for example, act in such cases if appealed to by certain authorities such as the Federal Government, the state governments, at least one third of the members of the Bundestag or by lower courts. To date, the Federal Constitutional Court has passed down rulings in over 141,000 cases. Approximately 125,000 related to constitutional complaints, but only about 3,360 of these were upheld (status as at December 31, 2002).

Repeatedly, the Court has concerned itself with matters of great significance as regards domestic or international policy and of considerable interest to the public. For example, the judges once ruled on whether it was in line with the constitution to deploy German soldiers out-of-area or whether the fundamental protection of life can be reconciled with the rulings under German criminal law on abortion. Independent of their political persuasions, the Federal Governments must bow to the decisions of the judges in Karlsruhe.

Domiciled in the city of Karlsruhe in Baden-Württemburg, the Federal Constitutional Court consists of two panels, each with eight judges, half of whom are elected by the Bundestag, and half by the Bundesrat. Each judge serves for 12 years and may not be reelected.

Information

www.bundespraesident.de
www.bundestag.de
www.bundesrat.de
www.bundesregierung.de
www.bund.de
www.bverfg.de

Parties and elections

A modern democracy cannot function without competing political parties. Elected for a specific term, the candidates these parties put forward either assume political leadership or keep a check on the government. The Basic Law allocates the parties a decisive role in shaping politics by decreeing in article 21: "The parties shall help to form the political will of the people."

The parties: Of the 36 parties that sought election to the first Bundestag in 1949 only six parties made it into parliament. Today there are five parties represented in the Bundestag, and one independent member. This concentration of parties is primarily the result of a debarring clause which stipulates that only parties which gain at least five percent of the valid second votes or at least three constituency seats can be represented in parliament (the "five percent hurdle"). The aim of this ruling was to avoid tiny splinter parties from entering parliament after the experiences of the Weimar republic and to allow for the kind of majorities that would make government possible.

Following the Bundestag elections in September 2002 the following five parties have been represented in the Bundestag: the Christian Democratic Union of Germany (CDU), the Social Democratic Party of Germany (SPD), the Free Democratic Party (FDP), the Christian Social Union (CSU) and Alliance 90/The Greens. The CDU has no party association in Bavaria, while the CSU puts up candidates for election in Bavaria only. In the Bundestag, however, the CDU and CSU have a joint parliamentary party.

The SPD, CDU, CSU and FDP were formed in the western states between 1945 and 1947. The SPD was a re-creation of the mainly labor-oriented party of the same name that had been banned in 1933. The other parties were completely new. Unlike the Catholic Center Party in the Weimar Republic, the CDU and CSU were aimed at both the Christian creeds. The FDP followed on in the tradition of German liberalism.

"The Greens" party was established at national level in 1979. In 1993, it merged with "Alliance 90", which put up candidates in the eastern states. The "Party of Democratic Socialism" (PDS), which was established when the Berlin Wall came down, is the successor to the former "Socialist Unity Party of Germany" (SED), the party of state in the former German Democratic Republic.

Party financing: The political parties running costs and their election campaign expenses are covered by contributions from party members, the income from party assets, donations, and state subsidies. The parties receive a "lump sum for election campaigns", whereby the amount depends on the number of votes the party in question received in the last European, Bundestag or state elections respectively.

The right to vote: Elections for all German parliaments are general, direct, free, equal and secret. Any German who is 18 years of age or older is entitled to vote. Upon fulfillment of certain conditions, Germans living

SPD

Party chairman: Gerhard Schröder
Membership: 734.693
www.spd.de

CDU

Party chairperson: Angela Merkel
Membership: 616.722
www.cdu.de

CSU

Party chairman: Edmund Stoiber
Membership: 181.021
www.csu.de

FDP
Die Liberalen

Party chairman: Guido Westerwelle
Membership: 62.721
www.liberale.de

BÜNDNIS 90 DIE GRÜNEN

Party chairpersons:
Reinhard Bütikofer, Angelika Beer
Membership: 46.631
www.gruene.de

abroad can also vote in elections ("active voting entitle-ment"). In principle, anybody who has possessed German nationality for at least one year is eligible to stand for election as long as he or she has reached the age of 18 on the day on which the election is held and has neither been disenfranchised nor lost the eligibility to stand for election or hold public office as a result of a ruling by a judge ("passive voting entitlement"). As a rule, the election candidates are nominated by their parties; how-ever, individuals with no party affiliation may also run for office.

Electoral system: Elections for the German Bun-destag are based on a combination of majority vote and proportional representation. Each enfranchised citizen has two votes, the first of which is given to a candidate in his constituency. The successful candidate is elected ac-cording to a relative majority vote, i.e., on a first-past-the post basis. The second vote is cast for a list of candidates for a particular party, with the parties in all states listing their candidates at state level in a particular order. Both the first and the second votes are then taken into account when determining election results. The Bundestag is made up of the seats that have been won directly in the 299 constituencies plus a further 299 seats where the members have been elected via the state lists.

In the polling booth

What basically determines the distribution of seats in the Bundestag is the balance of power between the parties as expressed in the results of the second vote in every individual state. But if one party in one state has more successful candidates from the first vote than its proportion of second votes would justify, then every directly elected member still maintains his seat. This party then has a number of "overhang" seats in this state. This is why the 15th German Bundestag elected in 2002 has a total of 603 instead of 598 seats.

The object of having the electorate vote for state lists is to ensure that the strengths of all parties in parliament reflect their share of the votes obtained. At the same time, the direct constituency vote gives people the opportunity to opt for a particular candidate. As a rule, the people take a keen interest in elections. The turnout for Bundestag elections is regularly around 80 percent or higher. However, the turnout for state and local elections fluctuates considerably.

According to a representative election sample, the 2002 Bundestag elections revealed the following trends: men favored the CDU and CSU, whereas women tended to vote for the SPD. The SPD achieved its best result in the second vote category among young female voters between 18 and 24 years of age, and its worst with men aged between 25 and 34. For the CDU and CSU alliance, the best results in the second vote was with men over 60, the worst with women in the youngest age group (between 18 and 24). The Greens and the FDP had more support from the younger voters than from the older age groups.

Information

www.bundeswahlleiter.de

Flags of the federal states in front of the Reichstag building

Federalism and self-government

As its name suggests, the Federal Republic of Germany is a federation consisting of several individual states, (the Länder). The federal nature of the system of government in the Republic is reflected in the fact that these 16 Länder are not mere provinces but states endowed with their own powers. They have their own state constitutions which must be consistent with the principles of a republican, democratic and socially responsible constitutional state as laid out in the Basic Law so that all Germans may enjoy uniform rights and duties and the same living conditions. Within this framework, the Länder largely have a free hand as to what they particularly wish to stress or specify in their individual constitutions.

This form of federalism is one of the sacrosanct principles of the German constitution. But this does not mean that the boundaries of the constituent states may not be changed – as long as the citizens affected by any such changes or amalgamations are in agreement. Provisions have been made in the Basic Law for boundary adjustments within the Federal Republic.

Federalism: The federal system has a long constitutional tradition in Germany. As experience here has shown, a federal structure takes account of regional characteristics and problems much better than would a centralized administration. Similarly to the United States or Switzerland, for example, Germany's federalism combines external unity with internal diversity. Federalism is a much better way of preserving regional diversity and makes it easier for the citizens in the individual regions to identify with the political administration and geography of their local environment.

Distributing authority between central and local state government is also a fundamental element in the system of sharing and balancing power. This includes involving the states in political decision-making at central, federal level, where they are involved in government through the Bundesrat. Furthermore, the federal system opens up the opportunity for competition between the states and for experiments on a smaller scale. A single state can, for instance, try out innovative methods in education which may serve as a model for nationwide reform.

The Bundesrat in session in Berlin

Culture falls under the ambit of the individual states:
Dance theater in Wuppertal...

Subsidiarity: The constitution emphasizes the core idea behind federalism, which also includes the principle of subsidiarity. Accordingly, matters should only be submitted to the next highest authority if the previous one is not as well equipped to handle them. This means that there is a progressive scale of authority, extending upwards from each individual, via his family, his neighborhood, his district and town or village, right through to the state and central government, and continuing on into the European Union and the United Nations.

Legislation: In the case of federal legislation, this principle is stated in article 70 of the constitution. Accordingly, the states have the right to enact legislation as long as the Basic Law itself does not empower central government to do so. Consequently, in principle, federal legislation is in the hands of the individual states – unless it is expressly stated that responsibility at the federal government level appears more appropriate. For this reason, responsibility for legislation is divided into three categories, name-

... the Semper opera in Dresden

ly exclusive, concurrent and framework legislation at federal level. Areas of legislation that fall exclusively within the purview of the Federal government, for example, are foreign affairs, defense, monetary matters, aviation and some areas of taxation.

In the case of concurrent legislation, the states have the right to pass their own laws on matters not governed by federal law. Simultaneously, in such cases, the Federal government may only legislate here if this is in the common interest in order to ensure equal living conditions for all or to maintain a uniform legal or economic situation. Areas which fall into the category of concurrent legislation include, amongst others, civil and criminal law, commercial law and nuclear energy, labor and land law, as well as the laws concerning aliens, housing, shipping, road transport, refuse disposal, air pollution and noise abatement. Since, in practice, the constitution has shown that uniform laws are necessary for these matters, the states have practically ceased to have any jurisdiction in these areas.

There are other areas which fall, in the first instance, under the jurisdiction of the states, but where the Federal government can issue framework regulations. This applies, for instance, to higher education, nature conservation, landscape management, regional planning and water management. There are also a number of supra-regional tasks which, though not mentioned in the Basic Law, are jointly planned, regulated and financed by the Federal government and the individual states. These were incorporated in the Basic Law in 1969 as "joint responsibilities" and cover the construction of new higher education institutions and the extension of existing ones, the improvement of regional economic structures, agrarian structures and coastal protection.

Administration: Direct federal administration is basically limited to the Foreign Service, the labor offices, customs, the Federal Border Guard and the Federal Armed Forces. Most administrative tasks are dealt with by the states independently. The Federal government's scope is basically limited to the Federal Constitutional Court and the supreme courts. These courts ensure uniform in-

The state parliament in Düsseldorf

terpretation of the law. All other courts come under the jurisdiction of the individual states.

The individual states are responsible for those areas of legislation not covered by the Federal government or which the Basic Law does not place within the ambit of the Federal government. Thus, they enact legislation on education and cultural policy almost in its entirety, as a manifestation of their "cultural sovereignty". They are also in charge of local authority government and police law.

The real strength of the states lies in their administrative functions and in their participation in the legislative process at federal level through the Bundesrat. The states are responsible for all internal administration and their bureaucracy actually implements most federal laws and regulations. State administration performs a threefold task: it handles matters that fall exclusively within its jurisdiction (such as schools, police and regional planning). It implements federal law in its own right and on its own responsibility (for example, the laws on the planning of building projects, trade and industry and environmental protection). And finally, it implements federal law on behalf of the federal government (for instance: construction of national highways, promotion of youth training). Thus, in constitutional practice, in the course of its development the Federal Republic has become a state where most legislation is enacted centrally, whereas the bulk of administration is conducted at the state level.

Local self-government: Local self-government also has a long tradition in Germany. It is an expression of civic liberty and can be traced back to the privileges of the free towns in the Middle Ages, when civic rights freed people from the bonds of feudal serfdom (which explains the origins of the German saying "town air makes people free"). In modern times, local self-government has primarily been linked with the reforms initiated by Baron von Stein, in particular the Prussian Municipal Code of 1808.

The Basic Law follows on in this tradition, expressly guaranteeing local self-government in towns, municipalities and counties. The latter accordingly have the right to regulate all the affairs of the local community independently within the framework of the law. All towns, municipalities and counties must have a democratic structure. Municipal law falls within the ambit of the states. For historical reasons, municipal constitutions differ from state to state, but in practice the administrative system is by and large the same in all states. In particular, self-government embraces local transport, local road construction, electricity, water and gas supply, sewerage and town planning as well as the construction and maintenance of schools, theaters and museums, hospitals, sports facilities and public baths. Other local responsibilities are adult education and youth welfare. The towns and municipalities discharge these duties largely independently and are very much responsible for their own actions. As a rule, any monitoring of self-government by the states is restricted to assessing the legality of theses actions.

Many such measures are beyond the means of smaller towns and municipalities and can be assumed by the next highest level of government, the Kreis, or county. The county, with its democratically elected bodies, is likewise part of the system of local self-government. Larger towns do not belong to a county, and are independent entities.

Local self-government and independence are, however, bound to suffer if the municipalities are unable to finance their programs. Appropriate financing for the municipalities is a repeated subject of public debate. Local authorities raise their own taxes and levies. These include real estate tax and trade tax. They are also entitled to raise local excise duties and consumption taxes. However, this revenue does not suffice to cover their financial needs. For this reason the municipalities receive, for example, a proportion of the revenue from income taxes

Petra Roth, President of the Standing Conference of German Cities

and value-added tax from the federal and state governments. They also receive allocations under the financial equalization arrangement which applies to every state. Furthermore, the municipalities charge fees for certain services.

Local self-government gives citizens an opportunity to become involved and exert a controlling influence. They can talk to elected councilors at town meetings, inspect budget estimates or discuss new building projects. The towns and municipalities are the smallest units in the political system. They need to thrive and develop in order to safeguard freedom and democracy within the state and society.

Information
www.staedtetag.de

The legal system

The law of the Federal Republic of Germany applies to virtually all aspects of life; as a result, legislation today consists of adjustments and amendments to existing laws to take social developments into account and to cope with social problems. Germany's legal system has been shaped by constitutional law but is also influenced by the law of the European Union and by international law. The body of federal laws now encompasses approximately 1,900 acts and 3,000 statutory instruments. Laws are passed by the Bundestag, and decrees on the basis of laws are enacted by the Federal government. State law is mainly concerned with such matters as schools and universities, the press, radio and television, as well as the police and local government.

Historically speaking, German law in part goes back to Roman law and in part dates back to numerous other legal sources in the various German regions. A uniform system of private law was created for the entire German Reich for the first time in the 19th century. To this

day, the Civil Code and the Commercial Code have preserved the liberal spirit of those times. Their underlying
principle is the freedom of contract.

Guarantees afforded by the democratic state:
The guarantees afforded by a democratic state are manifest both in substantive and procedural law. Criminal law
proceeds from the constitutional premise stated in the Basic Law that no act is punishable unless declared so by
law before it was committed. Another principle embedded in the constitution is that no one may be punished
more than once for the same offense. Restrictions to personal liberty are only possible on the basis of a formal
law. Only a judge may decide on the admissibility and
length of a prison sentence. Whenever a person is de-
tained without a judicial warrant, the matter must be
brought before a judge without delay.

Although the police are allowed to hold prisoners
in temporary custody, they do not have the authority to
detain anybody longer than the end of the day following
their arrest. Everybody has a right to a court hearing –
this, again, is guaranteed by the constitution and is a fundamental principle of the rule of law. The administration
of justice is entrusted to independent judges who are an-
swerable to the law only. As a matter of principle, these

Judges enter a court room

Local Court in Springe (Lower Saxony)

judges may not be dismissed from office or transferred against their will. Special tribunals are banned.

Nearly all of the foundations of this constitutional legal system in Germany were laid down in judiciary laws in the 19th century. Its major pillars are the Courts Constitution Act, which governs the structure, organization and jurisdiction of the courts, the Code of Civil Procedure and the Code of Criminal Procedure. The Civil Code, which came into force in 1900, and the Codes of Civil and Criminal Procedure were wrested by liberal and democratic forces from the Imperial government in the last 30 years of the 19th century. The German legal codes have also set an example for the legal systems of other countries.

The administration of justice in the Federal Republic has been organized into five categories:

Ordinary courts: These are responsible for criminal matters, civil matters (such as disputes arising from contracts under private law, e.g., sale or rental agreements), matrimonial or family proceedings and non-contentious legal proceedings, for instance, guardianship matters.

There are four levels: the local court (Amtsgericht), the regional court (Landgericht), the higher regional court (Oberlandesgericht) and the Federal Court of Justice (Bundesgerichtshof).

In criminal cases, each of the first three courts may have jurisdiction, depending on the nature and seriousness of the crime. In civil proceedings, either the local or the regional court can be court of first resort. Appeals may be lodged with up to two higher courts. There are two types of appeal. Berufung or an appeal on questions of fact or law represents a second instance both in legal terms and in terms of fact. In other words, it is also possible to bring new facts before the court in this kind of appeal. On the other hand, Revision, or an appeal on questions of law applied in court, only allows petitioners to question in legal terms whether substantive law has been applied correctly and the fundamental procedural regulations have been observed.

Labor courts: These handle disputes under private law arising from employment contracts and between management and labor force as well as matters covered by the Works Constitution Act. Here, there are three levels of appeal. The labor courts decide, for instance, whether an employee has been dismissed fairly or unfairly.

Lawyer and his client in court

Proceedings in the Federal Administrative Court

Administrative courts: The jurisdiction of the administrative courts extends to offer legal protection against all administrative acts and other administrative proceedings. The administrative courts handle all trials under public administrative law that do not fall under the jurisdiction of the social and finance courts or, in exceptional cases, the ordinary courts, or do not involve disputes which fall under constitutional law. Administrative courts also have three levels.

Social and financial courts: The social courts rule on disputes from all areas of social security. They also go to three levels of appeal. With only two levels, the financial courts deal with taxation and related matters.

Separate from the above-mentioned five types of court is the Federal Constitutional Court which rules on constitutional disputes. There are also state constitutional courts which handle disputes regarding the interpretation of the state constitutions. Even in such cases, appeals to the Federal Constitutional Court are not automatically excluded.

Judges: In the Federal Republic of Germany, there are approximately 21,000 professional judges, most of whom are appointed for life. More than three quarters of all judges are assigned to the ordinary courts. In exercising their profession, they are bound only by the spirit and the letter of the law. At local court level, most non-contentious legal proceedings are handled by judicial officers, who are not judges but higher intermediate-level civil servants in the judicial service. In several types of court, lay judges also sit with the professional judges. Their specialist knowledge in certain fields such as labor and welfare matters contributes to allowing the courts to make realistic decisions. They are also a manifestation of every individual citizen's direct responsibility for the administration of justice.

Public prosecutors: Numbering slightly more than 5,000, the public prosecutors are for the most part concerned with criminal proceedings and the enforcement of sentences. When a person is suspected of a crime, it is their duty to lead the investigations with the assistance of the police who, in such cases, are subject to the supervision and factual instruction of the public prosecutor's office. Following completion of investigations, the public prosecutor's office decides whether the proceedings should be terminated or prosecution instigated. In court proceeding they are the prosecuting council.

Attorneys-at-law: In Germany, there are more than 100,000 lawyers, who act as independent counsels and represent clients in all fields of law. By representing their clients in court they make a fundamental contribution to the administration of justice. They have special professional obligations, the fulfillment of which is monitored by bar associations and disciplinary tribunals. All professional judges, public prosecutors and, in principle, all attorneys-at-law must have the qualifications of a judge. In other words, they must successfully have completed the course of studies at law school and the subsequent compulsory course of practical training, each of which ends with a state examination.

Public finance

The task of financial policy is to ensure that the state can fulfill its central functions. One of the prerequisites for this – at least in the medium term – is a balance between revenue and expenditure.

Financial planning: The Promotion of Economic Stability and Growth Act that came into force in 1967 requires that the federal and state governments draw up their budgets in line with the principal economic policy objectives. These objectives are: price stability, a high level of employment, balanced foreign trade and appropriate, steady economic growth (the "magic square", as it is called). Both federal and state government must draw up financial plans for their areas of responsibility in which revenue and expenditure are projected over a period of five years. The purpose of this multi-annual financial planning is to ensure that public revenue and expenditure are commensurate with national economic resources and requirements. Proposed public spending must be listed in order of urgency and then balanced with ways of financing in view of the national economy.

The great importance of public budgets requires close coordination at all levels of the administration. The main body in this process of voluntary cooperation is the Financial Planning Council which was set up in 1968 and consists of representatives of the Federal and state governments, the municipalities and the German Bundesbank. In view of the budgetary stipulations of the Maastricht Treaty, which obligates participating EU countries to limit their national debt and national deficit, the coordinating function of the Financial Planning Council is taking on additional importance. There is also a Business Cycle Council with coordinating and advisory functions.

Taxes: In order to fulfill their functions, the Federal, state and local governments must have the necessary financial resources. The sources of revenue are as varied as are the wide-ranging public responsibilities. The main source of revenue is taxation. Total tax revenue for central, state and local government in 2002 was € 441.7 billion. Federal government's share was 43.5 percent, the state governments' 40.4 percent, the municipalities' 11.9 and the European Union's 4.2 percent.

Tax revenue has to be distributed in accordance with the responsibilities of the various levels of government. Income tax and sales tax are "joint taxes", and the revenue from them is distributed between the Federal and state governments according to specific formulas (taken from the sales tax which is renegotiated at intervals). Part of the revenue from income tax also goes to the municipalities. In return, they have to surrender to the Federal and state government a portion of the revenue they receive from trade tax, which used to be a purely local government tax. The municipalities are entitled to a proportion of the revenue from sales tax. Germany's payments to the budget of the European Union are financed from central government's tax revenue.

Other taxes apply to only one level of administration. The Federal government is entitled to revenue from

Advice at the tax office

insurance tax and all excise taxes with the exception of beer duty (for example mineral oil and tobacco duties). State government receives the revenue from motor vehicle tax, inheritance tax, beer duty, real estate transfer tax, betting and lottery tax as well as fire protection tax.

The municipalities obtain revenue from trade tax (minus the share taken by central and state government), real estate tax and local excise taxes. The single largest section of tax revenue comes from taxes on income including corporation tax, which accounts for 45 percent of the total.

The individual states have very different financial capabilities due to their great differences in size and economic structure. A national financial equalization arrangement helps balance out these differences.

For the average man on the street, the income taxes are particularly important. Employers deduct it from the wages and salaries of all employees, i.e., wage- and salary-earners as well as government employees, and remit it to the tax office. In 2003, the basic rate exempt from income tax remains € 7,235 for single persons and twice this amount for married persons. The rate of tax subsequently increases depending on income from 19.9 percent to 48.5 percent. This upper tax bracket is reached at an annual income of € 55,007, or double the amount in the case of married persons. The tax reform will continue to introduce other, noticeable forms of tax relief for all those in gainful employment until 2005.

Public borrowing: In addition to tax revenue, another means of financing public spending is to borrow money. As in the 1970s and since unification in particular, the federal and state finance ministers have had, despite drastic economies, to resort increasingly to the capital markets. At the end of 2002, the country's total public debt came to € 1.2 trillion, or some € 15,100 per inhabitant. In 2002, new borrowing by central government totaled € 31.9 billion. The medium-term goal of the Federal government's financial policy is to balance the budget without new borrowing requirements.

Limiting the public debt is also in accordance with the commitments Germany has made within the European Union. Through joint efforts to achieve a solid long-term financial position in Euroland, a basis can be created for lasting monetary stability and favorable overall economic conditions.

Federal Audit Office: Auditing of federal and state administration of budgets and public finances has been assigned to the Federal Audit Office and the 16 state audit offices. This is in keeping with Germany's federal structure and the constitutional principle that federal and state governments shall be autonomous and mutually independent in their budget management. The Federal Audit Office, as an independent body of government auditing, examines the accounts of the Federal government to determine whether public finances have been properly and efficiently managed.

Modern civil administration: One of the Federal government's declared objectives is to reduce bureaucracy. The aim is in this way to promote innovation and stimulate investment while relieving the average citizen of superfluous administrative tasks. The salient features of this plan to cut red tape are: to concentrate on a few, particularly important fields of activity, to focus on tangibly lightening the burden of as many citizens and companies as possible and to use modern technology to simplify business processes. The reduction of bureaucracy is seen as a dynamic process that needs to be adapted constantly and reviewed on a regular basis.

On February 26, 2003, the Federal government approved the key points on an agenda to reduce bureaucracy entitled "Promoting Small and Medium-Sized Enterprises – Creating Jobs – Strengthening the Community". The aim is to accordingly abolish unnecessary rules and regulations, thus promoting innovation and stimulating investment. Any new laws and regulations will be designed with our citizens and with economic considerations in mind and, from the outset, new national legislation will avoid an unnecessary burden of bureaucracy. Other key items on the agenda are the optimization of bureaucratic structures and business processes through restructuring and the use of IT as well as the delegation of responsibili-

Data protection for electronic information transmitted to the authorities

ty to other levels. The objective is to ease the load on small to medium-sized enterprises, to modernize federal administration and consolidate the public budgets.

Hand in hand with this focus on reducing bureaucracy, the successful processes of internal modernization under the terms of the "Modern State – Modern Administration" agenda will continue to be applied consistently. The constituent elements of modern administration management are: further improvements in the organizational side to the bureaucracy, the use of elements of business management such as controlling and cost and performance accounting, increased cooperation with private organizations (public private partnerships) and organizational aspects of greater, across-the-board use of new technologies.

With the help of ICT, administrative services can be provided more cost-effectively, rapidly and efficiently. With eGovernment the state and its administration can use the Internet to offer rapid, cost-effective and uncomplicated online services. eGovernment thus simultaneously contributes to a comprehensive modernization of the state and its administration and represents, for Germany, another step on the road to the information society.

Information

www.bundesfinanzministerium.de
www.bmi.bund.de

Pensioners on a park bench

Social security

In the Federal Republic, democracy and the state welfare system are closely interlinked. The fundamental principles of the welfare state are solidarity, on the one hand, and personal responsibility, on the other. In order to realize these principles the state has created a broad-based network of social services. The provisions of the welfare state complement the state's aim to safeguard its citizens' freedom by obligating the state to make a functioning social security system available. As well as the five branches of social insurance (pension, health, long-term care, accident and unemployment insurance) the social network also comprises services financed through taxation such as family benefits and social assistance.

A policy of state welfare really began with the 1883 Health Insurance Act, the 1884 Accident Insurance Act and the 1889 Invalidity and Pension Insurance Act. At the time, this legislation extended to only one fifth of all persons in gainful employment and one tenth of the population, whereas today some 90 percent of the population benefits from the provision of social security.

Pension insurance: The statutory pension insurance scheme is one of the pillars of Germany's social security system and, at the same time, represents the area to which the most public and private financial resources are committed. So that workers will be able to maintain an adequate standard of living after their retirement, a system has been put in place covering some 50 million insured persons and with an annual budget of over € 220 billion. Some 80 percent of persons in the working population belong to the statutory pension insurance scheme.

In 2003, employers and employees both pay one half of 19.5 percent of the latter's gross monthly salary up to a certain income level (€ 5,100 in west Germany and € 4,250 in east Germany). Any amounts over and above this ceiling are exempt from contributions and will not be taken into account when later calculating the size of the relevant pension. The pensions are not accumulated by investing these savings on behalf of the particular person, but are paid from current income from pension insurance by means of an allocation process. The pension scheme also covers expenses for rehabilitation, thus helping to restore the ability of those insured to pursue gainful employment, as well as providing support for people who must undergo vocation retraining for health reasons.

In west Germany, the average old-age pension for men is € 980, and for women € 644. In east Germany, men receive on average of € 1,030 and women € 830.

Since 2002, the statutory pension scheme has been complemented by a state-aided system of old-age provision funded by capital. Its aim is to compensate for the lowering of pension levels projected for the long term and to help to allow pensioners to maintain a living standard more closely resembling that of people still at work. State funding assists people on low to medium-sized incomes and families with children in particular to set up their own voluntary company or private old-age provisions.

The prerequisite for eligibility for a pension payment is having been through a certain "waiting period", i.e., having participated in the scheme for a minimum period of time. The pension is also not normally paid until the person in question has reached his 65th birthday. Persons drawing their pension earlier must expect deductions. Older employees can opt to work part time, i.e., gradually being phased out of employment and into retirement.

Health insurance: Almost everyone living in Germany has health insurance. Some 88 percent belong to a statutory health scheme and around nine percent are privately insured.

Up to a certain level of income (in 2003, € 3,825 gross per month or € 45,900 per annum), all employees are obliged to join one of the over 315 statutory health insurance schemes. Persons earning a higher gross amount than this are free to join a private scheme if they so desire. Subject to certain conditions, the statutory system also covers pensioners, the unemployed, trainees and students.

Employers and employees each pay half of the latter's health insurance contributions. These vary from company to company and in 2002 stood on average at 14 percent of gross earnings. However, there is an upper ceiling for the calculation of contributions. Even very high-income employees do not have to pay health contributions of more than seven percent of € 3,450. The employer pays the same amount. No contributions are payable for members of the family who do not work. From this point of view, employees with families are better off than single employees.

All insured persons have a free choice of panel doctors and dentists. The health insurance company pays the doctor's costs, as well as remedies, drugs, and appliances, hospital treatment and preventative health care. Patients have to pay a contribution towards medicines

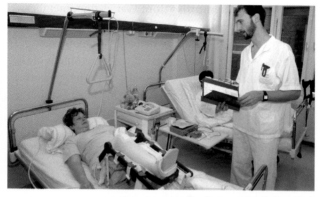

Doctor's round in hospital

and certain services (spectacles, dentures). The treatment of children is exempt from such charges. The health insurance company pays all or part of the cost of curative treatment at a spa. In the event of sickness employees continue to receive their salary or wages from their employer for up to six weeks. Some collective agreements provide for an even longer period. After this the health insurance company provides sickness benefits for up to 78 weeks.

Long-term care insurance: The principle behind this type of insurance is that everybody who has statutory insurance against the risk of illness automatically participates in statutory long-term care insurance. People with private health insurance must take out private long-term care insurance. As a rule, employees and employers each pay half of the long-term care insurance contributions.

At present, some two million people requiring care benefit from this type of insurance in the form of material or monetary support and receive care at home or in institutions. Some two thirds have opted for home care. As well as improving the position of those requiring care and their relations, long-term care insurance has also led to a marked improvement in the care infrastructure.

Social indemnification: War victims, members of the armed forces, persons performing civilian service, victims of violence, victims of damage caused by vaccines, victims of injustice at the hands of the government of the former German Democratic Republic and other persons for whom the community as a whole has a responsibility to provide are entitled to social indemnification benefits in the case of health damage. The pension entitlement varies depending on the severity of the health damage and is indexed to the general trend for wages and salaries. Such persons are also entitled to medical treatment and vocational rehabilitation measures. In the event of death as a result of damage to health, the victim's surviving dependents are entitled to survivors' benefits.

Accident insurance: Financial assistance after accidents at work is provided by the statutory accident insurance scheme. The contributions are paid by employers alone. Self-employed persons can take out voluntary insurance. Benefits can be claimed in the occurrence of an event insured against (accidents at work, occupational disease), leading to injury, illness or death. Accidents on the way to work are also insured. If an insured person sustains accidental injury the scheme bears the costs of treatment and pays injury benefits if, at the same time, the person in question is unable to work. If the insured person's working capacity is seriously diminished or he or she dies as a result of the accident insured against, the scheme pays a pension or a death grant and a pension to surviving dependents. These pensions are regularly adjusted to match changes in income levels. Vocational rehabilitation benefits above all cover vocational retraining measures designed to facilitate the injured person's reintegration into working life.

Safety at work: The aim of comprehensive safety at work provisions is to contribute to preventing work-related accidents, avoid occupational diseases, eliminate work-related health risks and to make work in general a

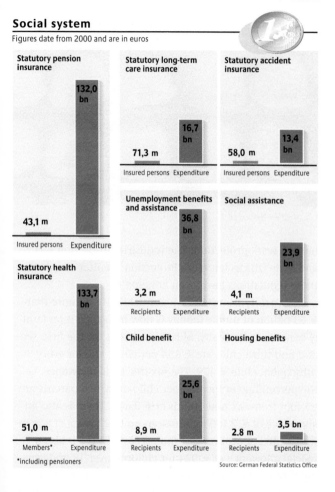

Social system

Figures date from 2000 and are in euros

Statutory pension insurance

132,0 bn

43,1 m

Insured persons   Expenditure

Statutory long-term care insurance

16,7 bn

71,3 m

Insured persons   Expenditure

Statutory accident insurance

13,4 bn

58,0 m

Insured persons   Expenditure

Statutory health insurance

133,7 bn

51,0 m

Members*   Expenditure

*including pensioners

Unemployment benefits and assistance

36,8 bn

3,2 m

Recipients   Expenditure

Child benefit

25,6 bn

8,9 m

Recipients   Expenditure

Social assistance

23,9 bn

4,1 m

Recipients   Expenditure

Housing benefits

3,5 bn

2.8 m

Recipients   Expenditure

Source: German Federal Statistics Office

more humane process. This includes regulation of working hours and special provisions for groups in particular need of protection such as young people and pregnant women. The employer bears the responsibility for the health and safety of his employees. He must make the necessary arrangements, verify their effectiveness and make improvements where necessary. For this, the employer can, depending on the size of his business, appoint a certain number of security experts and work doctors to advise

Protective helmets for work

him on work protection. The Industrial Inspection Boards and State Offices for Work Protection monitor whether these regulations have been adhered to.

Family benefits: An annual figure of more than € 53 billion of public money is now being spent on family benefits in Germany. Monthly benefits for the first, second and third child are € 154 per child, and for every subsequent child € 179. The tax-free child allowance, i.e., the percentage of income per child on which parents are exempt from tax now stands at € 3,648. There is also an allowance of € 2,160 for children up to 27 years of age towards care, education or training costs. There is also a special allowance of € 924 for children over 18 undergoing training but no longer living with their parents. For the first two years of a child's life, child-raising benefits of up to € 307, depending on income, may be disbursed. If the parents only wish these payments to run for one year, they can receive up to € 460. Alongside this financial support, the government is now attempting to make it easier to combine a family with working life. "Part-time work for parents" now means that both mothers and fathers are entitled to work part time, allowing them to spend more time with their child or children. Weekly working hours during the first two years of parenthood are accordingly 30 hours; the "third year" of these special arrangements can be taken until the child in question turns eight.

Particularly noteworthy is a considerable improvement in childcare services. The Federal government is now increasing its share in the joint financing of child benefits by the Federal and state government by over € 510 million annually, so that the individual states have more scope for extending childcare facilities. Provided that they fulfill certain conditions, all working parents can deduct work-related childcare costs from their taxes (see page 359).

Social assistance: In Germany, people who experience financial difficulties from which they are unable to recover independently or through support from the social insurance schemes, for example, are entitled to social assistance. As well as meeting the affected person's immediate living costs, this allows him or her to participate in the life of society. Anchored in the law, this type of assistance is intended to put its recipient back in a position where he is able to manage his life without help as soon as possible.

Social assistance can take the form of either money or material assistance. It consists of help with living costs or help with specific circumstances such as disability, illness or care. At the end of 2001, running payments to meet living costs were being paid to 2.7 million people. 1.5 million people received assistance for special circumstances.

Needs-oriented basic security: This service was first introduced as of January 1, 2003, guaranteeing that the living standards of persons over 65 without adequate incomes are brought up to the level of those receiving social assistance. The same applies to persons over the age of 18 who are not able to earn a living by employment owing to ill health and have no other source of income. As is the case with social assistance, material hardship

Family holiday on the beach

must be proven. However, unlike social assistance, in consideration of the entitled person's age and/or state of health, access to this kind of assistance is less complicated and calculation of benefits has been simplified.

Housing: Having a roof over your head is a basic human requirement. Accordingly, everybody in Germany who does not earn enough for adequate housing is entitled to housing benefits. Allowances to help cover rent or subsidies toward home ownership are dependent on income, the size of the applicant's family and on the relevant rent or house price. At the beginning of 2001, a good 2.8 million people were receiving housing benefits. In 2001, the costs of housing benefits, which are shared equally between central and state government, amounted to € 4.2 billion (see housing, page 380).

The state promotes house or apartment buying, particularly in the case of families and depending on personal income levels. The assistance is provided in the form of grants, cheap loans, tax benefits, and, in the capital-building phase, bonuses for personal savings.

Reform of the social system: Happily, as statistics indicate, in the future, as in the past, life expectancy will continue to rise. The residual life expectancy of a 65-year-old woman will increase from 19.5 years in the year

Application for social assistance

2000 to an estimated 20.8 years in the year 2010, and for men, over the same period, from 15.8 to 17.1 years. Coupled with a low birth rate, this will lead to an unfavorable ratio of working people to pensioners. Like other developed industrial nations, the Federal Republic of Germany is now faced with the twofold task of continuing to guarantee its citizens social security without making exaggerated demands on the capabilities of the working population through overly high taxes and contributions to social security. Consequently, reforms within the social state are inevitable.

Information
www.bmgs.bund.de
www.bmfsfj.de

Police officers in Berlin's government district

Internal security

Maintaining public security and order is one of the most important tasks of government. In the Federal Republic of Germany, this task is shared by the states and Federal government. For the most part, the police come under the jurisdiction of the states, but in certain areas the Basic Law assigns responsibility to the Federal government.

Police: Branches of the police force include the general police force, the criminal police, the emergency police force and the water police. Their duties range from averting dangers to prosecuting crime. Whereas the general police force is mainly concerned with petty crime and minor offenses, the criminal police deal with serious crimes and criminal offenses. In the prosecution of crime, the police are subordinate to the public prosecutor's office in charge of the relevant proceedings. The police have special units, which are deployed mainly in the case of hostage-taking, for protection purposes during special events, and for observation and searches.

Every state maintains organizationally separate emergency police force units within its police force. These are supplied with the necessary control structures and operational equipment by the Federal government.

The emergency police forces are responsible for dealing with exceptional circumstances including dangerous situations in the case of natural disasters or accidents that endanger the territory of more than one state. (art. 35 para. 3, 91 para. 2 of the Basic Law), for assisting other states in dealing with exceptional circumstances including the above-mentioned dangerous situations, as well as for assisting with individual police duties.

The state emergency police forces were fundamentally reformed between 1993 and 1997. They currently number 15,871 law enforcement officers.

Federal Border Guard: The Federal Border Guard (BGS) is a federal branch of the police force. Within the Federal Republic of Germany's internal security system it handles specific policing tasks and answers to the Federal Ministry of the Interior. The tasks performed by the Federal Border Guard include patrolling the borders and the railways and protecting aviation from attacks at most of the Federal Republic's major airports. Its brief as

Federal Border Guard

the border patrol is becoming ever more important with the rise of cross-border criminality on the country's eastern borders (such as smuggling of aliens, car smuggling and drug-trafficking). Since 1998, the Federal Border Guard has had an extended brief allowing it to check people's papers beyond the 30-kilometer zone, on railway stations and at passenger airports in order to prevent illegal immigration.

Furthermore, the BGS also has its own operational emergency forces departments. It also protects specific locations for selected constitutional bodies of the Federal government and the federal ministries. Moreover, it also discharges duties connected with environmental protection and policing shipping on the North Sea and the Baltic as well as being increasingly involved in international peacekeeping police missions abroad. The Federal Border Guard currently has some 38,500 members.

Federal Criminal Police Office: As Germany's central criminal police force, the Federal Criminal Police Office (BKA) is tasked with coordinating crime-fighting on a national and international level, thus ensuring a uniform approach to the problem. The BKA's most important partners in this process are the 16 State Criminal Offices.

The BKA is also the police's central body providing information and news, for police information management and for criminological and technical crime-related research.

Moreover, the Office collects large quantities of important information and evaluates it for the police's crime-fighting operations as well as collating strategic analyses of trends in criminal behavior.

As regards international police cooperation, the BKA has a pivotal function as the national central agency acting as the national counterpart for Interpol and Europol and as a matter of principle it is responsible for international policing to prevent or prosecute major criminal offenses.

The BKA performs policing functions in the prosecution of certain legally defined crimes. These include, for example, crimes relating to internationally organized gun-running, counterfeiting and drug-trafficking when matters need to be investigated abroad, as well as serious crimes against members of constitutional bodies or their guests, investigations against internationally active terrorist organizations and certain cases of computer sabotage. When it undertakes criminal prosecution, the BKA also affords its witnesses the necessary protection.

Furthermore, on request from another department, the BKA can conduct investigations in other areas of criminal activity. In the case of outstanding crimes against internal security in Germany the BKA is entrusted by the Federal Minister of the Interior or by the attorney general with prosecuting the crime. The protection of members of Germany's constitutional bodies is also the job of the BKA. Here, the BKA is assisted by the BGS (Federal Border Guard).

The BKA also comes under the auspices of the Federal Ministry of the Interior and currently employs some 4,800 staff.

Constitution-protection agencies: In order to be able to provide effective protection to the free democratic constitutional order, the federal and state constitutional protection agencies gather information about extremist activities and on other developments which constitute a threat to national security, and evaluate this on behalf of the Federal and state governments, executive authorities and courts. Another field of activity is counterespionage. The Federal Office for the Protection of the Constitution in Cologne reports to the Federal Ministry of the Interior. It collaborates with the state constitution-protection agencies. This agency has no executive police powers; in other words it may not interrogate or arrest anyone. Its activities are subject to close supervision on several levels: by the competent ministers, by the parliaments and the data protection commissioners. These controls are supplemented by the possibility of having individual measures which incriminate a citizen checked by the courts.

Terrorism: As the attacks on September 11, 2001 have shown, international terrorism has now evolved into a worldwide threat. The degree of violence to which terrorists are willing to resort, their logistical networks and the long-term planning that goes into their cross-border methods of attack have clearly demonstrated the dangers. In order to combat international terrorism more effectively, German parliament passed a number of amendments to existing laws. For example, the Federal Office for the Protection of the Constitution was granted the right to monitor activities directed against the peaceful coexistence of different peoples, since such activities spawn a favorable, dangerous seedbed for the spread of terrorism. The office also has the right to gather information on bank accounts and account-holders suspected of extremist undertakings or activities that might endanger security or are connected with secret service work.

In the case of certain serious forms of data network criminality, the Federal Criminal Office can initiate prosecution without having to submit a request to a pub-

Airport baggage checks

lic prosecutor and without receiving instructions from the Federal Minister of the Interior. The Federal Border Guard has clear instructions for the deployment of security forces in German airplanes (flight safety personnel). Changes to the Aliens Act now mean that persons who would endanger the free and democratic constitutional order or the security of the Federal Republic can be refused a visa or a residence permit for Germany. As regards the right of association, the "religious privilege", as it was termed, has been abolished. Religious groups that direct their activities against the constitutional order and come into conflict with penal law or disregard the principle of understanding between peoples can now be prohibited. Additionally, the conditions under which an organization can be banned under the law of association have been expanded: proceedings can now also be initiated against the kind of foreign associations that support violent foreign or terrorist organizations. In the passport and identification card law, the option for storing biometric features on such documents has now been included.

Data protection: Modern communication technologies have eased the workload of many companies and public authorities and are in the process of transforming our society into a global information society. But modern IT also entails risks. Stored data can be put to improper use and fall into the hands of unauthorized persons. Anybody with a sufficient quantity of data has access to a person's private life which must remain inviolable. To pre-empt such an abuse of privacy numerous federal and state laws have been enacted in Germany to protect personal rights.

The staff of departments that process data are required to maintain confidentiality. With few exceptions, people are legally entitled to find out what data concerning them are held by any body which processes data and can demand correction of incorrect data, have any that are disputed blocked or any that have been improperly obtained erased.

On the recommendation of the Federal government the German parliament elects a Federal Commissioner for Data Protection, whose function is to advise the Federal government and the parliament on points of data protection law pertinent to the legislative procedure, monitor the handling of personal data by federal authorities, providers of telecommunications and postal services and make recommendations to these agencies for improving data protection. Any person who feels that his data protection interests have been violated can lodge a complaint with the Federal Commissioner. Every two years, the Commissioner reports to parliament in writing on his work. At the level of state administration, State Commissioners perform this monitoring function. In a number of states it is the State Commissioner's job to monitor data processing by the private sector, in others this function is performed by special supervisory authorities concerned with the legal aspects of data protection.

Environmental protection

Active environmental protection is important for survival.
An increased number of natural disasters have height-
ened public awareness of the fact that only a sustainable
way of living and a sustainable economy have a future.
With this in mind, the protection of natural resources
essential for life is anchored in the Basic Law as an aim of
government. Thus, in accordance with article 20, one of
the present generation's obligations is "responsibility for
future generations." What this means with regard to an
active policy directed at safeguarding the future is that industry and agriculture, town planning and traffic must
handle limited natural resources such as energy, raw materials, land and water with such care that future generations will also be able to enjoy a stable climate, rich flora
and fauna, fertile soil and adequate water supplies.

To achieve this goal, state intervention is just as
important as the personal responsibility of commerce, industry and consumers. Over the past few years, Germany
has set an example and met with international approval
by introducing an ecological tax reform, by opting out of
its atomic energy program, and by switching to greater

The Reicherskreutzer Heide nature reserve

use of regenerative energies, with its impressive CO_2 reduction program and by establishing a recycling-based economy.

At the federal level, the Federal Ministry of the Environment, Nature Conservation and Nuclear Safety is responsible for environmental protection. Falling under its purview are the Federal Environmental Agency, the Federal Office for Nature Conservation and the Federal Office for Radiation Protection. Several of the states, too, have their own ministries for the environment. Cities, counties and municipalities perform important environmental protection functions at local level, too.

Nature conservation: Of great importance for sustainable development as regards nature conservation and the preservation of biological diversity is the international convention signed in 1992 in Rio de Janeiro which has the twofold aim not only of protecting and preserving biological diversity, but also of providing for its sustainable use. One of the foremost tasks of nature conservation is to protect existing natural or near-natural areas, reestablish them where necessary through restoration, link them together to form networks and minimize the impact of pollution.

In Germany, there are some 5,000 nature reserves and some 6,000 landscape protection areas covering around 2.3 percent and 25 percent of the country's total land area respectively. The switch over to ecological agricultural and forestry methods constitutes another important means of securing biodiversity. Consequently, the Federal government seeks to expand the scale of organic farming and other methods with low environmental impact. National and European Union grants will no longer be exclusively linked to productivity but will be linked more to ecological criteria. Germany is also involved in the creation of a pan-European ecological network with the objective, among other things, of making possible genetic interchange between individual conservation areas and is striving to create a network of ecologically valuable areas covering about ten percent of the land mass.

Climate protection: One of the key elements of environmental policy is climate protection. The Federal government will be honoring its international commitment to lowering greenhouse gas emissions as part of the Kyoto protocol. The latter calls for a 21 percent reduction in this kind of emissions between 1990 and the period 2008 – 2012. By the year 2002, a decrease of more than 19 percent had already been achieved. This includes all sources of greenhouse gas emissions – especially CO_2 emissions, which come from energy production, industry, buildings, private households and traffic. The ecological tax reform pursues the aim of encouraging people to use energy economically by gradually raising energy prices

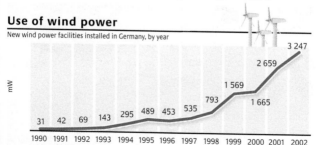

Use of wind power

New wind power facilities installed in Germany, by year

mW

1990	1991	1992	1993	1994	1995	1996	1997	1998	1999	2000	2001	2002
31	42	69	143	295	489	453	535	793	1 569	1 665	2 659	3 247

Source: DEWI, the Federal Wind Energy Association

for all those who cause these emissions. Moreover, under the terms of the ecological financial reform, there are plans to axe subsidies and change regulations that are detrimental to the environment.

The use of regenerative energies and the increased deployment of combined heating and power plants are now being promoted vigorously. These two measures are expected to lead to a decrease in CO_2 emissions by ten million tons. In the fields of private and household energy consumption, special energy-saving regulations will lower the energy requirements of new buildings by another 30 percent compared with the existing standard. Thru 2005, the Federal government will be allocating an additional € 1 billion for this purpose. Another important focus is traffic, where measures such as tax breaks and additional federal funds will be used to promote rail travel and low-energy-consumption cars, in particular.

Keeping the air clean: In Germany, too, the air is polluted, mainly by emissions produced by commerce and industry, road traffic, heating and power stations. Damage to the forests and outdoor monuments manifestly show the extent of environmental pollution.

A comprehensive program has been developed to counteract air pollution. For instance, filters and catalytic converters effectively reduce pollutants that enter the atmosphere from power stations, district heating systems

Environmentally friendly gas turbine

Keeping the air clean

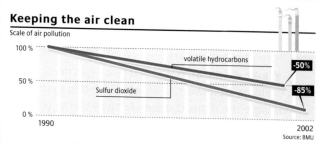

Scale of air pollution

100 %

volatile hydrocarbons   **-50%**

50 %

Sulfur dioxide   **-85%**

0 %

1990

2002

Source: BMU

and car exhausts. Technical regulations have compelled power station operators and industry to swiftly modernize their plant. Indeed, the results are something to be proud of: since 1990 air pollution through sulfur dioxide has fallen by 85 percent and that through volatile hydrocarbons (or PSOs, precursors of surface ozone) has dropped by half. In mid-March 2003 the federal government launched a broad-based national program to further reduce emissions of sulfur dioxide, nitrogen oxides, ammonia and PSOs.

Noise protection: In high-population areas, in particular, noise has become a serious inconvenience to the population. Accordingly, noise abatement is always a firm fixture on the agenda when planning residential areas, traffic networks and industrial installations. Traffic-reduced zones, speed restrictions for vehicles, noise-absorbing paving materials and quieter airplanes help to reduce noise levels. An Ordinance on Noise from Equipment and Machinery dating from September 2002 lists seven different types of machines and sets certain sound levels which may not be exceeded. Included on the list are concrete mixers, hydraulic hammers, concrete mixer trucks, sweeping machines, chainsaws, leaf collecting equipment and lawnmowers. As of 2006, the loudest of these will have to meet even stricter requirements. There are also special regulations regarding sensitive areas and times of day. For example, in purely residential areas, or districts where there are only health resorts and/or hospitals, such equipment may not be used at all on Sundays and public holidays and not after 8 p.m. or before 7 a.m. on working days. Additional restrictions apply to particularly loud equipment, even on working days.

Waste disposal: A good 20 years ago, many people in Germany were worried about suffocating in their own garbage. The refuse tips seemed to be on the verge of overflowing, and there were only a few garbage incineration plants. Spurred on by citizens' initiatives, the politicians began to issue ordinances on the treatment of the various forms of waste, to strictly limit the emissions from garbage incineration plants and to draw up regulations for refuse tips. Billions were invested in environmentally friendly waste disposal.

People soon realized that safe disposal is not enough, as full advantage needed to be taken of existing resources by reprocessing waste material. And what is more, waste avoidance had to be the order of the day. The best way to do this was by making the actual producers of waste material face up to their responsibilities. In 1991, the Federal Ministry for the Environment produced a Packaging Ordinance, anchoring in law the manufacturers' obligation to take back used packaging. The result was the Dual System ("Green Dot") established in 1992. Today, over 36 million tons of sales packaging has been collected separately and passed on for recycling.

Today, the policy on waste in Germany is to avoid the latter wherever possible, to process it in an environmentally sound way, and to dispose of it in an environmentally friendly manner. In 1996, the Closed Substance Cycle and Waste Management Act implemented this with regard to all manufactured and consumer goods. This law establishes the manufacturer's responsibility for his product and accords top priority to the avoidance of waste material. If waste cannot be avoided, then highest priority is given to its reuse in terms of substance or energy (recycling). Only the residual matter which can no longer be used may be disposed of in an environmentally friendly way.

On January 1, 2003, a mandatory deposit on non-reusable bottle packaging came into force. Accordingly, a deposit of 25 cents is payable on mineral water, beer and other fizzy drinks in this kind of packaging, which is refunded upon return of the empty packaging. If the packaging contains more than 1.5 liters, the deposit is 50 cents. There is no deposit on fruit juice, wine, sparkling wine, spirits and milk. The purpose of the deposit is to promote reusable bottle systems and make for a better use of valuable raw materials.

In accordance with the manufacturer's responsibility for his product there are now other ordinances on batteries, used cars and used oil. Among other things, there is also an ordinance on electric and electronic equipment in the pipeline. Moreover, trade and industry have made commitments regarding such items as used paper and left-over building materials.

Rivers and lakes: In recent years, the quality of Germany's water has improved considerably thanks to the introduction of extensive regulations on the discharge of waste water. Some 50 different industry sectors must comply with limits on pollutants and nutrient levels in waste water. Moreover, charges are levied for waste water discharge, which are then used for water protection. This has led to the construction of new sewage treatment facilities and the introduction of industrial processes involving low or zero-level waste water discharge. As a result, the pollution of many rivers such as the Rhine, Main and

Water protection

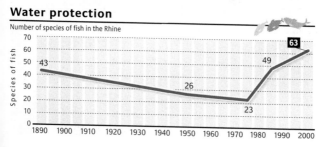

Number of species of fish in the Rhine

Elbe has fallen dramatically and the diversity of the species they contain has improved. The last inventory for 1996 to 2000 revealed that there were once again 63 different types of fish in the Rhine. Between 1951 and 1975, the figure had dropped to only 23 different species. Today, the focus of water protection is on further decreasing water pollution through the discharge of various different substances, especially by agriculture, and on the improvement of the morphology of Germany's waters. Most importantly, this is instrumental in implementing the EU directives on water.

Nuclear power: Given the high risks and the unsolved issue of the disposal of nuclear waste, the Federal government has decided to stop using atomic energy. An agreement has been reached with the energy utilities on discontinuing the use of nuclear power without having to pay compensation (see page 306). There are plans for a single final storage depot for radioactive waste deep inside geological formations by the year 2030. As a matter of principle, the nuclear power station operators must set up temporary storehouses at the power stations or nearby.

Radiation protection: On the basis of the Atomic Energy Act, the Radiation Protection Ordinance and the X-Ray Ordinance regulate the safe handling of ioniz-

Control room in Stade nuclear power station

ing rays. Stringent regulations protect persons, goods and the environment against damage. The key principle is to minimize radiation exposure as much as possible. Accordingly, in an amendment to the X-Ray Ordinance in 2002, the maximum exposure to radiation allowed for persons operating X-ray equipment (particularly in medical treatment and dentistry) was cut to around one fifth of the previous figure. Since 1997, protection has also been provided against non-ionizing radiation ("electrosmog") by an ordinance specifying limits for electromagnetic radiation.

International cooperation: Pollutants do not stop short at national borders, which is why international cooperation is important for environmental protection. Germany supports the process of international environmental and development partnership ushered in Rio de Janeiro in 1992. This led, in September 2002 in Johannesburg, to modest but tangible progress in the harmonization of national environmental protection objectives and to a global commitment by some 190 nations. Germany also supports the institutional strengthening of environmental protection at United Nations level and greater attention to environmental considerations by those engaged in world trade. Detailed agreements exist regarding the environmental sector, mainly with neighboring European countries. The fact that the EU is expanding eastwards offers an opportunity to export the European Union's strict limits to a large neighboring area and thus to cut pollution coming from this direction, too. Consequently, the number of countries that also see sustainability as their political objective will rise.

Organic farmer with chickens

Consumer protection

The first case of BSE in a cow born in Germany in November 2000 badly shook consumer confidence in the safety of foodstuffs, the production methods used in the agricultural and food industries, the ways laws are drafted and in official checks. Many consumers were deeply upset, feeling that they were at the mercy of others and that their health was under direct threat.

The discussions regarding BSE highlighted consumer fears and worries that went far beyond the question of how safe it was to eat beef and there was a vigorous public debate about such topics as the acceptability and quality of food in the globalized markets and modern production methods in the agricultural and food industries.

In view of the heated debate in society about the role of consumer protection and food safety, in January 2001 Federal Chancellor Gerhard Schröder established consumer protection as an independent field of politics, thus laying the foundations for a new political approach to consumer, agricultural and nutrition-related policy-making and ensuring new staff were deployed in this context. Irrespective of the specialist political responsibilities of the other federal departments and those of the states, the establishment of the Federal Ministry for Consumer Protection, Nutrition and Agriculture created a federal ministry with extensive political responsibility for all questions relating to consumer politics.

This new focus on consumer politics by the Federal government is linked to a strengthening of institutional consumer structures. The Federal government is thus expressly stating that consumer interests need to be taken more seriously than was previously the case and that within the framework of the social and ecological market economy the state must play an active part in safeguarding consumer interests.

The objectives of national consumer policy correspond with the main thrust of European consumer policy. These are:

- Protection of consumer health and safety
- Protection of the economic interests of the consumer
- Consumer information and education
- Stronger representation of the rights of the consumer

Information

www.verbraucherministerium.de

Joschka Fischer and Kofi Annan

Foreign policy

Priorities

In the early days of the 21st century Germany is actively engaged in securing peace, safeguarding human rights and combating terrorism around the world. Germany supports a system of global cooperative security within the framework of the United Nations, and in light of the historic expansion of the EU through 2004 now finds itself at the center of a union of neighbors closely interconnected by friendship as well as political and economic ties. The transatlantic relationship remains one of the cornerstones of German foreign policy. Germany will benefit considerably from the enlargement of NATO and the related extension of the zone of stability. Germany's policy towards Russia contributes to stronger European integration and helps secure stability and peace in the world in a spirit of cooperation. Development aid policy remains a core element of German foreign relations and part of the Federal government's political commitment to peace and cooperation based on partnership.

Information

www.auswaertiges-amt.de

Germany in Europe

When the EU is expanded to include 25 member states in
2004, the repercussions of the Cold War and Europe's division into two camps will have finally been eliminated.
Today, the advantages of European unification are already a reality for hundreds of millions of Europeans:
They can travel within countries that have signed the
Schengen Agreement – from North to South and East to
West – without needing to show their passports at borders. Within Euroland, all Europeans have the same money in their pockets, and no longer need to convert or exchange currencies. The citizens of the EU member states
are free to choose their place of residence, work and education. No obstacles impede the cross-border passage of
goods, services or capital. A joint constitution is being
drafted. Since its foundation, the Federal Republic of Germany has been a driving force for European unification,
and works especially closely in the field of integration
with France and other partners.

Integration and expansion

The foundation of the Federal Republic of Germany on May 23, 1949, took place against a background of mounting enthusiasm for Europe. Mindful of the terrible consequences of World War II, support for the pro-Europe movement swiftly grew. It was strongly promoted by parliamentarians, government members and former resistance fighters, and as early as May 5, 1949 led to the establishment of the Council of Europe.

Following the quashing of the violent Nazi tyranny, Germany adopted reparations, strong ties to the West and an embedded position in Europe as the key tenets of its raison d'etre. These objectives were already reflected in the first version of the Basic Law drafted in 1949, which limited Germany's sovereign rights in order to "bring about and secure a peaceful and lasting order in Europe, and between the nations of the world" (Article 24 of the Basic Law), in a system of mutual, collective security.

Coal and steel union and the EEC: On April 18, 1951 Belgium, Germany, France, Italy, Luxembourg and the Netherlands set up the "European Coal and Steel Community" (ECSC). This process was moved forwards in the Treaty of Rome signed on March 25, 1957: this created the European Economic Community (EEC) and the Eu-

Signing of the Treaty of Rome

ropean Atomic Energy Community (EURATOM), and the six founding member states of the coal and steel union agreed to operate a free market by eliminating all trade barriers, adopting a joint economic policy and harmonizing the standard of living in the member states. Germany's Walter Hallstein was appointed the first President of the EEC Commission in Brussels.

The special relations between Germany and France as were enshrined in treaties were an integral part of the EEC. By overcoming their long-standing enmity and augmenting consensual understanding between them, the two countries became a motor of European integration. When the Élysée Treaty was signed in 1963 it placed the Franco-German friendship on a basic footing that extended way beyond the political level, and through such things as youth exchange programs made the respective general public the basis for mutual understanding.

Simultaneously, the joint security architecture had also been fleshed out. When the extensive plans for a European defense community were rejected by the French National Assembly in 1954, the Federal Republic of Germany joined the West European Union (WEU) and NATO. In 1955, the Treaty of Paris accorded the Federal Republic of Germany full sovereignty.

The Elysée Treaty

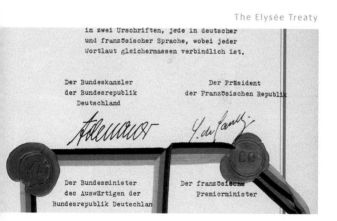

in zwei Urschriften, jede in deutscher
und französischer Sprache, wobei jeder
Wortlaut gleichermassen verbindlich ist.

Der Bundeskanzler
der Bundesrepublik
Deutschland

Der Präsident
der Französischen Republik

Der Bundesminister
des Auswärtigen der
Bundesrepublik Deutschlan

Der französische
Premierminister

However, certain restrictions remained in place relating to Germany as a whole, the stationing of troops and the status of Berlin. Germany's newly-founded Armed Forces, the Bundeswehr, were integrated into NATO structures. And the Federal Republic of Germany declared itself willing to forgo the development of nuclear, biological and chemical weapons.

The original six members of this core of European states were joined in 1973 by Denmark, Great Britain and Ireland, then, in 1981 by Greece, and in 1986 by Spain and Portugal, taking total membership to 12. And the tally climbed to 15 in 1995, when Austria, Finland, and Sweden joined. By that time, many changes to the original treaties had taken place. In 1967, the ECSC, EEC and EURATOM were merged to form the European Community (EC), and one year later the customs union came into force. In 1972, a first step was taken towards a single currency when the currency union was formed, followed in 1979 by the European Monetary System: Henceforth, the ECU (European Currency Unit) was the official unit of currency for trade between the Member States. The Single European Act signed in 1987 effectively harmonized legal directives. And in 1990 the first stage of the Economic

Border checks are disbanded

and Monetary Union (EMU) came into effect with the aim of achieving price stability by greater coordination of economic, financial and monetary policy.

Abolition of border controls: On June 14, 1985, Germany, France and the Benelux countries convened in Schengen, a border town in Luxembourg, to resolve that: "Internal borders can be crossed without the need for passport checks". Since then, other nations have joined this treaty: Denmark, Greece, Italy, Portugal and Spain, but also new EU members Austria, Finland, and Sweden. Norway and Ireland are associated Schengen members.

The euro as single currency: During a summit meeting at Maastricht in Holland in February 1992, the way was paved for stronger Community ties. The Maastricht Treaty set out the timetable for the launch of the euro as a single currency, to be introduced by the signatory states on January 1, 2002. The euro swiftly emerged alongside the dollar as a new, global currency. The population of Euroland totals 303 million (compared to United States: 276 million, Japan 127 million); the Eurozone generates 16 percent of total global GDP (United States: 22 percent, Japan: 7.3 percent), while it accounts for 19.1 percent of the world's exports

Euro coins

(United States: 10.7 percent, Japan: 11.1 percent), and 18.7 percent of global imports (United States: 14.4 percent, Japan: 9.7 percent).

In order to secure the stability of the new single currency, the Maastricht Treaty stipulates that the national budget deficit of each member state may not exceed three percent of its GDP, and national debt should not exceed 70 percent of GDP. Thanks to Germany's insistence, the European Stability and Growth Pact was passed in 1997.

EU expansion: In 1993, the European Community, which had altered its name to the European Union, signed European treaties, as they were known, with the countries of Central and Eastern Europe, and these then served as the basis for the accession procedure initiated in 1998. To qualify for membership, nations must have a democratic, constitutional order, protect human rights, as well as respect minorities and provide adequate protection for them. Two other essential aspects are a viable market economy, and the capacity to withstand competitive pressures within the Union.

Member states are also expected to embrace and adopt the duties and obligations arising from EU membership, including translation of EU law (as set out in some 80,000 pages of legal regulations) into national law.

On December 13, 2002 at the Copenhagen summit meeting of the Heads of State and Government – the Council of Europe – accession negotiations were completed with ten EU candidates, namely Cyprus, the Czech Republic, Estonia, Hungary, Latvia, Lithuania, Malta, Poland, Slovakia, and Slovenia. In the cradle of democracy – Athens - the 15 EU Heads of State and Government and the ten new members signed the relevant accords on April 16, 2003. Following a ratification process in all the member states and acceding nations as well as referendums in the latter countries, accession is scheduled for May 1, 2004.

From a community of six to a Europe of 25 nations

Both sides stand to reap economic benefits from EU expansion eastwards. In 2002, German foreign trade with the acceding nations once again increased far faster than Germany's overall external trade, of which it now makes up nine percent.

Germany has been instrumental in pressing the expansion negotiations forward ever since they first began. As it shares borders with Poland and the Czech Republic, and is a key trading partner with the acceding nations, Germany has a special interest in EU expansion.

Negotiations are continuing with Bulgaria and Rumania with a view to these nations joining the EU in 2007. In December 2004, a decision is to be taken on the future of negotiations with Turkey based on a special report to be prepared by the European Commission. From Germany's point of view it is vital that the Commission report confirms Turkey does indeed fulfill the political criteria, which include safeguarding human rights as well as full protection of minorities.

A prerequisite for expansion of the European Union is that its present structures are first altered. The Union has made progress in this difficult task as regards its common agricultural and structural policy, its own budget and institutions.

EU agricultural and structural policy:
Agenda 2000, which was passed in 1999, represents one of the most comprehensive reforms the European Union has undertaken in its entire history. The package of measures comprises wide-reaching reforms to the common agricultural and structural policy, as well as changes to the system of EU financing. Indeed, in view of the liberalization of world trade it had become indispensable to bring EU guaranteed prices for agricultural products into line with the prices on global markets. The implementation of the Agenda made this easier by authorizing direct payments to farmers. A central element of the reform package was expansion of the policy for rural districts, including greater support for eco-sound farming methods. Agricultural spending was increased by an average of € 40.5 billion a year in real terms for market measures, while an extra € 13 billion was committed for rural development. In other words, agricultural spending was stabilized at the 1999 levels.

It is the key objective of EU structural policy to eliminate the wide gap between prosperous and weaker economic regions. One look at the EU's eastern neighbors suffices to make one realize that the Union will

Farmer in Württemberg

have to provide financial support if the Central and East European states are to catch up financially.

In order to ensure successful eastwards expansion, the EU has also had to re-organize its own financing. The expenditure scheduled in budget plans is markedly lower than the previous budget ceiling of 1.27 percent of the EU's GDP. As a result of re-financing, total financial resources will drop from around € 92 billion in 2000 to € 90.3 billion in 2006. Moreover, greater consideration was given to the financial capacity of the individual member states. Consequently, German net payments will decrease from 0.54 percent of Germany's GDP in 1999 to 0.42 percent in 2006.

Institutions: The Treaty of Nice, which came into force in 2003, is intended to secure the EU institutions' capacity to act following expansion. The national right of veto has been abolished for a number of crucial decisions, and the timetable has already been set for other areas in which majority voting will be adopted. After that time, individual members will no longer be able to exercise vetoing rights should a group of states opt to push ahead with a project relating to integration policy; in this way, the real strengths of deeper cooperation can now come into their own.

Another aspect was to strengthen the role of the Commission President. In future, he can bring greater influence to bear, and take a stronger political lead in communicating views. The right of the European Parliament to bring litigation before the European Court of Justice has been expanded, and it is also given co-decision options in more fields.

A re-weighting of votes in the Council comes into effect on January 1, 2005, strengthening the weight of the large member states. A qualified majority decision must be supported by a majority of member states. In addition, a member state can insist that the Council reviews a resolution supported by member states who together constitute 62 percent of the total EU population. The size and composition of the Commission will alter in November 2004 when each member state will be represented by one Commission member only; the goal: to reduce the size of the Commission despite the fact that the Union will then comprise 27 member states.

European Parliament: At the same time that government cooperation has been intensified, the rights of the European Parliament have also been strengthened. Since 1979, members of the European Parliament have been selected by general, direct elections every five years, with the next elections scheduled for 2004. Not least of all owing to this direct legitimization the European Parliament has evolved from being an advisory assembly to constituting a parliament with legislative powers and controlling authority on a par with that of the national parliament. The 626 MEPs, of whom 31 percent are female, are elected according to the principle of national election regulations. Following EU expansion, at the next election in 2004 the number of seats per member state will be redistributed.

In December 2001, the Council of Europe in Laeken convened the European Convention on the Future of Europe. This Convention was appointed to devise suggestions on three issues, namely to bring the mechanisms of the European project and the European Union bodies

The European Parliament in Strasbourg

Valéry Giscard d'Estaing and Gerhard Schröder

closer to European citizens, to structure political life and the European political arena in an expanded EU, and to make the EU a model for others to follow and a factor ensuring stability in the new world order.

Reaching its resolutions on a consensus basis, the European Convention adopted a draft European constitution and submitted this to the President of the Council of Europe in Rome on July 18, 2003. The draft constitution will be the subject of deliberations by a government conference as of October 2003 and the findings are expected to be published in spring 2004.

Together with France, Germany has made numerous proposals to the Convention for a reform of the EU. In 2002, the year marking the 40th anniversary of the Elysée Treaty, Franco-German cooperation proved particularly fruitful and pioneering in this context.

Common Foreign and Security Policy: The EU Common Foreign and Security Policy (CFSP), which includes European Security and Defense Policy (ESDP), is moving forward. The establishment of permanent political and military structures in Brussels in 2001 has further stimulated the ongoing integration of European foreign policy. In the process, the so-called Political and

Joschka Fischer and Javier Solana

Security Committee (PSC) is increasingly developing into a central management and coordinating body of CFSP After the Treaty of Nice came into force on February 1, 2003 the Council of the European Union (generally speaking the Foreign Ministers) can authorize the PSC to take appropriate decisions relating to the political control and strategic management of EU operations for the purposes of crisis management. In addition, Javier Solana, the High Representative for EU Common Foreign and Security Policy, is increasingly providing key stimuli for the formulation and implementation of European foreign policy.

The EU has set itself the goal of being in a position as of 2004 to deploy a rapid-response force of up to 60,000 soldiers for peace-keeping, peace-maintaining and human-itarian tasks. As regards civilian operations, the aim is to supply up to 5,000 police officers and 200 legal experts, i.e., judges and attorneys, to form a pool of civilian admin-istrative experts, and be able to dispatch disaster preven-tion teams of up to 2,000 persons at short notice.

The EU and NATO see themselves as strategic part-ners in the prevention of international conflicts and crisis management. Conferences at ministerial level are supplemented by regular meetings of the EU policy and security policy committee and the NATO Council, as well as meetings of the military committees. It was also thanks to the insistence of the German Federal government that, at the end of 2002, agreement was reached between the EU and NATO that the EU be given access to NATO capabilities, especially planning capacities. This created a decisive prerequisite for the EU to be able to undertake peace missions in the Balkans after consultation with NATO – and to relieve NATO. In 2003, Germany shouldered NATO tasks in Macedonia, as well as United Nations policing assignments in Bosnia and Herzegovina.

Judicial and domestic policy: Under the terms of the Amsterdam Treaty, which came into effect in 1999, important areas of national judicial and domestic policy were ceded to the authority of the EU, which increased the latter's ability to combat organized crime, and laid the foundations for a common visa, asylum and immigration policy. The European Parliament was also granted substantially stronger rights. In order to clearly delineate the tasks of the Union from those of the Member States ("who does what"), greater emphasis was placed on the principle of subsidiarity.

Efforts continue to implement the aim of the Treaty, namely to create a European area characterized by liberty, security and jurisprudence. Germany has made significant contributions in this context. For example, the asylum procedure has been rendered much more efficient, and agreement has been reached on the minimum standards for the acceptance of persons applying for political asylum. Further regulations are intended to create a common platform of minimum regulations for a European asylum and refugee act.

The tragic events of September 11, 2001 greatly influenced collaboration with the United States in the field of criminal justice and police matters. The EU is continuing its carefully targeted efforts to improve cooperation in

German-Polish cooperation for border patrols

combating cross-border crime. One example: the lengthy and often complex extradition procedure has been replaced by a system of handing over suspects on the basis of a European arrest warrant. The Federal Government is particularly pleased that in the cases of 32 defined misdemeanors, the requirement that the crime be a criminal offense in both nations has been dropped.

The foundation of a European agency for judicial cooperation known as Eurojust has spelled a marked improvement in fighting serious crime. At present headquartered temporarily in The Hague, Eurojust will considerably facilitate requests for judicial assistance between national prosecuting offices, as well as initiating and coordinating Europe-wide investigations. In addition, a European network was set up comprising agencies charged with bringing to justice persons who have committed genocide, war crimes, and crimes against humanity.

In future, combating serious crime such as terrorism, human trafficking, child pornography and the sexual exploitation of children will be handled on a uniform basis throughout Europe. Moreover, concerted efforts continue to be made against corruption and organized crime.

The European police agency Europol was set up in The Hague in 1999 and has to date largely served as a database for serious cross-border crime. It has now been granted extensive new powers. Among other things, Europol can participate in joint investigation groups set up by member states or request individual member states to initiate investigations.

Franco-German cooperation: A decisive condition for progress in the European consolidation process has always been the functioning of the Franco-German powerhouse. Celebrations in January 2003 to mark the 40th anniversary of the Élysée Treaty demonstrate how much relations between the two former arch-enemies have improved in the post-War decades.

On January 22, 2003 at a joint Council of Ministers Meeting in Paris to mark the 40th anniversary of the Élysée Treaty, both sides agreed to cooperate closely in all policy fields – especially in foreign, security and defense policy, economic and finance policy, as well as on legislation. When drafting bills, ministers consult their respective partners. The Franco-German summit meetings which are regularly held take the form of a Franco-German Council of Ministers which is prepared by the foreign ministers.

In each country an authorized representative (Secretary General) is appointed for Franco-German cooperation. This person prepares the meetings of the Council of Ministers and coordinates implementation of the joint resolutions. January 22 is to be celebrated henceforth as "Franco-German Day". Over seven million young people have taken advantage of the services of the Franco-German Youth Association to familiarize themselves with their neighboring country. More than 2,000 town-twinning arrangements and 3,000 school exchange programs are in place. There are also close economic ties between the two nations for whom each is the other's foremost commercial partner.

Charles de Gaulle visits Konrad Adenauer

CSCE and OSCE: On August 1, 1975 the CSCE final accords were ratified in Helsinki by seven Warsaw-Pact states, 13 neutral countries and the 15 NATO states (including the United States and Canada). They thereby committed themselves to the inviolability of borders, the peaceful settlement of disputes, non-intervention in the domestic matters of other states, as well as the protection of human rights and basic freedoms.

Following the dramatic upheavals in East Europe, the CSCE born of the Charter of Paris emerged in 1995 as the Organization for Security and Cooperation in Europe (OSCE). Its prime objectives include complete security, conflict prevention and post-conflict reconstruction. This positioned the OSCE as a global model for conflict-solving.

The 55 Member States participating in the OSCE include all the states in Europe, the successor states to the Soviet Union, as well as the United States and Canada. OSCE decision-making bodies are the Heads of State and Government, the Council of Ministers that convenes annually, the Permanent Council that convenes at least once a week, as well as the Forum for Security Cooperation, that is empowered to take its own decisions on political and military matters, and likewise meets once a week.

40 years of the Élysée Treaty

The highlight of celebrations to mark the 40th anniversary of the Franco-German friendship agreement was the first joint parliamentary assembly of both nations. The 900 or so MPs met in the Palace of Versailles

OSCE representative monitoring the parliamentary elections in Kosovo.

The Minister of Foreign Affairs of the OSCE participating State selected for one year to chair the OSCE bears overall responsibility for executive action. He/she is assisted by the Secretary General (who also heads the OSCE Secretariat), as well as the person preceding and succeeding as Chairman-in-Office.

OSCE structures and institutions include the Office for Democratic Institutions and Human Rights, the Representative on Freedom of the Media, the High Commissioner on National Minorities, the Court of Conciliation and Arbitration, and the Coordinator of OSCE Economic and Environmental Activities. The Representative on the Freedom of the Media is an institution spawned by a German initiative. Special importance is accorded to the freedom of expression and the role of free, pluralistic media by the OSCE. In this context, the Representative on the Freedom of the Media (currently former German MP Freimut Duve) has an early-warning function. If he suspects there may have been serious breaches of OSCE principles he can contact the member state directly as well as other parties, in order to form an idea of the situation, and assist in finding a solution to the problem.

Germany makes a substantial contribution to the OSCE's work, both in financial terms and as regards human resources. It contributes some ten percent of the OSCE budget totaling around € 185 million (2003). Moreover, German staff members are involved in almost all long-term OSCE missions.

Council of Europe: In 1950, Germany became an associated member of the Council of Europe, (which now numbers 45 states), and since 1951 has been a full member. The Council comprises the Committee of Ministers as its decision-making body, the Parliamentary Assembly, as well as the Congress of Local and Regional Authorities as consultative bodies. Two main areas of the Council's work are to advance the protection of human rights and to bring the states of Central and East Europe into line with European structures. A so-called monitoring system is in place to ensure member states meet the obligations they accept on joining the Council. If a state seriously breaches Council principles, sanctions can be passed which may even result in expulsion from the Council. Since November 1998 it has been possible to bring violations of human rights before the European Court of Human Rights, which is permanently convened. The Council of Europe has also created the office of a Commissioner for Human Rights.

Conventions passed by the Council (and they now number 186) also include the European Convention for the Protection of Human Rights and Fundamental Freedoms, the European Convention for the Prevention of Torture and Inhuman or Degrading Treatment or Punishment (Anti-Torture Convention), the European Social Charter, the European Cultural Convention, as well as the Convention on Human Rights and Biomedicine. Milestones in the field of protection for minorities include the Framework Convention for the Protection of National Minorities as well as the European Charter for Regional or Minority Languages – Germany played a pivotal role in the formulation of these initiatives.

The Council of Europe in Strasbourg

As such, the Council of Europe combines pan-European membership with a legally binding (and enforceable!) framework as well as a highly diverse series of programs for supporting democratic reform processes. Some 800 million people in 45 European states have recourse to an unprecedented means of appeal before the European Court of Human Rights. For the young states of Central and East Europe, membership in the Council of Europe counts as a first democratic seal of approval prior to their admission to further Western organizations. However, the Council of Europe not only acts as a guardian but also to efficiently support a value community that extends beyond the European Union. As such, it plays a key role in stabilizing democratic and constitutional structures in Central and East Europe.

For these reasons, the Federal Republic of Germany accords the Council of Europe a pioneering role en route to creating and maintaining a single European juridical zone and a European value community. Accordingly, Germany has always promoted the Council of Europe through active and generous support – and this has included voluntary assistance. Furthermore, Germany is actively involved in Council of Europe programs at all levels, and with 12.7 percent is one of the largest contributors to the Council of Europe budget donating almost € 170 million. The German government continues in its efforts to place stronger emphasis on the role of the German language – alongside the official languages of English and French – in the daily work of the Council. Its aim is to create stronger influence for the scope of the Council through greater use of the German language in Council publications as well as translations of verdicts passed by the European Court of Human Rights into German.

Information

http://europa.eu.int
www.eu-vertretung.de
www.eu-kommission.de
www.europarl.eu.int
www.europarl.de
www.dfjw.org
www.europarat.de

Slovenia: Voting on EU and NATO accession

The reform process in Central and East Europe

In tandem with international economic and financial institutions and other bilateral sponsors, Germany has, from the outset, supported the establishment of democracy and market economies in the emerging democracies of Central and East Europe.

From the end of 1989 until the end of 1999, Germany committed some € 40 billion to East Central Europe and € 77 billion to Russia and the newly independent states on the territory of the former Soviet Union. In other words, Germany has contributed roughly one third of total assistance. Since 1993, the Federal government has operated the TRANSFORM program, which provides valuable help in this context. It offers assistance and advice to Belorussia, Bulgaria, the Czech Republic, Estonia, Hungary, Latvia, Lithuania, Poland, the Russian Federation, the Slovakian Republic and the Ukraine in the establishment of democracy and a social market economy. Assistance totaling € 30.7 million was committed in 2002.

South East Europe: The objective of Germany's South East Europe policy is the long-term stabilization of the entire region. German efforts are aimed at consolidating and connecting stable zones with the aid of the Stability Pact for South East Europe. The goal is to create a solid foundation for the transition of the entire region to a peaceful, democratic future. Those regions primarily targeted are the states of former Yugoslavia without Slovenia but including Albania. In addition, the neighboring states of Bulgaria and Romania are to benefit from the project funds. Moldavia was admitted to the Stability Pact in autumn 2001. Employing an integrative approach, the political, economic and social causes of conflicts are to be addressed: i.e., active crisis prevention is pursued. Simultaneously, the countries of this region are to be offered the chance to join the Euro-Atlantic organizations. Slovenia's accession to the EU was confirmed as early as April 2003, Croatia applied for EU membership in February 2003.

The Stability Pact created in 1999 largely as a result of Germany's initiative provides the international community with a framework for the following objectives:

- foster democratically legitimized governments,
- create open and pluralistic civilian societies,
- strengthen human rights and the rights of minorities,
- support free, independent media,
- establish market economy structures and promote economic prosperity,
- intensify cross-border cooperation,
- fight organized crime and corruption,
- create conditions that allow the return of refugees.

A package of tasks for swift implementation were put together as "lighthouse projects", as they have been called. Sponsor coordination and the mobilization of resources for the region remain a central task. At the regional Conference in Bucharest in October 2001 the international community made a further € 3 billion available for Stability Pact projects. Germany is making a contribution of € 1.2 billion for a period of four years (2000-2003). However, since the Federal government believes the Stability Pact will continue to play a pivotal role after 2003, it will continue to support it.

Not least of all Germany also participates in stabilizing the nations formerly engaged in civil war in the Balkans by deploying military and military police. In April 2003, a total of 1,368 soldiers from the German Armed Forces were deployed in Bosnia and Herzegovina (SFOR), 3,783 in Kosovo (KFOR), and 72 in Macedonia (CONCORDIA) – in each instance their stay will probably be of a longer-term nature.

SFOR: The mission of the German SFOR contingent, which is responsible for Sarajevo and its surroundings, is to secure the Dayton Peace Agreement, to deter the various ethnic groups from hostilities, and guarantee the freedom of movement of its own forces, international organizations and NGOs. In addition, SFOR monitors compliance with the arms control agreement for Bosnia and

German SFOR helicopter over Sarajevo

Herzegovina. It is also the brief of the German contingent to operate a field hospital for all SFOR members. What is more, the SFOR supports the International War Crimes Tribunal in its work in Bosnia and Herzegovina. The general framework for the SFOR mission is set by UN Security Council Resolution 1088 of December 12, 1996 taken in connection with the Dayton Peace Agreement of December 1995.

KFOR: It is the mission of the 37-nation KFOR force to help with the establishment of a multi-ethnic, peaceful, constitutional and democratic Kosovo subject to autonomous self-government, and to ensure its safety by military means if necessary. It must heed the territorial integrity of the Federal Republic of Yugoslavia in the process. To this end, the region must be de-militarized and stabilized. Key tasks are to provide humanitarian aid, to foster the return of all refugees and displaced persons, not to mention supporting the administration and international aid organizations. Moreover, KFOR assists the work of the International War Crimes Tribunal in Kosovo. The general framework for the deployment of the Kosovo Force is provided by Resolution 1244 passed on June 10, 1999 by the World Security Council.

KFOR convoy run by the German Armed Forces in Skopje

CONCORDIA: The European Union has been on its first military operation in Macedonia since March 31, 2003. Known as CONCORDIA, it involves 350 soldiers whose task is to secure the peace agreement of Ohrid, which ended the fighting with UCK rebels in Macedonia. In effect, it continues the work of NATO's "Allied Harmony", "Amber Fox" and "Essential Harvest" operations. The deployment is considered to be a test case prior to possible EU command of peace-keeping troops in Bosnia and Herzegovina.

Germany in NATO

As a consequence of the changes brought by the end of
the Cold War, the Alliance faces ever more complex
dangers to stability and security, and must contend with
particular challenges as regards the creation of new and
improved capabilities of NATO members. Through its firm
stance and cooperation, the North Atlantic Alliance has
contributed substantially to the far-reaching reform
process in Central and East Europe. As such, the expansion of NATO, (from which, owing to its position at the
center of Europe, Germany, in particular benefits) has also extended the zone of stability.

North Atlantic Treaty Organization (NATO):

The North Atlantic Treaty originally signed in 1949 by
12 European states and North America, now numbers
19 members: Belgium, Canada, Czech Republic, Denmark,
Germany, France, Greece, Iceland, Italy, Luxemburg, the
Netherlands, Norway, Poland, Portugal, Spain, Turkey,
Hungary, the Unite Kingdom, and the United States.
The accession of seven further states – Bulgaria, Estonia,
Latvia, Lithuania, Romania, Slovakia and Slovenia – is
scheduled for 2004.

In April 1999, the NATO summit in Washington, marking the defense organization's 50th anniversary, fundamentally redefined the role, mission and self-image of the Alliance. NATO's new strategic concept places the focus of its mission firmly on security and stability of the entire European-Atlantic region: in the form of alliances and cooperation, conflict prevention and crisis management.

In the 1990s, NATO employed various forms of alliance and cooperation to integrate the states of Central and East Europe as well as Russia into the European-Atlantic security structures. The Partnership for Peace set up in 1994 was followed in May 1997 by the NATO Russia-Founding Act, and the NATO-Russia Permanent Joint Council first convened on May 28, 2002.

The Czech Republic, Hungary and Poland were welcomed as new members in April 1999. The seven afore-mentioned states can join NATO as of 2004. Likewise, NATO has emphasized the principle that the door is open for Albania, Croatia and Macedonia as candidates for membership. At the NATO summit in Prague in November 2002, NATO members made it clear that expansion of NATO was not directed against the security interests of Russia or other partner states.

Following the September 11, 2001 terrorist attacks NATO responded for the first time in its history by invoking Article 5 of the Washington Treaty declaring the attack against the United States an attack against all 19 allies. It is an important task of the Alliance to respond appropriately to risks that often originate from regions with unstable government structures.

Specifically, NATO must be prepared to avert the threat of dangers from non-state actors including acts of terrorism, sabotage and organized crime, not to mention interruptions to the supply of essential resources. It must prevent the proliferation of weapons of mass destruction (biological, chemical and nuclear weapons), and missile technology by implementing decisive non-proliferation and arms-control measures.

As part of creating new capabilities, plans envisage establishing a NATO Response Force. The latter brings together ultramodern mobile land, sea and air regiments ready to move quickly to where they are needed as decided by the NATO Council and to work together when deployed.

NATO states

NATO member states:

- previous
- joining in 2004
- prospective members

Canada

United States

ATLANTIC OCEAN

Iceland

Norway

Estonia

Latvia

Great Britain   Denmark

Lithuania

Netherlands   Poland

Belgium Germany   Czech Republic

Luxembourg   Slovakia

France   Hungary

Slovenia   Romania

Croatia

Bulgaria

Portugal   Spain   Albania   Macedonia

Italy

Turkey

Greece

German Armed Forces: Formed following Germany's accession to NATO on May 9, 1955, the German Armed Forces comprise some 290,000 male and female soldiers in 2003. The present target structure is approx. 285,000 soldiers, of whom some 202,000 are professional or temporary conscripts, while 53,000 are doing their basic military service, and 27,000 are volunteers performing additional service. The German Armed Forces are divided into the classic arms of army, air force, and navy, as well as the two military organizational segments of troops, on the one hand, and the central medical corps, on the other.

The German Armed Forces' mission and tasks derive from its constitutional mission, and the objectives of German security and defense policy. The German Armed Forces guarantee the nation's ability to implement its foreign policy, make a contribution to stability at the European and global level, ensure national security and defense, and assist with defense of its allies, as well as promoting multinational cooperation and integration. Its mission includes international conflict prevention and crisis management; it assists the Alliance partners, protects Germany and its citizens, conducts rescue and evacuation operations, partnership and cooperation, and support.

George Robertson and Joschka Fischer

Young recruits take their oaths

The comprehensive reform of the German Armed Forces initiated in 1999 was largely precipitated by the radical changes in the security policy environment, the enlarged scope of deployment, NATO restructuring and the need to develop Europe's capability to act within the EU framework. The objectives of the reform are to restore a balance to German Armed Forces tasks, capabilities, equipment and funds, while also placing it in a position to continue its participation in international peacekeeping missions in cooperation with the forces of its allies and partners.

The speed at which the German Armed Forces has had to address new challenges is abundantly clear if one considers the changes that took place between 1998 and 2002. € 178 million was allocated to international missions in 1998 – a sum which had risen almost ten-fold to over € 1.5 billion in 2002. Between 8,000 and 10,000 troops are constantly deployed on out-of-area missions. As part of German Armed Forces restructuring, the number of troops in deployment will be increased steadily in coming years to 150,000 to maintain the present deployment level and allow for preparation, debriefing as well as ensuring service members a minimum stay with their family.

The German Armed Forces' defining characteristic is its embedding in the multi-national theater. It is the visible expression of international solidarity, joint assumption of responsibility and shared burdens. In future, German forces will as a matter of principle only be deployed on a multi-national basis under the auspices of the United Nations, NATO or the EU. In addition, the German Armed Forces is integrated into many multi-national associations; these include the First German-Dutch corps in Münster, the Eurocorps in Strasbourg, the German-Danish-Polish corps in Stettin, and the Franco-German brigade in Müllheim.

Though changes have been radical, two typical features of the German Armed Forces have remained unchanged: the incorporation of soldiers into society as citizens and the concept of inner leadership. Liberty and responsibility are the political and moral points of reference underlying the concept of inner leadership, and shore up German soldiers' role as citizens in uniform.

The German Armed Forces is subject to the primacy of the political system. It is an army in a democracy and championing a democracy. In this context, the Defense Commissioner of the German Bundestag plays an important parliamentary supervisory function, protecting the constitutional rights of servicemen. Every member of the armed forces has the right to complain directly to the Defense Commissioner, who can request information and access to files from military units and visit any German Armed Forces facility unannounced.

German men who have completed their 18th year are required to do basic military service for a period set on January 1, 2002 at nine months. For the German government, there is no feasible alternative to compulsory military service in terms of the deployment capabilities, performance levels and economic viability of the troops. The German constitution stipulates that nobody can be forced to do armed military service against their conscience.

German battalion for biological, chemical and nuclear defense deploying to Kuwait

Conscientious objectors to military service can, however, be obliged to perform other service for a period set on January 1, 2002 at ten months. Typically, work is assigned in the social sector, in environmental protection, restoration or conservation of the countryside.

As part of its equal opportunities policy starting on January 1, 2002 the German Armed Forces became an option for women wishing voluntarily to pursue a career in any of its divisions. In January 2003, the number of women serving in the German Armed Forces stood at 8,365. Female soldiers have the same rights and obligations as their male colleagues, and are inspected, trained, supported, promoted and paid according to the same criteria.

Information
www.nato.int
www.bundeswehr.de

Female airforce recruits take their oaths

Gerhard Schröder and George W. Bush

Transatlantic relations

The transatlantic orientation is one of the constants of Germany's foreign policy. Outside of the European Union the United States and Canada are Germany's closest allies and partners. NATO forms the main cornerstone of the transatlantic alliance.

With no other region in the world do Europeans share as many values, ideals and interests. The EU and North America are the two economic regions with the strongest mutual ties in the world. Each region sees daily turnover with the other in excess of € 1.25 billion. And in both cases, transatlantic trade constitutes some 20 percent of total foreign trade. Mutual investments contribute even more strongly to the linkages between the two economies: More than 60 percent of foreign investments in the United States originate in the EU, while some 45 percent of U.S. foreign investment is committed to the EU. Given the intensity of the business relations, it is hardly surprising that transatlantic trade conflicts occur. Often disputes arise from a difference of opinions on individual matters such as consumer protection, EU import prohibitions on beef treated with hormones, or genetically modified organisms. But the controversies over trade policy should not be seen out of proportion: In fact, only two percent of products and services are affected by them, while 98 percent of trade is free of hitches.

In 1990, the EU and the United States signed the "Transatlantic Declaration" in which they agreed to put a regular and close consultative network in place. Following this, in 1995 both sides undertook to put their reciprocal relations on a broader footing in society in the "New Transatlantic Agenda". The objective is to involve social groups more strongly in transatlantic decision processes.

Transatlantic relations have also always encompassed Europe's relations to Canada. Like the United States, after World War II Canada was committed in and to Europe. Canada is a close EU partner when it comes to addressing numerous global issues.

As of 1999, the tasks of the German-American coordinator in the German Foreign Ministry have been expanded to include Canada. This coordinator develops new initiatives, extends the framework for cooperation and ensures programs are properly coordinated. In addition, the coordinator nurtures the contacts with the decision-makers in all areas of US and Canadian society, and fosters encounters at all levels of society – this includes a large range of exchange programs.

The transatlantic dialog is also complemented by the regular summit meetings of the G 8 nations (Canada, France, Germany, Great Britain, Italy, Japan, Russia, and the United States).

UN General Assembly

Global issues

United Nations: A crucial element of German foreign policy is its involvement in the United Nations, to which Germany has belonged since 1973. Indeed, UN membership has become a major cornerstone of the nation's peace, security and human rights policy. The United Nations provides a forum for discussion of solutions for global problems affecting mankind – from the preservation of peace and questions of the global economy or development through to issues relating to the environment or the population explosion. Germany contributes just under ten percent of the regular UN budget, which amounted to some US$ 1.3 billion in 2002, making it the third largest contributor to the United Nations.

Germany, which has been a member of the UN Human Rights Commission almost without interruption, and was highly instrumental in 1993 in creating the office of a High Commissioner for Human Rights, emphasizes the importance of human rights policy in the United Nations. It likewise makes concerted efforts in the field of disarmament and arms control, which has, among other things, led to the creation of a UN weapons register on the flow of conventional weapons.

The high standing this active UN work has brought Germany is reflected in its being elected a member of the Security Council on four occasions – namely in 1977-8, 1987-8, 1995-6 and 2003-4. Moreover, the fact that it was elected most recently by 180 of the total of 183 votes indicates the special recognition its efforts have brought it. In February 2003, Germany was elected to chair the Security Council.

In line with the UN Charter, the Security Council carries the main responsibility for the preservation of world peace and international security. Its resolutions are binding for all members. It has five permanent and ten non-permanent members who meet on an almost daily basis at UN headquarters in New York to discuss current conflicts and debate on means of their settlement. The German government has set itself the goal of using German membership of the Council to strengthen the Council's function in keeping world peace. It takes its cue here from a comprehensive understanding of security that also takes into account human rights, development

Meeting of the UN Security Council

policy and economic aspects. The German government favors cooperative approaches when solutions to regional problems are being sought. It is necessary to take existing concepts for conflict prevention and follow-up strategies forwards.

Germany has developed a concept to complement multilateral peace efforts by measures taken at a national level. This includes projects to foster democracy and assistance with equipment. For instance, assistance in the form of democratic monitors is provided to developing nations in the process of organizing free elections or setting up armed forces. Germany also plays an important role in training and preparing civilian staff for international peace missions by the United Nations, the OSCE or the EU. The Federal Foreign Office has run the corresponding programs since 1999. In 2002, it set up the ZIF Center for International Peace Missions in Berlin. It is ZIF's goal to better prepare civilian personnel for missions, and to make Germany more capable of acting in the field of crisis prevention.

International Criminal Court: A significant new instrument of international law in the punishment of genocide, crimes against humanity and war crimes, and

Inauguration of the International Criminal Court

thus the prevention of such criminal acts is the International Criminal Court, which has its headquarters in The Hague. The Statute of Rome, which led to its establishment, came into force on July 1, 2002. From the start, Germany has been one of the strongest supporters of the Court, and makes the single largest financial contribution to its operations. In future, those responsible for war and expulsion will no longer be able to avoid punishment by hiding under the protection of national sovereignty. Since the objective is to ensure perpetrators of such crimes do not feel safe anywhere, the Court will make a positive contribution to national criminal law systems and national support for rights.

Environmental protection: Environmental protection has likewise become an essential part of German foreign policy. After all, environmental damage extends beyond national borders. Changes to the climate, the hole in the ozone layer, the extinction of flora and fauna, not to mention marine pollution, the spread of the deserts and destruction of the forests all have global consequences. As a result, environmental protection is one of the most important tasks facing the international

Convention on the World Climate in Bonn

community. Apart from protecting the basis for life, it is also conflict prevention and proactive security policy all in one.

Germany is actively involved in negotiating and implementing international agreements, and in preparing conferences for the protection of the environment. Milestones include the Conference on the Environment and Development in Rio de Janeiro (1992), and the World Summit for Sustainable Development in Johannesburg (2002). Via its diplomatic missions the Federal Foreign Office fosters the export of modern German environmental technology especially to developing and threshold countries. Furthermore, Germany is keen to attract international environmental organizations to Germany. Bonn – a UN location – is also home to the Secretariat of the Framework Convention on Climate Change, the Secretariat of the Convention to Combat Desertification, and the Secretariat of the Convention on Migratory Species. The UN's International Tribunal for the Law of the Sea set up in 1996 is located in Hamburg.

Development policy cooperation

Development policy is an independent pillar of German foreign relations and in terms of the objectives part of the German government's global policy aimed at peace, cooperation based on partnership and the fight against poverty. If we are to offer upcoming generations a future worldwide, we must foster sustainable development in all nations. The core problems of many developing nations have reached a level that affects the future prospects of the world as a whole. In this sense, development policy is instrumental in securing a joint future for nations. Through its development policy the German government seeks to help reduce poverty, secure peace, and contribute to a fairer form of globalization. In the

Millennium Declaration issued in September 2000 the United Nations stated its goal of halving the number of people living in absolute poverty by 2015.

The German government cooperates on development policy in the following areas:

1. Improvement of political structures: The precondition for successful and sustainable development is a nation's willingness to adopt a good, responsible form of governance. Consequently, this forms the foundation for contractual agreements between donor and receiving nations. We can conclude by saying that respect for human rights, democracy, rule of law, the involvement of the civilian society, but also the equality of men and women are all part of the development process.

2. Improvement of economic structures: Institutional stability and economic growth are basic prerequisites for a nation's economic progress. This also includes restructuring measures at a national level aimed at enabling primarily small and mid-sized companies to prosper financially. Yet it is essential at the international level also to regulate world trade by creating the requisite international finance and trade framework, if developing nations are not to become the losers in globalization.

3. Improvement of social structures: Only by altering the social structures of a society is it possible to ensure that the disadvantaged groups also benefit from economic growth. For this reason, basic welfare provisions are a prime objective of development policy. By this we mean above all adequate medical care, educational and training opportunities together with social security systems.

4. Improvement of ecological structures: It is in everyone's interests to secure basic conditions that will ensure the future survival of all people. Environmental disasters such as floods and drought repeatedly show that man's influence on his environment can cause horrendous problems. It follows that preserving the natural environment is always an integral part of development policy

projects. Maintaining a global ecological balance is also the prime aim of international conventions and agreements.

In 2002, Germany donated a total of 5.68 billion Euro to developing nations as official development assistance - or ODA for short. ODA covers all financial contributions from state bodies including the federal states and communities such as are made available to the developing countries and multilateral institutions. ODA funds are always granted as subsidies or have favorable repayment terms, distinguishing them from private or public assistance where repayment is governed by market conditions.

The German government continues in pursuing the goal of increasing ODA to 0.33 percent of GDP by the year 2006, from a figure of 0.27 percent in 2002. In 2003, the budget for the Federal Ministry for Economic Cooperation and Development was raised once again to € 3.77 billion. The long-term aim is for ODA to account for 0.7 percent of German GDP. This will be necessitated by growing EU development aid (including the German contribution), as well as debt relief.

Development Minister Heidemarie Wieczorek-Zeul

German cooperation on development policy consists of financial, technical and personnel cooperation. In 2003, Germany made € 1.05 billion available for financial cooperation. Such assistance provides developing nations with the money to finance certain projects – for example in the form of loans at highly favorable terms – and create structural preconditions for sustainable development. In such cases, it is important to scrutinize the development policy effect of the planned investment closely, and to ensure the money actually does benefit the people it targets.

A total of € 705 million was committed to technical cooperation in 2003. Such assistance is made in the knowledge that developing nations often do not have what is needed to launch urgently needed projects such as establishing a health system solely from their own resources. They rely on specialist know-how and material from abroad, yet these would be too costly if they were to acquire them on the free market. This is where technical cooperation comes in: it provides specialists, consultants and advisors, trainers, and experts who make available or finance the equipment and material. To qualify as sustainable, a project must fit into existing structures, and be such that the host nation can continue it afterwards.

Then there is personnel cooperation: it helps compensate for the often inadequate education systems in developing countries, particularly as regards the qualifications of specialists or those with leadership or management functions. A number of German organizations run seminars and courses to train specialists in developing countries to handle a wide range of tasks in the local economy or administration.

Furthermore, German experts are sent to the host country to act as development aid workers or consultants, for example in a ministry where they can be integrated into the existing staff.

Efforts by the private sector, intended ultimately to result in investments, are becoming increasingly important. Under the terms of public private partnerships (PPP), public development cooperation and private firms collaborate – for instance in training specialists or initiating measures to enhance infrastructure. In 2003, there were already over 800 partnerships with companies which support projects in more than 60 nations. The goal is to forge joint ventures or other forms of cooperation with companies in the host nation.

Many private organizations are engaged in the field of development policy, from churches via political foundations through to NGOs. Alongside the large aid organizations which are highly experienced in working abroad, there are younger, smaller associations which rely strongly on advice and support in order to make an effective contribution to sustainable development in the nations of the South. In this regard, Germany's diplomatic missions see themselves as points-of-contact, providing consular support to those Germans posted to the host nation, but also offering advice in finding suitable partners and projects.

German know-how in Thailand

Development
cooperation

Children in a refugee camp managed by the German
Organization for Technical Cooperation (GTZ) in
Kabul. More than one million refugees have returned
to Afghanistan after the end of the war. Work has
begun rebuilding society there.

In 1999, at the G7 Summit in Cologne the leading industrial nations agreed to a comprehensive debt remission initiative for 37 of the poorest developing nations. To date, 26 highly indebted developing nations have qualified for extensive debt relief: In other words, they no longer need to pay back a large portion of their debts. Today, firm approval has been forthcoming for over two-thirds of the planned debt relief packages. For the nations in question, this means they can halve their debts – and there is the additional relief granted by bilateral creditors. In return, the debtor nations agree to employ these funds to fight poverty by committing the money to schools, hospitals, water provision projects or professional training.

Foreign cultural and education policy

Given that it emphasizes creating understanding among nations, securing peace, preventing conflict, and protecting human rights, foreign cultural and education policy is an integral part of German foreign policy. The international conflicts of recent years have clearly demonstrated the need for understanding between different cultures. This dialogue is assisted by fostering youth exchange programs, university and academic exchange schemes, grants, German schools abroad, theater, music and film projects, as well as language courses.

In 2002, a total of € 566.9 million was set aside for foreign cultural and education policy projects and programs. The most important areas were: German schools abroad, to which € 174 million was committed, university grants and academic exchanges which totaled € 136 million, and operating funds and program financing for Goethe Institute Inter Nationes, which came to € 164 million.

Intercultural dialogue: International exchange in the fields of theater, music and the fine arts conveys an up-to-date snapshot of artistic life and work in Germany. In recent years, greater emphasis has been placed on dialogue with representatives of foreign cultures. The most important elements of this cultural exchange are the support of guest performances by musical ensembles but also theater and dance groups, not to mention the promotion of art exhibitions.

In 2002, the Federal Foreign Office allocated some € 12.7 million of its cultural policy budget to guest performances (music, theater, dance), exhibitions and artist exchanges. Project assistance is made dependent on prior consultation with those organizations that translate foreign cultural policy into activities on the ground, and which also contribute to projects; especially worthy of mention here are Goethe Institute, the Institute for Foreign Relations and the Liaison Office for International Relations of the German Music Council.

Awarding of Goethe medals for services to the German language and culture

German language: Promoting the German language outside Germany is a particularly enduring form of foreign cultural and education policy. It is, after all, primarily through a knowledge of the German language that people become familiar with the culture of German-speaking countries. Instruction in the German language is supported on all continents, with the emphasis on the EU and those nations aspiring to become members of it. As European integration continues, ever greater importance is attached to competence in foreign languages. In Germany, teaching foreign languages is accorded great importance, and it is equally in Germany's interest that the teaching of German as a foreign language is treated in a similar vein in our EU partner nations.

Another regional focus for support for German language instruction is Russia and the CIS states, where some eight million people are learning the language. The young generations in Germany and Russia are each keen to learn the other's language. In 2002, the German-Russian Youth Forum drew attention to its activities by conducting Russian and German language competitions in Berlin and Moscow respectively.

German cultural intermediaries: The largest organization, Goethe Institut e.V., maintains 125 cultural institutes in 76 nations as well as 16 institutes in Germany. Its tasks include providing German instruction, providing specialist support for foreign German teachers, conducting and arranging cultural events such as poetry readings, theater guest performances, film festivals etc., as well as communicating a comprehensive image of Germany by furnishing information on the cultural, social and political life in Germany.

In enabling the international exchange of students and academics, the German Academic Exchange Service (DAAD), makes a valuable contribution to global mobility. It develops friends and partners for Germany among foreign academic elites, and promotes cosmopolitan educa-

Goethe Institute in Tunis

tion and training for German students. Such activities help make German universities more international, and consequently go towards increasing the attractiveness of Germany as an academic location.

The Alexander von Humboldt Foundation (AvH) awards research fellowships and grants to highly-qualified up-and-coming academics as well as top academics. It nurtures the establishment of international academic networks, and international research cooperation, and cultivates the latter through intensive follow-up activities.

Other important organizations that translate cultural policy into practice are the Institute for Foreign Relations, which among other things organizes art exhibitions, the Liaison Office for International Relations of the German Music Council (guest performances by amateur ensembles and choirs), not to mention Deutsche UNESCO Kommission e.V. The German Archaeological Institute (DAI) teams up with international partners to explore the historical roots of today's civilizations. Moreover, the activities of the Deutsche Welle also form part of foreign cultural and education policy. Worldwide 210 million people tune in to Deutsche Welle radio programs, and 97 million watch their TV programs. More than 4,200 partner stations run all or part of DW programs.

Schools abroad: In 2002, there were 117 German schools abroad, with a capacity of 70,000 pupils (of whom 53,000 are not German nationals). Dispatching teachers to 370 state schools meant another 180,000 pupils were reached – in other words 250,000 pupils worldwide. Schools abroad are an excellent example of successful collaboration between the state and private sector. Private sponsoring associations manage the schools independently, and contribute considerable services via school fees and donations from the business community. The German Foreign Ministry also supports such schools in the form of teaching staff, and financially via operating grants.

As perhaps the most intensive communicators of German culture and language, the foreign schools are equally attractive for native pupils, German students, or children from other nations. The majority of pupils come from host nations. Many later attend German universities and on graduating remain in Germany in pursuit of their careers. This creates networks which represent valuable foundations for foreign policy, the export industry and culture. In order to fully exploit this potential, in 2001 the Federal government began to offer up to 60 full grants for university studies to the most successful foreign pupils. First indications are that these young students are amongst the best in their specialist area.

Cultural assets: Since 1981, Germany has supported nations in the Third World in retaining their cultural heritage. Thus far, some € 30 million has been devoted in over 100 developing countries on more than 1,000 projects, with an emphasis on restoration and conservation measures in the broadest sense of the word. The most important requisite for all projects is that the host nation is a partner country willing and able to also assume responsibility for the project.

Angkor Wat: Cultural preservation with German assistance

The German government makes a concerted effort to secure the return of German cultural assets which are abroad as a result of war. All such efforts by the Federal government are conducted with the awareness of German responsibility for World War II, particularly the extensive damage which the Third Reich inflicted on the museums, archives and libraries in those nations occupied by German troops.

Information

www.bmz.de
www.goethe.de
www.daad.de
www.humboldt-foundation.de
www.ifa.de
www.deutscher-musikrat.de
www.unesco.de
www.dainst.de
www.kulturportal-deutschland.de
www.deutsche-kultur-international.de
www.dw-world.de

Federal Foreign Office

Both within Germany and abroad, the Federal Foreign Office is increasingly developing into a sought-after service provider. One example of this is in the realm of tourism. For those traveling to other countries the Federal Foreign Office makes up-to-date information on the security situation in the individual nations available on its home page www.auswaertiges-amt.de. On the ground, consular officials ensure that the consequences of mishaps, misfortune, illnesses and other incidents are kept within reasonable limits.

The global network of 218 diplomatic missions (in 2003), not only serves diplomatic relations, the analysis of developments in various nations and regions which government policy must respond to. It is also concerned with economic promotion. After all, even in the age of the Internet, intergovernmental agreements and assistance in initiating contacts remain indispensable. Germany is a nation which depends heavily on its exports. In this regard, thanks to its global presence, the services it offers German companies, and its work in identifying foreign investors, the Federal Foreign Office makes an important contribution to securing Germany's future prosperity.

Information

www.auswaertiges-amt.de

Federal Foreign Office in Berlin

Computer-assisted production of car parts

The economy

Exporting underground railway carriages to China

Germany's position in the world economy

Ranking third in terms of total economic output, Germany is one of the world's leading nations. With regard to world trade it places second. The country continues to be an attractive market for foreign investors, offering a superbly developed infrastructure and a highly motivated, qualified work force. Top-notch research and development projects are additional hallmarks of the country.

The social partnership between trade unions and employers ensures a high degree of social harmony. Reforms to the social security system and structural reforms to the labor market are intended to reduce ancillary labor costs and rejuvenate economic growth, which, in comparison with other EU countries, is at a low level.

Compared with other industrial nations, the German economy has an almost unprecedented international focus. Companies generate almost a third of their profits through exports, and almost one in four jobs is dependent on foreign trade. The high level of international competitiveness is most evident where companies vie with others in the international arena. Despite the slump in world trade, the share of exports expanded at a higher than average rate. In addition, the continuous rise in direct investments by international companies in Germany and by German companies abroad underscores the strong position of the German economy in comparison with its international competitors. It is buttressed at the national level by a favorable inflation rate and unit labor costs as well as by a stable society.

Foreign trade: Over the past few years the German economy was able to expand its position in the world market. According to data from the International Monetary Fund, ever since 1997 the price-adjusted figures for exports of German goods and services have grown more strongly than the volume of world trade. Even in 2001, when the volume of world trade dipped 0.2 percent, German exports increased 6.7 percent and as such significantly outperformed the other major European economies. In terms of world trade, Germany managed to hold on to its second ranking, behind the United States but ahead of China.

Between 1991 and 2002, the German trade surplus soared. From a good € 11 billion in 1991 it increased to around € 84 billion in 2002. Imports totaling € 665 billion were offset by the export of goods and services totaling € 749 billion. The year before, the trade surplus had reached a record € 87 billion. Exports from the German economy are thus on a par with the total output of Spain. In 2001, a balance of trade surplus was achieved for the first time since unification.

The increased competitiveness of German companies is illustrated by the marked improvement in export ratios in the most important export sectors. The export ratio shows the share of sales outside Germany in relation

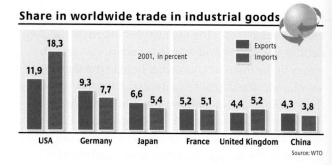

Share in worldwide trade in industrial goods

2001, in percent

Exports
Imports

USA	Germany	Japan	France	United Kingdom	China
11,9 / 18,3	9,3 / 7,7	6,6 / 5,4	5,2 / 5,1	4,4 / 5,2	4,3 / 3,8

Source: WTO

to overall sales. Between 1991 and 2002 the export ratio for mechanical engineering soared from 52 percent to almost 69 percent, in the chemicals industry from 50 percent to almost 70 percent, in the automobile industry from 43 percent to 69 percent, and in the electronics industry from 31 to 42 percent.

The western industrialized countries are Germany's most important trading partners. The closest trading relationships continue to be those with EU member states, with whom more than half of all foreign trade is conducted. In 2002, the most important partner was once again France. In terms of imports, the Netherlands and United States followed next. Following France, the main importers of German goods and services were the United States and Great Britain.

The curve for trade with central and east European countries also has also been rising steadily. Whereas in 2001 total foreign trade rose by just 4.6 percent, trade with these countries increased by 12.8 percent. Poland was the most important market for German goods and services in central and east European countries. The Czech Republic and Hungary are also important trading partners for Germany in the region. All in all, trade with Central and Eastern Europe accounted for 11.9 percent of overall foreign trade, surpassing even trade with North America. This is a clear indication of just how strong the role of the region is for German foreign trade and the importance it will have for Germany in light of EU expansion eastwards.

Foreign trade is exceedingly important for both growth and employment. In Germany, roughly one job in four depends on the export trade. The figure for manufacturing is even higher, with 25 percent of all produce being exported. Income and the standard of living in Germany would be lower were the country not to have such close ties with the world economy. In addition there would be fewer resources available for public services such as education, health care and provisions for old age. Needless to say, efficiency and competitiveness are also a fundamental basis for relations with other countries. Trade and economic links help stabilize international relations.

Foreign investments: At the end of the 1980s, there were regular debates in Germany on the qualities of the country as a magnet for foreign investors. At the time, foreign companies were hesitant to invest in the country, whereas German companies were considerably increasing their commitments abroad in the form of direct investment. As a result, many skeptics came to the

Cars being exported from Bremerhaven

Germany's foreign trade partners, 2002

Imports		Exports	
France	49,4	France	69,8
Netherlands	43,1	USA	66,6
USA	40,0	United Kingdom	54,2
United Kingdom	33,7	Italy	47,4
Italy	33,6	Netherlands	39,5
Belgium	27,0	Austria	33,3
Austria	21,2	Belgium	31,2
China	21,1	Spain	29,7
Switzerland	19,5	Switzerland	26,6
Japan	19,0	Poland	16,1

figures in € billion

Source: German Federal Statistic Office

conclusion that Germany was no longer an attractive place for investments and that hence German jobs would be lost to foreign competitors.

The situation today is totally different. German investments abroad continue to outweigh the inflow of direct investments into the country appreciably, but this is normal in the case of an economy that is heavily export-oriented. After all, investments abroad are made in order to penetrate new markets and build up marketing and service networks. On the other hand, what is particularly striking is the trend for the annual inflow of investments into Germany from abroad between 1992 and 2002. In 2002 alone, the amount invested in Germany by foreigners was greater than for the entire 1990-97 period (a good € 35 billion). In the four years 1998, 1999, 2001 and 2002 – in other words excluding the takeover of Mannesmann by Vodafone in 2000, which bumped the figure for investments in Germany to over € 220 billion – foreigners invested € 153 billion in Germany, or three times as much as in the five years before.

According to a study by the International Institute for Management, in terms of investment inflows into the country, Germany ranks second worldwide following the

United States. As a result of these healthy inflows of capital, the scale of foreign investment in Germany has almost tripled since the beginning of the 1990s, from around € 100 billion to € 280 billion at the end of 2000. The government commissioner for foreign investments in Germany advises foreign investors in all related matters.

The scale of German direct investments abroad almost quadrupled over the same period, namely from € 150 billion to € 570 billion. The larger share of this sum was most probably committed to penetrating foreign markets. Globalization means that companies have to show their presence throughout the world.

The German business world has realized this and is acting accordingly. What is more, foreign investments also secure jobs. Worldwide, around four million jobs are maintained as a result of German investment commitment. It also impacts positively on the German economy. Estimates suggest that three jobs outside Germany maintain one job in the country.

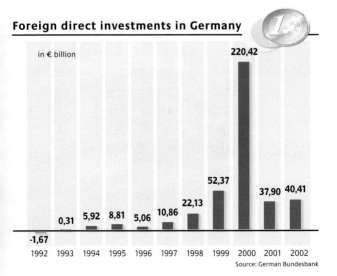

Foreign direct investments in Germany

in € billion

Year	Value
1992	-1,67
1993	0,31
1994	5,92
1995	8,81
1996	5,06
1997	10,86
1998	22,13
1999	52,37
2000	220,42
2001	37,90
2002	40,41

Source: German Bundesbank

Foreign economic policy: Germany welcomes free world trade, opposes any form of protectionism, and is committed to further liberalization measures with regard to world trade under the proviso of adherence to more strictly ecological and social standards with regard to sustainable development. International negotiations and organizations are geared to devising rules for trading, making foreign markets more transparent and dismantling trade barriers. Furthermore, in order to overcome the alarming prosperity differential between wealthy and developing nations it is also necessary to integrate the latter into the world economy to a greater extent than at present.

By promoting foreign trade (for example by the government's Hermes coverage and guarantees for investment) the position of German companies, especially small and medium-sized businesses with limited human and financial resources in international competition, are strengthened. Support for this commitment abroad on the part of German companies is one of the most impor-

tant tasks performed by the German Federal Foreign Office. The names of contacts at representative offices outside Germany can be found on the Federal Foreign Office Web site. These provide information on markets and conditions for investment and broker contacts with the governments of host nations. Whenever it appears to be necessary and sensible, concrete projects can be shored up with political arguments.

In order to balance out the economic and political risks from investments in developing countries and those still emerging as market economies, the Federal Government offers special promotional measures. To this end, it has signed treaties with 124 developing countries and emerging market economies in Central and Eastern Europe on the protection and promotion of investments. As a protection against political risks, the federal government pledges guarantees for investments deemed worthy of being promoted in said countries.

Deutsche Investitions- und Entwicklungsgesellschaft mbH), the German investment and develop-

A containership in Hamburg Harbor

ment company founded by the federal government, promotes direct investments in the Third World and in emerging market economies. Small and medium-sized German companies are entitled to low-interest loans and grants from the Kreditanstalt für Wiederaufbau.

In future, the support of German companies engaged in exporting new technologies such as renewable energy will become a focal point in the promotion of exports.

Information

www.invest-in-germany.com
www.ixpos.de
(For bodies involved in promoting foreign trade)
www.ahk.de
(Information about the network of German Chambers of Foreign Trade)
www.ihk.de
(Chambers of Commerce and Industry)
www.bfai.com
(German Office for Foreign Trade, with among other things data bases and publications)
www.bmwi.de
(The Federal Ministry of Economics and Labor among others with promotional programs)
www.auswaertiges-amt.de/aussenwirtschaft
(German Federal Foreign Office provides information on specific countries)

Mechanical engineer at work

The German Economic System

Trademarks of Germany as an economic location are its innovative and internationally competitive companies, qualified and motivated staff, an internationally recognized training system, a superbly developed infrastructure, and peak performance in research and development, not to mention a high degree of social harmony due to the social partnership between unions and employers. The plan is to stimulate economic growth, which is lower than the rest of Europe - 0.2% in 2002 - in particular by structural reforms in the labor market and the social insurance systems.

Germany as an economic hub

Germany is one of the world's leading industrial countries. Between 1991 and 2002, GDP, that is the total value of all manufactured goods and services in a year, increased from € 1,710 billion to € 1,984 billion – expressed in 1995 prices. Needless to say, the weak world economy also affected Germany. This led to growth in Germany in 2002 being limited to 0.2%. However, the country ranks third internationally in terms of its total output. Germany has maintained this exceptional position even though in the past few years the country and its citizens have had to master considerable economic changes brought on by unification.

Competitiveness: In recent years German industry has become substantially more competitive and has asserted and expanded its leading market position on German, European and international markets. German industry's value added (in other words its profit margin) increased further. In real terms, in 2000-1 it regained the level achieved in 1991 totaling around € 410 billion, whereas through 1995 it had decreased 8.2% in real terms.

The classic sectors of mechanical engineering, the automobile industry, electrical engineering and the chemical industry contributed particularly to the renewed increase in industrial output. But new industrial fields such as biotechnology also played a role. German industry was able to further expand its existing strong position in important sectors – on a European stage, too.

High-vacuum manufacture of Microsystems

Economic output – an international comparison

GDP 2002, 1995 price levels

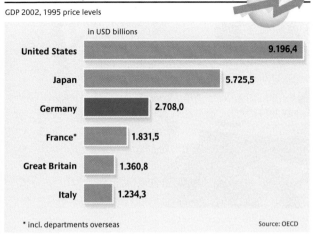

in USD billions

United States	9.196,4
Japan	5.725,5
Germany	2.708,0
France*	1.831,5
Great Britain	1.360,8
Italy	1.234,3

* incl. departments overseas   Source: OECD

Between 1995 and 2001, Germany's share in EU automobile industry production climbed from 48.2 percent
to 52.6 percent, in engineering from 42.3 percent to
44.4 percent and in the field of manufacturing office machines and IT devices from 24.9 percent to 29.7 percent.

Founding of new companies: The past decade
has seen an appreciable upturn in the number of new
companies founded, an important prerequisite for successful labor-market policy. During this time, approx.
420,000 to 500,000 companies were established in Germany per year. Even given the fact that there was a considerable pent-up demand in east Germany to increase
the number of new companies, there was also a significant increase in west Germany. In the 1970s, approximately 150,000 new companies were established per year,
in the 1980s the figure was approximately 300,000, reaching between 350,000 and 450,000 in the 1990s. The balance between new companies being established and
those being closed remained at the high level of 80,000
to 120,000, clearly above that of the 1980s.

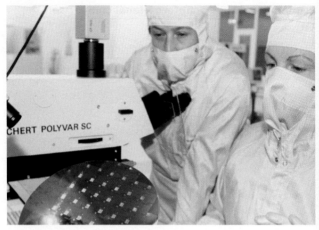

Research into semi-conductors

R&D: Germany occupies a strong position world wide in R&D. Above all, large trade or industrial corporations are active here.

Their R&D outlays have risen appreciably in recent years. Despite the difficult economic situation, companies increased their spending between 1995 and 2002 by € 10 billion to a total of € 36.9 billion. Within this period, total German spending on R&D rose from € 40.7 billion to € 52.8 billion.

Since 1997, some 90,000 additional jobs have been created in sectors involving intensive research. As for knowledge-intensive (commercial) services, the number of jobs increased by a good 400,000 between 1998 and 2000. Specifically the automobile industry is of great significance in the general field of R&D and has succeeded in improving its already strong position. It accounted for almost 40 percent of expenditure in the industry. In the last ten years the mechanical engineering sector increased R&D outlays by 40 percent to more than € 40 billion.

Patents: A significant sign of the high level of research in the German economy is the trend for patent registrations. Research intensity (i.e., the number of patents per million residents) increased by a double-digit figure. In past years, a continuous increase in the number of German patent applications with international participation has been recorded at the European Patent Office. The share of German applications climbed from 8.5 percent in 1998 to just on 10 percent in 2000. Germany occupies a leading position in Europe in this regard alongside Sweden and Finland. As for triad patents (i.e., inventions registered in Europe, the United States and Japan), Germany has roughly the same intensity as the United States.

Infrastructure: Another advantage Germany has as an economic hub is its very well developed supply and transport infrastructure. The road and rail network is very extensive, and along with the modern telecommunications infrastructure this means that goods, services and information can be swiftly exchanged. More is invested in the infrastructure thanks to the introduction and great acceptance of ultramodern technologies. For example, in

Patented pipe connector for spark-free welding

Transportation hub: Halle/Leipzig

2002, almost half the population was using the Internet and approximately two thirds of the population were using mobile telephones (see p. 286).

Liberalization: The appeal of Germany as an economic hub has also risen considerably due to liberalization in the telecoms sector, in the postal service, electricity generation and, most recently, in the gas market. In other words, Germany has swiftly opened these markets both by international comparisons and in terms of the deadlines set in the relevant EU directives and has assumed a pioneering role within Europe. This is a cost advantage for the entire economy. The end-user draws benefit from the availability of greater choice and less expensive offers.

Taxes: By virtue of the reforms to the German tax system in 2000, the tax burden on companies and private households in Germany has clearly dropped. A married employee with two children in this country generally does not pay more tax than in the United States. Also for the average, representative company the tax load in Germany is almost identical to that in the United States.

Employee qualifications: Well-qualified and flexible employees create another advantage for Germany. According to the most recent survey, 84 percent of employees have vocational qualifications, 16 percent of this number have a degree from a technical college or institute of tertiary education: the dual system of vocational training which splits responsibility for training between educational institutions and firms is particularly practice-orientated and successful (see p. 320).

The fact that the economy is little burdened by labor disputes on an international comparison is an indication of the high performance motivation of employees and the good social climate which is based on a social partnership between unions and employers. From 1990 to 1998, the number of strike days averaged 4.8 per 1,000 dependent employees in Germany, while for example in Great Britain, the number of working days lost through labor disputes totaled 26.4, in the United States 42.5, in Denmark 44.6 and in Italy 177.1.

Mainz's weekly market

Economic System and Economic Policy

The German Constitution (the Basic Law) does not pre-scribe a certain economic system but excludes a purely free market economy by insisting on adherence to the principle of a welfare state. The concept of the "social market economy", from which German economic policy has taken its cue since the middle of the 20th century, is secured by placing market forces in a framework set by social policy measures.

Social Market Economy: Ludwig Erhard was the main mind behind the social market economy and the German economic miracle, as it is known (in other words, the post-War German economic upturn). He was the first economics minister in the German Federal Republic and later was also Federal Chancellor for a few years. He takes historical credit for devising the concept of the social market economy and implementing it in the actual economic system of West Germany.

This was fundamentally supposed to enable the free play of forces on the market by raising consumer opportunities, motivating providers to achieve innovations and technical progress, and distributing income and profit according to individual achievement. But above all, it limits too much accumulation of market power. The state's duty is to create the framework for functioning competition. At the same time, the state must promote the readiness and ability of people to trade responsibly and to be more independent. It must not hinder either of these by taking over too much responsibility itself, for government action burdens the economy and society in the form of taxes and duties. This is detrimental to the work factor and limits freedom in the disposal of earned income.

Over a long period, a social system has emerged in Germany which internationally is considered exemplary - it hedges against risks incurred from unemployment, disability or a person's inability to work in his/her chosen profession, accident, illness, age and other social conditions. A special feature of the German system is the cooperation of employers and employees, expressed in the equal financing of contributions to pensions, medical and long-term care and unemployment insurance. Moreover, the social partnership of unions and employer associa-

Ludwig Erhard

tions is subject to the institutionalized settlement of conflicts as outlined in the collective labor law. The German Basic Law guarantees, in article 9, autonomy in negotiating wages, i.e., the right of employees and employers to bear the responsibility themselves for deciding on working conditions in contracts resulting from collective bargaining. The law covering collective bargaining and the Industrial Democracy Act, both of which were influenced in their wording by industry and the trade unions, play a considerable role in determining work regulations.

By reforming labor law and in particular the protection against unlawful dismissal and the social insurance system, the plan is to lower ancillary labor costs and boost economic growth.

Trade unions: The largest trade union organization is the Deutsche Gewerkschaftsbund (DGB), the German Trade Union Federation, which at the end of 2002 had approximately 7.7 million members. The DGB is based on the principle of one industrial sector, one trade union: unions include workers and employers within an entire industry, trade or other economic sector independent of their professional position within the business. Thus, for example, a chauffeur and a bookkeeper who work in an automobile factory would join the IG Metall trade union.

A total of eight unions have joined forces under the aegis of the DGB. These include the VERDI services trade union, which was founded in 2001 and which unites the Deutsche Angestellten Gewerkschaft (DAG; German Salaried Employees Union), the German Postal Union, the Union of Retailing, Banking and Insurance, the IG Medien (media union) and the Public Service, Transport and Traffic Union. With its 2.8 million members, VERDI is the largest single union in the world. The second largest union in the world is the IG Metall with its 2.7 million members.

Michael Sommer, Head of the DGB

The Deutsche Beamten Bund (DBB or German Civil Servant's Federation) with approx. 1.2 million members is the most important organization for public-sector employees. It does not conduct wage negotiations due to the special situation of laws covering public-sector employment and therefore, for example, cannot call members out on strike. Otherwise, however, it has all the characteristics of a union and considerable influence. The Christliche Gewerkschaftsbund Deutschlands (CGB, Christian Trade Union Federation of Germany) with its affiliated unions, numbers about 306,000 members.

The German trade unions are not connected with any particular political party or church. Nobody is forced to join a union; the closed shop system, which according to agreements between employers and unions allows only union members to be employed, is unknown in Germany. The rate of unionization, that is the proportion of workers who are members of unions in certain industries, varies greatly, but averages less than 50%.

Employers: Employers have joined to form regional associations which - as with the DGB unions - are based on the principal of one industry, one association. The central organization of the employers' association is the Bundesvereinigung der Deutschen Arbeitgeberverbände (BDA;

BDA President Dieter Hundt

Confederation of German Employers' Associations). Like the DGB, it does not conclude collective wage bargaining agreements but instead functions as a coordinating body representing the basic interests of its members. The BDA covers all branches of business – from industry, commerce and crafts, banks, insurance and agriculture to transport. It represents companies, however, only in their function as employers, in other words as the negotiating partner of the unions. All other interests, for example all matters of economic and tax policy, are represented by other associations. For example the Bundesverband der Deutschen Industrie (BDI; Federation of German Industries), the Zentralverband des Deutschen Handwerks (ZDH; National Federation of German Skilled Crafts and Trades) and the Bundesverband des Deutschen Gross- und Aussenhandels (Federation of German Wholesale and Foreign Trade).

Collective Agreements: There are two basic types of collective bargaining agreements which unions negotiate with the employer's association or with individual employers. Wage and salary agreements regulate the pay of workers and employees. In most cases they are agreed upon for a short time span. General agreements which as a rule run for several years govern general issues such as working hours, length of holidays, terms of notice and overtime rates. In addition there are special wage contracts which include special regulations such as vocational training, supplementary retirement benefits and protection against rationalization measures.

In principle, labor and management can negotiate their wage contracts freely. They must, however, abide by the constitution and the statutes. The average statutory maximum number of working hours per week in Germany is 48 hours. However, almost all employees work fewer than 40 hours a week and some only 35. Similarly, the law prescribes a minimum paid holiday of 24 working days, but collective agreements generally provide for a holiday of 30 working days. Nearly all workers receive additional holiday money and a Christmas bonus on the basis of collective agreements. In many cases, actual wages, salaries and other payments in many sectors of industry are considerably above collectively agreed rates.

Industrial Action: In particular, the German system of setting wages contributes to wide reaching social harmony compared with other countries. In Germany, industrial action can only be taken in connection with collective wage agreements. It is therefore restricted to the parties to which the agreement concerns. During the life of a collective wage agreement the parties thereto are obligated to maintain industrial peace. This means that industrial action cannot be called on matters covered by agreements still in force. In order to prevent industrial action, provision has been made for arbitration in which independent arbitrators can make suggestions on how to resolve the wage issue. Under the trade unions' statutes, moreover, union members are required to vote on whether a strike be called, and the latter only occurs if passed by a qualified majority. A union's right to strike is counterbalanced by the employer's right to lock them out. With this instrument which is publicly controversial but legally permissible, workers can be locked out of their work places and thus prevented from working.

Arbitration in a public-sector service dispute

The state remains neutral in labor disputes. Strikers and locked-out workers thus receive no unemployment benefit from the social insurance system. Union members receive strike pay from the union strike funds for loss of earnings while non-members receive nothing.

Workers and entrepreneurs are not in opposition to one another all the time however, but collaborate in many areas. Apart from everyday cooperation on the shop floor, representatives of both sides' organizations also meet on many other occasions, for example, on apprentice examinations committees. In the labor courts, which rule on employment-related disputes, there are lay judges involved on both sides at all levels. Within the framework of self-administration, as it is known, the management boards and representative assemblies of social insurance schemes (unemployment insurance, health insurance, accident insurance, pension insurance) are made up in equal part of employer and employee representatives.

Works constitutions and co-determination: Worker's participation in the business is one of the basic pillars of the German economic system. The Works Constitution Act, which was amended in 2001, governs the collaboration between employers, staff, works councils, unions and employees' associates. The act centers on the participation of the works councils and thus the staff in business decisions. The right of co-determination hinges on issues such as working hours, organization of work and even extends to configuration of workstations. One of the important co-determination rights ensures that the employers must consult the works council before a dismissal. Failure to do so would result in the dismissal being declared null and void. Tasks of the works council include ensuring adherence to valid legislation, decrees, accident prevention, regulations, wage agreements and works agreements.

Co-determination in the company enables employees to influence company management through their members on the supervisory board. This co-determination on the supervisory board makes certain that staff participate in important corporate planning and decisions. For example, the supervisory board appoints the members of the management board. The number of staff representatives and business representatives on supervisory boards of co-determined companies depends on the legal form of the company. The Co-Determination Act of 1976 prescribes that supervisory boards be composed of equal numbers of shareholders and staff representatives. Co-determination rests on the conviction that democratic rules cannot be limited to government but must also be effective in all walks of life.

Economic Policy: The overall aim of German economic policy is to secure stable prices, a high rate of employment and a balanced foreign trade along with steady economic growth. The central task of economic policy is to limit unemployment. New jobs which are assured in the future can only be created through investment and innovation.

The approximately three million self-employed individuals as well as small- and medium-sized enterprises (SMEs), businesses involved in retailing, the craft trades, services and independent professions are important target groups of government support. Tens of thousands of medium-sized manufacturing companies, particularly those involved in mechanical engineering, component suppliers, and in the new industrial fields such as biotechnology or the nano-industry form the basis for the competitiveness of the German economy. In order to create more jobs in SMEs, conditions and particularly those for starting up new businesses and small companies need to be substantially improved.

An important prerequisite for a well-functioning German economy is free competition which is guaranteed by the Law Against Restraints of Competition (Cartel Act). It prohibits agreements harmful to free competition. The Office for the Control and Supervision of Cartels in Bonn and the cartel authorities of the federal states monitor compliance with the law. The European Commission plays an increasingly important role in the supervision of the European laws governing competition. The federal government not only supports competition in the domestic market but also rejects any form of protectionism in world trade. Germany is interested in open markets owing to its traditional focus on exports. For the German economy it is important to expand the European single market and to maintain old markets outside the European Union as well as opening new ones.

Devising and coordinating economic and fiscal policy is the joint task of the federal government, states and municipalities. They work together in various committees: the Business Cycle Council consists of the Federal Ministers of Economics and Finance, one member of each state government, and representatives of municipalities and associations of municipalities. The German Bundesbank may also take part in the consultations which occur at least twice a year. The Business Cycle Council endeavors to ensure that processes involving all participants in economic policy are as uniform as possible.

The similarly composed Financial Planning Council has the task of coordinating financial planning on all levels of government. The federal and state governments are obliged to draw up multi-annual financial budgets so that public revenue and expenditure can be geared to the demands and capacities of the national economy.

Furthermore, the federal government is advised by independent economic experts. These include the Council of Economic Advisors for the Federal Ministry of Economics and the Council of Economic Advisers for the Federal Ministry of Finance, scientific research institutes and the Council of Experts on the Assessment of Economic Trends which was set up in 1963. Comprised of five independent economic experts, this body presents a report every autumn which discusses the overall economic situation, future trends and economic policy. Every January, the federal government presents an annual economic report to the Bundestag and the Bundesrat. It describes among other things the federal government's economic and financial targets for the current year and outlines the plans as regards economic and financial policy.

Craftsmen at work on a building site

Employment and the labor market

In modern society employment is of fundamental importance for ensuring a living, being able to enjoy general living standards and as a basis for both governing one's own life and self-expression. In 2002, despite the upheaval that had to be contended with in the east German labor market, the number of people employed rose by almost two million to 38.7 million. At the same time, there were however around four million without gainful employment. Reforms already introduced and further structural reforms are intended to achieve an enduring reduction in unemployment.

Employment: Two thirds of those in employment worked in the service sector, a figure that has grown substantially over the past few years. Conversely, the number of people working in industry decreased from almost 30 percent in 1991 to 21.6 percent at the present time. By far the majority of those in gainful employment, namely 34.6 million, worked for somebody else, a good four million were self-employed with family members helping out.

Unemployment: This employment figure is offset by the fact that on average in 2002 there were more than four million people without work. The unemployment rate among all civilians available for work stood at 9.8 percent, an increase of 0.4 percent on 2001, meaning that almost one in ten people able to work was without gainful employment. In west Germany, the unemployment rate stood at 7.6 percent and in east Germany at 17.7 percent.

On the one hand, this is the result of far-reaching changes in economic structures, and on the other hand, the consequence of an ongoing weak economy. Reducing unemployment is the federal government's no. 1 task.

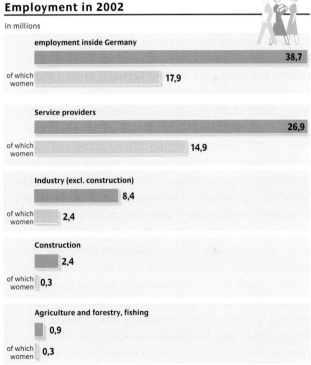

Employment in 2002

in millions

employment inside Germany

38,7

of which women

17,9

Service providers

26,9

of which women

14,9

Industry (excl. construction)

8,4

of which women

2,4

Construction

2,4

of which women

0,3

Agriculture and forestry, fishing

0,9

of which women

0,3

Source: German Federal Statistics Office

It is endeavoring to help more people find employment by reforming the labor market and the social security system.

Following unification in 1990, Germany was suddenly faced with a divided labor market: In the west German states, the unusual economic conditions prompted by unification had a positive effect on the labor market. Once this had run its course, the west suffered a far-reaching weakening of the economy, which impacted with a lag on the labor market.

In the east German states, the transition from a socialist command economy to a social market economy has cost large numbers of jobs. Between 1989 and 1993, the number dwindled by around 3.6 million to approximately 6.2 million. This meant that immediately following unification there was a sharp increase in unemployment, with a rebound then emerging. This came about in part as a result of the increasing integration of the economies in east and west Germany and the enormous transfers of funds paid by West Germans in the form of taxes to the east German states.

In 2002, the situation worsened once again. The worldwide economic downturn in 2001 impacted negatively on the German economy. The situation was characterized by weak demand at home, the crash on the stock markets, and the escalating crisis in the Middle East. The result was an increase in average annual unemployment to more than four million. The average length of time spent unemployed was 34 weeks.

A particularly serious problem in both parts of Germany is the high number of long-term unemployed, in other words those who have been looking for work for more than one year. For the most part, these include workers with insufficient vocational qualifications, the elderly, those with health-related restrictions and east German women. Having been considerably reduced in the preceding years, in 2002, as a result in particular of

Wheel-chair users employed archiving documents

trends in east Germany this figure rose again, with the annual average standing at 1.31 million.

The rule of thumb for the labor market in both East and West continues to be: the fewer qualifications candidates have, the less chance they have of finding a job. Almost 40 percent of those unemployed have no vocational qualification. On the other hand, those in the West with qualifications from a higher education institute practically enjoy full employment. According to the Federal Institute for Employment their position in the labor market has been strengthened even further and is surprisingly impervious to swings in the economy.

The physically challenged: The federal government pays particular attention to finding occupations for the physically challenged. On October 1, 2000 the Act To Reduce Unemployment among the Physically Challenged came into effect, improving equal opportunities for the physically challenged in everyday working life. Between 1981 and 2000, the number of physically challenged without work rose from 93,809 to 184,089. As a result of increased efforts on the part of the federal government, in 2001 the figure was trimmed by 6.9 percent, and in 2002 by a further eight percent to 156,900.

The elderly and employment: Given demographic trends – in future there will be more elderly and fewer young people in employment – and bearing in mind the increasing financial problems of the pension systems, elder segments of the population still working have become increasingly the focal point of attention. Politicians, business and society today concentrate even more on enabling elder citizens to pursue some form of occupation. Among other things, the Federal Institute for Employment provides financial support to this end. Its efforts have resulted in the number of those unemployed over the age of 50 dropping considerably in 2001 and 2002.

Apprenticeships: Given the importance of vocational qualifications in later working life, it is important that there is a sufficient number of apprenticeships on offer through the Dual System (see p. 320). However, only one in three companies actually offer such apprenticeships.

In 2002, the number of new apprenticeship agreements signed dropped from the previous year by around 42,000 to just over 572,000. On September 30, 2002 the number of unsuccessful applicants nationwide increased by 2,921 to a total of 23,383.

Training in the new profession of mechatronics

That said, by December 31, 2002 supply and demand were almost completely balanced. The federal government continues to pursue a policy aimed at halting the decline in the number of apprenticeships offered by companies and encouraging more companies to offer training opportunities.

In order to increase the number of apprenticeships, businesses and the self-employed with an annual turnover of up to € 500 million receive low-interest loans of up to € 100,000 for every additional apprentice. Furthermore, companies offering the training are released from the obligation to prove their knowledge of professional educational matters in a course followed by examination for a period of five years. They are, however, still subject to the usual examination with regard to suitability by the Chamber of Commerce and Industry and the Chamber of Craftsmen. This measure is aimed at encouraging small businesses in particular to offer apprenticeships.

Due to the particularly difficult situation in east Germany, in 2003 the federal government once again financed around 14,000 training opportunities there, and an apprenticeship drive is ongoing to create additional training opportunities.

Training to be a chemical lab technician

Both business and the trade unions support the emergency program for reducing youth unemployment, "JUMP", through which by the start of 2003 around 514,000 youths had received assistance. In both 2002 and 2003, more than € 1 billion was made available in the form of grants to cover additional wage costs and measures for gaining qualifications.

The Federal Institute for Employment: The promotion of jobs, job placement, and the payment of unemployment benefit all fall within the ambit of the Federal Institute for Employment. It also administers the statutory unemployment insurance, which was introduced in 1927. It is obligatory for all employees as a matter of principle. Contributions are paid half by the employee and half by the employer. The Federal Institute for Employment has branches throughout Germany: the employment exchanges.

Labor promotion: The main task in active labor promotion is to prevent unemployment before it occurs. It also involves ensuring that the unemployed are re-integrated into the world of work as quickly as possible. To this end, the FIE grants those youths and grown ups with insufficient resources their own allowances towards apprenticeships. It can also assist with further vocational training of the unemployed, or those threatened with unemployment through providing living costs and covering the costs involved in the training scheme. Such people are likewise entitled to vouchers financing further training measures. Furthermore, the Federal Institute for Employment supports the integration of the physically and mentally challenged into everyday working life.

Job placement: An important task performed by the employment exchanges is matching up the unemployed with job vacancies. In 2002, a reform of the law meant that greater stress is now placed on the unemployed taking a more proactive role in the search for new employment. In future, an agreement will lay down legal-

Simulating a job interview

ly binding duties and activities for employment exchanges and those seeking employment. The unemployed
may also make use of private employment agencies,
which, if successful, are rewarded with vouchers from
the employment exchanges.

Benefits for the unemployed: Anybody who is
unemployed, registered with an employment exchange,
and over a period of three years has paid unemployment
insurance contributions, is entitled to unemployment benefit, which is however paid for a limited period only.
Those who are still unemployed after exhausting their entitlement to unemployment benefit may apply for unemployment assistance. However, this involves an assessment
of whether the person really is in need. To this end, a
means test is carried out (see p. 151.).

Alliance for Jobs: In 1998, in view of the growing problems on the employment front, the Federal Government teamed up with representatives of the industrial
associations and trade unions to create the "Alliance for
Jobs, Training and Competitiveness" as a platform for dis-
cussing measures aimed at job creation. The alliance has
made several important decisions, for example the hiring

of up to 20,000 IT experts from outside Germany without the normal red-tape ("Green Card"). In 2003, however, as a result of unbridgeable differences between the trade unions and the industrial associations, the talks were broken off until further notice.

Reforms: In 2003, a wide variety of measures aimed at invigorating the employment market came into force. These are aimed at opening up new job creation opportunities and to improve and speed up job placements. The Federal Institution for Employment will cease to be structured as a public-sector employee and develop into a service provider for both companies and those in search of employment.

An important element of the reforms is to set up staff service agencies covering all branches of employment at all the employment agencies. These agencies, for the most part operated by private job placement companies, can place people who were previously unemployed and who are registered with them in companies for a limited period. The state subsidizes anyone unemployed becoming self-employed. This system of "One Person Companies" is subsidized from unemployment insurance for the first three years of self-employment, provided that annual income does not exceed € 25,000. An unbureaucratic revision of the system with regard to small, already existing self-employed outfits will open up new opportunities for job creation in tandem with the "One Person Companies".

In addition, there are to be subsidies for job creation opportunities in private households. To this end, employing a house-help will to a certain extent be tax-deductible. A further step is subsidies of "mini jobs", as they are known, in the low-wage sector, whereby the employed make very low or even no social contributions, and employers only have to pay a flat-rate contribution. The federal government anticipates that solely by subsidizing "mini jobs" it will succeed in creating 320,000 new jobs. Further new measures will improve employment opportunities for older employees. These new measures however go hand in hand with expectations of the unemployed. As such, young unemployed people will be expected to become more mobile: Anyone refusing an offer of employment will be required to provide reasons for doing so.

These reforms were accompanied by a program entitled "Capital for Work" aimed at small and medium-sized companies. If a company offers an unemployed person an unlimited contract it may be rewarded with a low-interest loan of up to € 100,000. This is in the interests of SMEs in particular, which frequently have difficulties in financing investments because banks have become more cautious in the granting of loans. In this way there is an incentive for companies to employ those without work.

Information

www.bmwi.de
(Federal Ministry of Economics and Labor)
www.bmbf.de
(Federal Ministry of Education and Research)
www.dgb.de
(German Trade Union Association)
www.bda-online.de
(Federal Union of German Employers Associations)

Income, assets, prices

Income: In 1962-63, private households in West Germany had disposable income of DM 907 (€ 463). Of this figure, DM 730 (€ 373) was used for private expenditure, almost two thirds for food, clothing and accommodation. In 1998, monthly disposable income stood at DM 5,448 (€ 2,786), with DM 4,192 (2,143) utilized for private expenditure. There is an unequal distribution of assets and disposable income. The average income for the self-employed form the pinnacle of the income pyramid, followed by public-sector employees, company employees and pensioners.

   Assets: Since 1980, financial assets held by private households – which include, for example, cash, savings, securities and life insurance policy claims – have more than tripled. At the end of 1998, the figure stood at € 2.91 billion in Germany, as opposed to € 0.77 billion in West Germany at the end of 1980. In addition to this sum there is the value of property, for the most part owner-occupied accommodation or accommodation that is rented out. In 1998, 48 percent of private households in the west

German states and 33 percent of those in the east German states held real-estate assets. Since the 1950s, the formation of financial and tangible assets such as one's own property has been subsidized in the Federal Republic through state premiums, bonuses and tax rebates. In addition to these general subsidies for all citizens, since the beginning of the 1960s there has been a special subsidy for creating assets for employees in the form of a state savings bonus.

Prices: The standard of living depends both on the level of income and that of prices. For this reason trends in consumer prices are an important political issue. Compared with other countries, the Federal Republic boasts above-average price stability. At the beginning of the 1990s, however, high consumer demand as a result of unification, greatly increased wage rates and tax increases to finance the reconstruction of the economy in east Germany, which had suffered enormous damage over the previous 40 years, all contributed to a rise in prices. Over the past few years the rate of inflation has once again dropped. In 2002, it was up 1.3 percent on the previous year, the lowest rise since 1999.

The glass Volkswagen factory in Dresden

"Aufbau Ost", the agenda for economic recovery in east Germany

When Germany celebrated unification on October 3, 1990 large sections of the east German economy were highly unprofitable. In the eastern states a modern economic structure is emerging that is geared to the future. In particular, ongoing industrial growth, higher export levels, increasing innovation and the establishment of internationally recognized high-tech centers all bear witness to the fact that this is an area with a strong future. Scarcely a decade after unification, it stands up well in comparison with national and international competition.

Growth: Until 1995, the economy in east Germany grew by up to ten percent. This high rate of increase can be attributed first and foremost to the buoyant building sector. This trend has panned out and since 2001 the economy in eastern Germany has also been unable to escape worldwide economic problems. As in 2001, economic performance in eastern Germany also dropped slightly in 2002.

On the other hand, industry in the new states grew by 4.4 percent in 2002, a difficult year, thus following on from the high levels of previous years, which had posted an average of six percent growth. In 2002, east German industry, which at the beginning of the 1990s was at rock bottom, achieved its highest share of the gross value added since 1991. Industry and services closely related to production seized the opportunity to build on their role as the growth drivers.

Exports: Increasing sales by east German industry in national markets, in particular in international markets are a reflection of its increasing competitiveness. Between 1992 and 2002, the ratio of exports to total sales increased considerably, namely from 13.9 to 23.9 percent, though in terms of exports east Germany still trails behind west Germany (around 39 percent).

Economic recovery in the East in figures

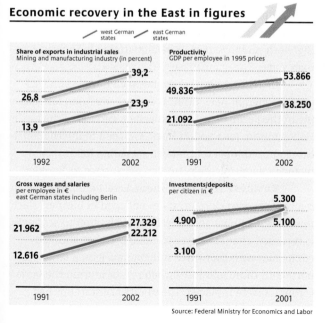

west German states / east German states

Share of exports in industrial sales
Mining and manufacturing industry (in percent)
39,2 | 26,8 | 23,9 | 13,9
1992 — 2002

Productivity
GDP per employee in 1995 prices
53.866 | 49.836 | 38.250 | 21.092
1991 — 2002

Gross wages and salaries
per employee in €
east German states including Berlin
27.329 | 22.212 | 21.962 | 12.616
1991 — 2002

Investments/deposits
per citizen in €
5.300 | 5.100 | 4.900 | 3.100
1991 — 2001

Source: Federal Ministry for Economics and Labor

Economic recovery in the East in figures

Investments excl. buildings in € billion

1991	1992	1993	1994	1995	1996	1997	1998	1999	2000	2001
21,7	24,2	26,3	28,6	29,5	29,8	28,5	30,4	32,0	33,7	32,6

Source: Federal Ministry for Economics and Labor

Innovations: With regard to innovations, industry in the east German states is again closing the gap on the west German states.

In east Germany, medium-sized companies make up for the lack of large companies engaged in research, which in west Germany account for around 84 percent of all research work. 7.4 percent of all SMEs make an impression with new products and production processes, considerably more than corresponding companies in west Germany (4 percent). One in five companies active in high-tech research work is headquartered in the east German states.

Increasing networking between business and science resulted in new business centers emerging for example in the Berlin district of Adlershof, Dresden, Erfurt, Halle/Leipzig, Jena and Rostock, engaged in internationally recognized top-level research including fields such as biotechnology, microelectronics and surface technology.

Business start-ups: Immediately after unification many in the east German states engaged in business start-ups, thus making a considerable contribution to economic recovery. Thanks to over 530,000 newly established companies with over three million new jobs, a large proportion of those jobs lost through restructuring the large combines were replaced. The number of start-ups has since reverted to normal.

Foreign investments: The advantages that the new states offer are reflected in the fact that almost 2,000 foreign companies from more than 50 countries have invested in them. In the ten years following unification, almost € 16 billion in foreign investments flowed into eastern Germany. These have included, for example, the AMD and Motorola microelectronics projects in Dresden as well as chemical production lines in the Halle–Leipzig–Merseburg triangle and in parts of East Brandenburg.

Infrastructure: Foreign investors are presented with a modern infrastructure. The degree of training, the motivation and the flexibility of the workforce are recognized as being exemplarily high. Compared with other European countries, investors receive a high degree of support for investments. In addition, east Germany possesses a telecommunications infrastructure that has been completely modernized over the past few years, state-of-the-art road and rail systems and several international airports.

The airports in Dresden, Leipzig, Erfurt, not to mention the three Berlin airports Tegel, Schönefeld and Tempelhof, offer international investors a choice of airports with international connections. The interstate system and in particular the major East/West road arteries have been modernized and can accommodate a large volume of traffic. Rail connections between the east and west German states have been extended, with the capital city Berlin becoming a well-functioning railway hub. Any gaps between the previously separate railway systems have been filled.

Income: Since unification, considerable progress has been made in creating equal living standards for both East and West Germans. Since 1991, gross income for each employed person in the east German states has risen from 50.4 percent of the level in the West in 1991 to 77.4 percent in 2002. Disposable income in the eastern states is around 90 percent of the level in the West.

Pension payments from the statutory pension insurance scheme to those in the East have also risen. Since July 2003, the pension of an average wage earner after 45 years employment is € 1,176 in the west German states and € 1,034 in the east German states. In other words, the theoretical pension in the east German states amounts to almost 88 percent of that in the West.

Accommodation: Since 1990, with financial aid from the federal government, more than half the apartments in eastern Germany have been either modernized or restored. This has resulted in considerable improvements in the quality of their lives. Average living space per individual rose from 29.5 sq. m. in 1993 to 32.8 sq. m. in 1998. Whereas in 1993 only 57 percent of apartments had a central heating system, this figure had increased to almost 83 percent by 1998. Bathrooms and sanitary facilities are now standard in 95 percent of apartments.

In a representative poll in the spring of 2001, the majority of east Germans surveyed had a positive view of their own standard of living and let there be no doubt that reunification had increased their affluence. 54 percent were of the opinion that unification had led to an improvement in their financial situation. A mere 17 percent were of the opinion that they were economically worse off than before unification.

Solidarity Pact: The first Solidarity Pact, as it is known, since 1995 resulted in the east German states being included in the federal state financial equalization scheme. The Solidarity Pact is a method whereby the federal government and the federal states support the reduction of the special burdens shouldered by the east German states, including Berlin, which came about as a result of the division of the country. Solidarity Pact II, which was passed in 2001, ensures the continuation of financial support. Initially scheduled to last until 2004 it will now run until 2020. It offers the east German states a total of € 156.5 billion in federal government funding.

There continues to be a particular focus on the promotion of investments, with particular attention being paid to industrial companies and production-related services. Special attention is paid to structurally weak regions. The joint efforts by federal government and the federal states to make "improvements in the economic structure" has proved its worth, and over the past few years has played a substantial role in shoring up the east German states. Tax bonuses on investments are another instrument of promotion, benefiting industry and production-related services.

The federal government places particular importance on supporting R&D, especially in the corporate sector. It is particularly concerned in strengthening the ability of east German companies to successfully market new products and processes. With regard to promoting innovation and technology, particular attention is paid to close cooperation between business and the academic world.

Restored houses in Rostock

Given the surplus supply of accommodation, where further promotion is concerned the federal government is concentrating its efforts on consolidation of the markets for residential accommodation and creating urban structures. The program entitled "Stadtumbau Ost" (Urban Reconstruction East), for which federal government, the federal states and municipalities have earmarked around € 2.7 billion until 2009, will further increase the quality of life. Investments in town planning result in high levels of public and private investments and increase demand for goods and services. The protection of monuments in historical town centers also forms part of the support for town planning.

The most important business sectors

In Germany, as in other countries, there has been a shift in the importance of individual business sectors over the past few years. The service sector has become considerably more relevant, and its role is by now almost on a par with that of industry. The German IT and biotech sectors are both international leaders, as are technology for the use of renewable energies and environmental protection. The crafts trades continue to be an exceptional German feature and will in future remain at the core of the country's business life.

Industry

Industry continues to form the mainstay of the German economy and is the hub for all business activities. In comparison with other EU countries and the United States, its share of the economy as a whole is relatively large. In 2001, there were almost 6.4 million employees in around 49,000 industrial corporations. Sales totaled almost € 1.35 trillion. Exports accounted for more than a third of all products manufactured. Almost 98 percent of all companies had a payroll totaling less than 500 and as such belonged to the SME sector, which provides around 40 percent of all jobs in industry and whose sales account for some 33 percent of all industrial sales.

The importance of industry in the German economy has dwindled considerably over the past few years. As a result of long-term structural changes, between 1970 (in the former West Germany) and 2001, industry's contribution to the gross value added of all business sectors fell from 51.7 to 23.8 percent. By contrast, the contribution public and private service providers make to overall economic output has increased considerably. In 2001, these produced 20.2 percent of gross value added. Commerce, the hospitality industry and transportation account for 18.7 percent. Financing, leasing and corporate service providers have a share of 31 percent. In the industrial sector, rapidly expanding branches such as IT and communications technology and the aerospace industry have failed to make up the ground lost by the decline of such "traditional" branches as textiles and steel.

In Germany, 2.6 million industrial workers are employed by large corporations with a payroll of more than 1,000. All in all, the small group of large companies account for some 51 percent of total turnover. Many of these firms are known throughout the world and have branches or research facilities overseas. They include the carmakers Volkswagen, BMW and Daimler-Chrysler, chemical corporations such as Aventis, Bayer and BASF, the electrical equipment manufacturer Siemens AG, the energy corporations E.ON and RWE, and the Bosch Group.

The automobile industry: This is one of the most important branches of the German economy. Germany is the world's third largest producer of automobiles, following the United States and Japan. Of the 5.12 million motor vehicles manufactured in the Federal Republic in 2002, more than 70 percent were exported.

The automobile industry has a long tradition in the east German states as well. Following unification however, the models produced under the old GDR regime stood no chance against international competition, and production of models which were technically obsolete was phased out. Several large carmakers from western Germany have now opened new plants in Saxony and Thuringia. In 2001 alone, the automobile industry invested more than € 800 million in east German states. This figure represented more than ten percent of total investments in industry in eastern Germany that year. All in all, the west German automobile industry has invested around € 3.5 billion in east German states over the past few years. Once production is in full swing, around 370,000 cars a year will leave the modern assembly lines there.

Mechanical engineering and plant construction: Most firms in German industry are engaged in mechanical engineering and plant construction. Traditionally, SMEs have predominated, and it is thanks to their flexibility and technological efficiency that Germany is among the world's leaders here. More than 80 percent of companies engaged in mechanical engineering are highly specialized SMEs with less than 200 employees. As component suppliers to industry and an innovative field they play an important role in the economy as a whole. In the international arena, the spectrum of products they offer is unparalleled, encompassing more than 20,000 different items – from consoles, printing machines and agricultural machinery to machine tools.

The chemical industry: This is an important supplier of primary, intermediate and finished products for sectors such as health care, the automobile industry, the construction industry as well as for private consumption in Germany. Thanks to its state-of-the-art technology, innovative products and emphasis on research, it plays a leading role worldwide. In addition to the large firms in this branch, which rank among the world's most important corporations, there are also numerous small and medium-sized companies.

The chemical industry has a long tradition in the east German states. The aim of government policy has been to retain the core of the traditional chemical production regions in the East through a process of restructuring and privatization. The chemical industry is making considerable efforts to improve environmental protection, and has assumed a pioneering role in many areas.

Aerospace: The aerospace industry in Germany is a small branch, but nonetheless of enormous strategic importance. In proportion to sales, the amount the industry spends on R&D is considerably higher than in all other branches.

Aerospace is Germany's technology driver, combining almost all the high-tech of the information age: electronics, robotics, measuring and control technology, materials technology and regulatory technology. Innovations from the sector have proved to be an enormous boost for computer production and are put to use in several other branches of industry. Mobile communications systems, car navigation systems, live coverage of major

The Ariane 5 rocket engine at Daimler-Benz Aerospace in Bremen

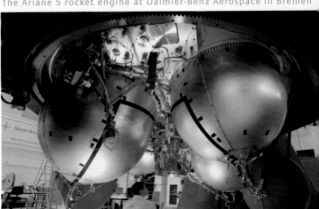

sporting and political events, video conferences with people in distant countries and global research into the environment and climate would all be impossible without aerospace.

Following a lull at the beginning of the 1990s, the German aerospace industry has enjoyed a period of considerable growth. In 2002, 69,950 employees in the sector generated sales of € 15.3 billion. That year, civilian aviation contributed 68.3 percent of total sales, military aviation 23.1 percent, and space operations 8.6 percent.

Biotechnology: Worldwide, German biotechnology and genetic engineering is second only to the United States. It is one of the most innovative German branches and posts above-average growth rates.

In 2001, the number of companies primarily engaged in commercializing modern biotechnology rose ten percent to 365. Sales posted by German biotechnology companies rose by 33 percent to over € 1 billion. A total of € 1.3 billion was invested in R&D, 71 percent more than in 2000. The number of employees in the sector rose by 35 percent to 14,408. Modern biotechnology methods and genetic engineering are used by a whole host of companies in what has become known as the life-science sector.

Cooling samples in a genetic engineering lab

Environmental technology: Be it technology for purifying sewage or for the use of renewable energies, German environmental technology is booming. The number of jobs in the renewable energy sector has risen considerably. Around 130,000 people are now employed in this sector, which has a bright future ahead. At the same time, the use of renewable energy is a welcome fillip for the economy in general: From 2000 to 2001 alone, total sales for the sector soared by 20 percent to around € 8.2 billion.

A portal for the transfer of environmental technology (www.cleaner-production.de) operated by federal government provides a whole host of information on German environmental technology and offers an opportunity for those involved in environmental technology inside and outside Germany to contact one another.

Electrical engineering: With around 881,000 employees, the German electrical engineering and electronics industry is one of the largest industrial employees in the country. In 2001, the predominantly SMEs generated sales of over € 160 billion and between 1996 and 2000 invested over € 30 billion in Germany. Moreover, with exports totaling around € 105 billion, the sector is one of the strongest German export branches, and places third worldwide behind the USA and Japan.

Further branches of industry: Other areas which continue to be of great importance are the food industry, the textile and clothing industry (including the leather goods industry), metallurgy and metal-processing industry, mining, precision engineering and the optical industry.

The Chambers of Industry and Commerce: The DIHT Association of German Chambers of Industry and Commerce is the national organization of the 82 German chambers of industry and commerce. All German firms within the country (with the exception of craft and trade enterprises, the independent professions, and agricultural operations) are by law members of the chambers of industry and commerce. They represent the interests of regional businesses vis-à-vis the municipalities, state governments and regional state authorities. They function as advisers for their member firms and as knowledgeable providers of information for business and industry. The chambers of industry and commerce are democratically organized and independent of government influence. The Association of German Chambers of Industry and Commerce represents the interests of business and industry at the federal level and at the European Commission in Brussels.

It also supports the approximately 110 offices of the German chambers of commerce abroad as well as the offices of delegates and representatives of German industry in more than 70 countries all over the world, providing support primarily for SMEs.

Presenting cell phones at CeBIT in Hanover

Service providers
IT

The liberalization of the telecoms markets and the accompanying acceleration in the speed of technological advance has, in the space of but a few years, considerably strengthened Germany's position with regard to competition from other industrialized nations. The contribution made to overall value added by the IT industry, and by telecommunications in particular, is growing at an above-average rate in comparison with other sectors. At the same time, this has resulted in an even more state-of-the-art infrastructure, significant price reductions, new services and thus greatly improved working and living conditions. This provides the requirements necessary for the country to make increased use of its economic advantages in the framework of globalization.

Telecommunications: Germany is already the largest and fastest-growing mobile telephony and online market in Europe. All in all, between 1998 and 2002 sales posted by companies engaged in providing telecoms services rose from around € 44.2 billion to € 60 billion, or an increase of three percent in comparison with 2001. Since 1998 the number of companies providing such services has rocketed from 1,066 to over 2,000.

In 2002, around € 8 billion was invested in the telecommunications sector. The number of calls via landlines has increased by 22 percent. Between 1998 and 2002 the number of connections rose from 46.5 million to 53.7 million. With regard to mobile telephony, the volume of calls, which are registered by the minute, surged by 17 percent to 32 billion minutes. There were three million new subscribers to mobile communications providers, taking the total figure to 59.2 million. This means that 71.7 percent of all Germans now have a cell phone, putting Germany clearly ahead of the United States, with 47.7 percent, and Japan, with 62.1 percent.

Cell phone users in Germany

in millions

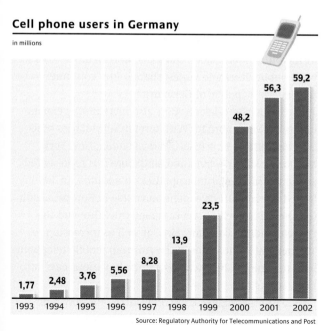

1993	1994	1995	1996	1997	1998	1999	2000	2001	2002
1,77	2,48	3,76	5,56	8,28	13,9	23,5	48,2	56,3	59,2

Source: Regulatory Authority for Telecommunications and Post

Until 1996, telephone services in Germany were provided exclusively by the Deutsche Bundespost or, later, by Deutsche Telekom AG. The Telecommunications Act of that year established the regulatory framework for liberalization of the telephony market as of January 1, 1998. Following the dissolution of the Federal Ministry of Posts and Telecommunications, a Regulatory Authority for Telecommunications and Post was established under the purview of the Federal Ministry of Economics.

Its main task is to act as a watchdog monitoring the dominant market role of Deutsche Telekom AG and Deutsche Post AG, which had previously enjoyed a monopoly and to assist new competitors by creating the necessary equal opportunities. It also awards licenses for the telecommunications and postal markets and manages these licenses and telephone numbers.

Deutsche Telekom: Deutsche Telekom AG is the largest telecommunications provider in Europe and the third largest carrier in the world. In 2002, it still provided 51.4 million of the 53.7 million telephone numbers registered. On January 1, 1995 Deutsche Telekom was transformed into a joint stock company. In November 1996 it went public. Its single largest shareholder continues to be the Federal Republic of Germany.

Deutsche Telekom AG is also increasingly expanding its activities abroad. With foreign subsidiaries of its own and offices in Brussels, Paris, London, New York, Moscow, Jakarta, Beijing and Singapore it is represented in the world's major metropolises. In addition, in 1999 it forged ahead with its expansion course in Europe, acquiring the British cell phone company One2One and the French landline company Siris, as well as increasing to 100 percent its holdings in the Austrian mobile telephony firm max.mobil. It also holds a stake in various east European companies.

Approximately 1,300 other firms are now registered with the Regulatory Authority for Telecommunications and Post, operating in any of the various branches of the telecom sector. In particular, the liberalization of the telephone market has attracted a large number of competitors who have already commenced local, regional or nationwide operations. In larger cities, big companies such as Mannesmann Arcor and Otelo are primarily responsible for ISDN connections. In addition, there is an ever greater number of local and regional competitors entering the market.

Transformation of the telecommunications sector into a free market has sparked fierce competition among the numerous new providers. Their many different rates are often bewildering, especially in the case of long-distance calls. In 2003, this competition is expected to extend to local calls, since, as is the case with long-distance calls, the possibility of using a "call by call" is also to be introduced here. This offers subscribers the opportunity to select the cheapest provider on an individual call basis. Several large companies such as T-Mobile, Vodafone, VIAG and VEBA are all jostling for a share of the cell phone market. This competition within the telecommunications sector has resulted in enormous advantages for customers. Since the end of 1997, prices for cell phoning, Internet access and long-distance calls have plummeted and are now among the lowest in Europe.

Internet: In the Federal Republic of Germany there is a broad spectrum of electronic information services. The Internet has by now penetrated almost all spheres of private life and almost the entire work world. It provides a quick, low cost method for transporting information throughout the world, and it can now be used for much more than just ordering books, films and CDs, for example tenders and orders, payments for bills and cash-free transactions. The Internet is increasingly becoming an important instrument for entrepreneurial activity.

More than 50 percent of Germans aged 14 or over use the Internet for private or business purposes. The Regulatory Authority estimates that at the end of 2002, 35 million, or roughly half of those over 14, go on-line, be it at home, at work, in Internet cafés or at friends' homes. The fact that the cost of this Internet access has dropped so dramatically has encouraged this extensive use.

With e-commerce sales of almost € 50 billion, Germany heads the European table for e-business transactions. Over the past few years the German market for IT and telecommunications grew disproportionately in comparison with the economy overall. In 2002, ICT sales accounted for 6.4 percent of gross domestic product (GDP), putting it in third place in terms of sales after automobile production and electronic engineering.

In 2002, Germany had a 21.1 percent share (€ 136 billion) of the European market, making it the market leader ahead of Great Britain, with a share of 20.6 per-

Surfing in an Internet café

cent. Despite the gloomy overall economic scenario, which also left its mark on the ICT sector, the number of employees grew from 710,000 in 1998 to 784,000 in 2002.

Banks exchanges and insurance companies

There are a wide variety of financial institutions in the Federal Republic of Germany. In addition to the "Big Four", Deutsche Bank, Dresdner Bank, Commerzbank and HypoVereinsbank there are public savings banks and the Land central banks (the central credit institutions of public savings banks), credit cooperatives (Volksbanken and Raiffeisenbanken), private banks as well as building and loan associations, central depositaries for securities and investment companies.

For years now, the banking sector has been undergoing pronounced concentration. Whereas in the 1950s, there were just under 14,000 independent credit institutions, by 2001 the number had shrunk to 2,695.

The large banks: In terms of business volume, the "Big Four" clearly head the list of all German insti-

The European Central Bank in Frankfurt

tutes. According to Bundesbank statistics, in terms of net worth as at year-end 2001, Deutsche Bank, HypoVereinsbank, Dresdner Bank and Commerzbank jointly account for a market share of 16 percent of the entire credit market.

Together, the land central banks and savings banks have a 36 percent share and the cooperative banks 12 percent.

In 2003, following a drastic drop in earnings in the banking sector, the German banking scene was in the throes of a far-reaching process of restructuring. The year before, Dresdner Bank had been taken over by the Allianz AG insurance group. At the beginning of 2003, the Association of German Banks was anticipating that over the course of the next 5-10 years the number of bank branches in Germany will have decreased by around 50 percent, corresponding to the size of the branch network in neighboring countries.

The Federal Financial Supervisory Office in Bonn and Frankfurt is responsible for supervising the activities of all credit institutions in Germany. Should a credit institute run into financial difficulties and savers suffer losses, compensation is forthcoming from mandatory state measures and establishments set up by the banking system itself to guarantee the safety of deposits.

Payment by card: Nowadays, every employee has a giro or salary account. In addition, in 2001 there were more than 52 million Eurocheque or Maestro cards in circulation in Germany. Credit cards are also becoming more and more popular. In 1980, 580,000 Germans had credit cards; in 2001 there were around 19 million of these cards in use. It has been possible to withdraw money from ATMs for more than 20 years now. Today, state-of-the-art machines accept a wide range of German and foreign check and credit cards. Electronic machines for changing international currencies into Euros can be found at airports and major train stations. The "electronic cash" system introduced in 1990, i.e. cashless payment transactions by check-card in conjunction with a PIN number, is becoming ever more important in retail stores and at gas stations. In 2001, this method of payment was used 489 million times, more than twice as often as in 1997.

Over the past few years scarcely any sector of the German economy has mushroomed as that of financial service providers. The volume of business conducted by German banks grew from almost € 2 trillion at the end of 1988 to € 6.38 trillion at the end of 2002. Whether it be savings deposits, securities, or cashless payments, over the past ten years the benchmarks for all German financial markets have rocketed.

Exchanges: In 2002, the turnover on German exchanges totaled € 4.4 trillion. The volume of contracts on the futures exchange, which has been growing continually since it opened in 1990, represented € 56 trillion in 2002, which meant that the EUREX futures market has maintained its position as the largest futures exchange in the world.

In Germany, securities trading is conducted on the one hand on one of the eight exchanges (Berlin, Bremen, Düsseldorf, Frankfurt/Main, Hamburg, Hanover, Munich and Stuttgart) and via the electronic trading platform Xetra. Most exchange trading takes place in Frankfurt and via Xetra. A significant slice of securities trading takes place over-the-counter via telephone and increasingly by means of electronic OTC trading platforms.

Deutsche Börse AG, which was founded in 1993, has emerged to become one of the leading providers of exchange and securities services worldwide and as such is competing directly with exchanges in centers such as London, Paris and the United States.

Insurance companies: Insurance is an important part of Germany as a financial hub. In economic and political terms, the going got tougher for them as well in 2002, though despite all the obstacles the sector managed to post growth. For the year as a whole, the Association of German Insurance Companies forecast a growth in contributions of 4.1 percent to more than € 141 billion. One year before, contributions had risen 2.7 percent to € 135.4 billion. In 2002, insurance claims totaled more than € 158 billion, a rise of 6.2 percent. The year before these had dropped by 2.4 percent. In 2001, insurance contributions amounted to ten percent of the disposable income of Germans.

Including 40 subsidiaries of foreign companies, there are more than 430 insurance companies registered in the Federal Republic of Germany, employing around 245,000 employees. Companies such as Allianz, Aachener und Münchener Lebensversicherung, the AXA group, Münchner Rück, Deutsche Herold and Deutscher Ring are among the biggest in the sector.

Commerce

Comprising 730,000 companies and a payroll of 4.4 million in Germany, commerce is one of the economic sectors in the country with proportionally more employees than any other branch. Almost 13 percent of the total workforce is employed in this sector. Despite the considerable trends to downsizing, commerce is still well and truly in the hands of SMEs, with seven out of ten companies having less than six employees.

Sales in commerce amount to more than € 1 trillion. In the Federal Republic the branch's contribution amounts to between nine and ten percent of gross value added. In terms of commerce in the European Union as a whole, the share of German commercial companies amounts to around 20 percent.

Trade fairs: Trade fairs are one of the leading service sectors of the German economy. The Federal Republic of Germany is the leading center worldwide for staging international trade fairs. Around two thirds of all leading trade fairs are held in Germany.

In terms of sales, five of the ten largest organizers of trade fairs are headquartered in Germany. Exhibitors and visitors spend around € 10 billion annually on trade fairs. Overall, trade fairs are worth € 23 billion to the German economy and ensure around 250,000 jobs.

Each year, some 140 national trade fairs and exhibitions are organized, attended by 160,000 exhibitors, make use of 6.5 million square meters to attract nine to ten million visitors.

From a global point of view, the number one point with regard to German trade fairs is their international aspect. Almost half the exhibitors come from abroad, and of those one third are from non-European countries. Almost one in five visitors to international trade fairs come from outside Germany, and of those around 20 percent from overseas.

Wholesale and retail trading: Retail trading, comprising 430,000 companies and wholesale trading with 120,000 firms form the backbone of this sector. In addition, there are some 70,000 intermediaries and around 100,000 car dealerships and gas stations.

Important trade fairs

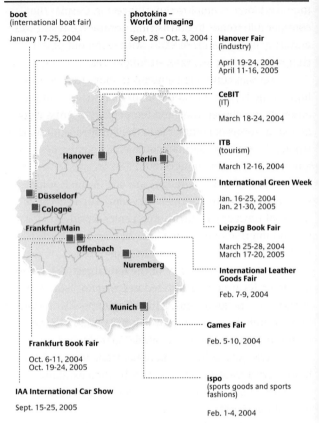

boot
(international boat fair)

January 17-25, 2004

**photokina –
World of Imaging**

Sept. 28 – Oct. 3, 2004

Hanover Fair
(industry)

April 19-24, 2004
April 11-16, 2005

CeBIT
(IT)

March 18-24, 2004

ITB
(tourism)

March 12-16, 2004

International Green Week

Jan. 16-25, 2004
Jan. 21-30, 2005

Leipzig Book Fair

March 25-28, 2004
March 17-20, 2005

**International Leather
Goods Fair**

Feb. 7-9, 2004

Games Fair

Feb. 5-10, 2004

ispo
(sports goods and sports
fashions)

Feb. 1-4, 2004

Hanover

Berlin

Düsseldorf
Cologne

Frankfurt/Main

Offenbach

Nuremberg

Munich

Frankfurt Book Fair

Oct. 6-11, 2004
Oct. 19-24, 2005

IAA International Car Show

Sept. 15-25, 2005

Furthermore, in line with the European system of
business segments, around 10,000 repair workshops for
consumer goods are included in this economic sector.

In 2002, there was a slight drop in sales in both retail and wholesale trading on the previous year. Retail
sales dropped by 1.9 percent from € 327 billion to € 321
billion. This development was even more drastic for
wholesale trading, which posted a slump of 3.4 percent to
€ 575 billion. In both sectors, the number of employees
remained for the most part stable, at 2.5 million and 1.2
million respectively.

The retail trade has undergone a profound structural change in recent decades. Sprawling retail complexes on the edge of town have multiplied. This trend is particularly evident in the east German states. As a result, competition has become even stiffer, and profit margins have shrunk accordingly. Rewe, Aldi and Metro are the groups with the largest number of stores and the highest sales figures. An increasing number of German retailers are stepping up their business activities abroad. Conversely, foreign competitors such as the US corporation Wal-Mart or the French retail group Intermarché are claiming a share of the German market.

The opening hours for German stores are increasingly coming into line with internationally accepted practice. In what is set to be the last step for the moment, in 2003 the Federal Government extended Saturday opening hours to 8 p.m. from 4 p.m. previously.

Increasing motorization and a trend towards more economical bulk buying have favored the spread of hypermarkets, self-service department stores and discount stores, which are becoming ever more popular with consumers. As a result, many small neighborhood retailers have gone out of business.

In a DIY store

In recent years, however, small and medium-sized retailers have managed to compete with large retailers by catering for individual tastes, specializing in certain types of products, and offering expert advice and personalized service. They have also increasingly joined forces to cooperate in the areas of purchasing, sales and marketing. The Federal Government supports SME-retailers through numerous promotional programs and forms of credit.

Public services

The public service continues to be one of the largest employers in the Federal Republic. By German law, public-sector employees are entrusted with the sovereign duties of federal government, the federal states and municipalities in matters concerning for example the police, financial authorities, the legal system and education. Their duties and rights are determined by public law. Judges and soldiers are likewise public-sector employees. In addition to these areas, federal government, the federal states and municipalities also employ a whole host of employees on a normal contract basis, many of whom work in health care and social establishments.

Carers with the children entrusted to them

In mid-2001, around 4.8 million people were employed by central government, the federal states, and communities. As such the number of public service employees had dropped dramatically over a period of just a few years. In 1991, there had still been as many as 5.6 million employees in this sector. Almost half those working in the sector are employed on a contractual basis, with civil servants making up just under 40 percent.

Tourism

Following commerce, tourism is the second largest service sector in Germany, contributing eight percent to the country's GDP. Almost three million people are employed either directly or indirectly in the branch and it provides apprenticeships for around 100,000. The hospitality industry, with more than 50,000 hotels and boarding houses, as well as 180,000 restaurants and inns, is the mainstay of the sector. Furthermore, there are also 18,000 tour operators and travel agents, 5,500 coach companies with 50,000 buses and 3,000 camping sites.

In 2002, more than 110 million guests spent a night in hotels, boarding houses or camping sites with

"Vacancies" on the island of Rügen

sleeping facilities for more than eight, a slight drop of two percent on the previous year. There were a total of 339 million overnight stays, a decline of three percent.

Skilled crafts and independent professions

The skilled craft sector is the most varied in the German economy and its SMEs form the traditional backbone of business in Germany. In 2001, there were almost 5.7 million employees working in around 851,000 firms, which was also training more than half a million apprentices. In other words, the skilled crafts sector accounts for almost 15 percent of all those in employment, and for around 34 percent of all apprentices. As such it trains far more apprentices than are actually required, thus providing other business sectors with a steady stream of qualified junior staff. In 2001, sales in the skilled crafts sector totaled € 509 billion.

In the Federal Republic of Germany, the skilled crafts sector is made up of all those firms which practice one of 94 trades, from bricklaying to violin building.

A qualified optician testing vision

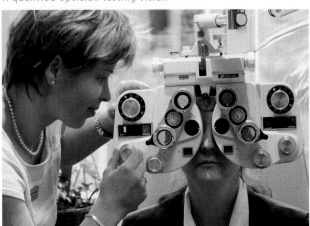

As opposed to most other European countries, in Germany being a skilled crafts company is not dependent on the size of the operation, the number of employees or the amount of sales generated.

Some provisions relating to the skilled crafts sector are anchored in law. As an example, a master craftsman's diploma entitles the holder to practice a skilled trade, providing him with the requisite practical and business skills to run such a firm. It entitles the holder to manage a company on his own and to train apprentices. In future, however, this particular provision will apply only to those trades in which insufficient skilled training could endanger the common weal, for example, electricians.

The independent professions form an important part of the German SME sector. At the beginning of 2002 there were around 761,000 self-employed persons in the independent professions in Germany. Those working in healthcare professions, in other words doctors, dentists, vets, pharmacists and therapists still formed the largest contingent, about 35 percent. The second largest group, comprising around 202,000 members, is made up of legal, business and tax consultants such as attorneys, tax consultants, certified public accountants and management consultants. With regard to technical independent professions, architects and consultant engineers made up the greater part of the 133,000 members. The some 161,000 members working in professions in the cultural domain make up the fourth largest group. Those registered as being self-employed themselves provide work places for some two million people. The more than 157,000 apprenticeships they offer make them the single largest provider of training opportunities following the skilled trades, industry and commerce.

Common to all independent professions is the fact that they provide the population and the business community with important services involving advice, assistance, care and representation, on their own responsibility and not under instruction from third parties. Over and above working for their own personal gain, the members of the independent professions are under a special obligation to serve the interests and welfare of society as a whole.

Transportation

The above-average quality of the transportation infrastructure is one of the biggest structural advantages the Federal Republic has to offer. A closely-knit network of interstates and highways, a railroad system that in many places uses the very latest in technology, conveniently located waterways and a whole host of airports provide a high level of mobility for private individuals and businessmen alike. Further expansion of this network and continued modernization of the transportation infrastructure are playing a decisive role in fostering Germany as an economic hub for the future. For this reason the federal government has greatly increased investment in this area. Whereas in 1998 investments in transportation totaled € 9.5 billion, in 2002 this figure had risen to € 11.5 billion.

Transrapid: Transrapid, the maglev railway, is one of the central projects being subsidized by federal government. There is no method of transportation faster than Transrapid, and in addition passengers enjoy the very highest standards in safety and comfort. Its environment-friendly technology also makes it very economical, as it is subject to almost no wear and tear and uses comparatively little energy, making it cheaper to operate than traditional railway systems. Investments required are roughly comparable. The federal government is subsidizing the first stretches in North Rhine-Westphalia to the tune of considerably more than € 2 billion. The first stretch went into operation, however, not in Germany, but in China, with the inaugural journey in Shanghai taking place at the turn of 2002-3 in the presence of the German Chancellor Gerhard Schröder.

Deutsche Bahn's ICE high-speed train

The railway system: The railway network is now equipped for high-speed trains traveling at up to 280 kilometers per hour. The gaps that existed between the divided railway systems in east and west on unification have now all been closed. In 1994, Deutsche Reichsbahn (in the east) and Deutsche Bundesbahn (in the west) merged to become Deutsche Bahn AG, a private company. Compared with other forms of transportation, railways are particularly environment friendly and thus indispensable. In 2002, almost two billion passengers traveled by rail in Germany. In total, there are more than 44,000 kilometers of rail tracks.

Roads: Outside built-up areas there were more than 230,000 kilometers of road surface available to motorists, of which almost 12,000 were interstates. As such, Germany has the fourth longest interstate system in the world following the USA, China and Canada. There are speed restrictions in place on most sections of German highways. On major roads the speed limit is 100 kilometers per hour, in built-up areas as a rule not faster than

50 kilometers per hour and in residential areas often only 30. At the beginning of 2003, there were more than 53 million motor vehicles registered in Germany, of which a good 44.5 million were cars.

Shipping: In 2002, there were 2,200 ocean-going vessels registered with German shipping lines in Germany (with its import and export focus). The fleet is one of the safest and most modern in the world, and each year more than 240 million tons of goods were turned around, meaning that German ports such as Hamburg, Bremen/ Bremerhaven, Wilhelmshaven, Lübeck and Rostock were able to maintain their position in the international market. German ports are "fast ports", in which even large ocean-going vessels can be turned around within a short space of time. Though the network of inland waterways totaling 7,500 kilometers in length is not particularly closely-knit it nonetheless serves most of the large cities and important industrial centers, thus making an important contribution to maintaining their attraction as business hubs.

Air traffic controllers in a control tower

Air traffic: Following the terrorist attacks on September 11, 2001 in the United States, air passenger levels at German airports also dropped slightly. In 2002, the number of air travelers boarding and alighting flights decreased by 3.2 percent to 113.7 million. On the other hand, the amount of air cargo transported increased by 4.5 percent to almost 2.2 million tons. Frankfurt's Rhine-Main Airport is the country's largest, and is also one of the most important in Europe. In 2001, it handled 48.56 million passengers and 1.49 million tons of air cargo. More than 120 foreign airlines fly to German airports, from where there are direct connections to around 300 destinations in more than 100 countries.

German carrier Lufthansa is one of the most important international airlines. In 2002, its fleet of more than 300 ultra-modern aircraft brought almost 44 million passengers to their destinations.

Goods transportation: The haulage and logistics business. Every year, around 4 billion tons of freight are transported by truck, rail, inland waterway, ocean-going ship and air. The haulage sector accounts for almost € 50,1 billion of business and provides employment for around 370,000, mostly in SMEs. With sales totaling € 39.3 billion in 2002 and a payroll of 376,000, the Deutsche Post World Net Group is Europe's leading logistics company and comprises sections providing letter delivery, express delivery, logistics and financial services. Its direct competitors are companies such as United Parcel Service, Deutscher Paket Dienst, TNT, and Hermes. The fact that over 92,000 new jobs were created by private companies operating in the goods delivery and courier markets was an important result of the liberalization of the postal sector.

High-voltage cables

Energy

Germany is one of the largest consumers of energy worldwide. Given the scarcity of raw materials and with consideration for the environment, since the 1970s the Federal Republic of Germany has been making massive efforts to save energy and put it to effective use.

This includes the use of renewable energy, which in the long term will source one fifth of all energy requirements.

With regard to the supply of energy and raw materials, Germany is heavily reliant on imports. Around two thirds of the necessary primary energy has to be imported, and it is heavily reliant on other countries for raw materials. Given this scenario, it has long sourced its energy and raw materials from a wide range of countries, thus ensuring a high degree of security with regard to supplies.

Domestic natural gas reserves cover up to a quarter of the country's requirements. Reserves of lignite, potash and rock salt are sufficient for decades. As a result of the unfavorable geological conditions in Germany, however, hard coal deposits cannot be mined competitively.

Energy-saving measures such as better insulation and energy-saving devices are promoted by the state. As a result, since the beginning of the 1970s specific energy consumption, i.e., the amount of energy required for the production of one unit of GDP, has been falling continually in west German states, and in the 1990s fell almost 16 percent for the country as a whole.

Renewable energy sources: In 2000, renewable energy had a mere 2.1 percent share of primary energy. The federal government intends to double this share to 4.2 percent by 2010. With regard to electricity production, the share is due to be increased from 6.25 percent in 2000 to 12.5 percent in 2010.

Calculations by the German Ministry of the Environment indicate that in 2001 the use of renewable energy in Germany had led to a reduction of almost 44 million tons of carbon dioxide (CO_2) emissions, which is more CO_2 than Berlin's population of 3.4 million generates in a whole year.

The federal government's long-term aim is for renewable energy to cover roughly fifty percent of all energy requirements by the middle of the century. In 2020, it is

Checking a solar energy panel

due to have a ten percent share of all primary energy requirements and ten percent of electricity consumption. (also see p. 163.)

Lignite: Lignite is the principal domestic source of fossil fuels in Germany. The largest deposits are in the Rhineland, southern Brandenburg and in Saxony. Economically viable reserves total around 43 billion tons. In 2001, lignite accounted for some 11.2 percent of primary energy consumption in Germany.

Hard coal: The main hard coal deposits are in the Ruhr region (North Rhine-Westphalia) and in the Saarland. Reserves total about 24 billion tons. In 1950, hard coal accounted for 73 percent of the old Federal Republic's primary energy consumption. By 2001, its share had fallen to around 13.1 percent.

Oil: Oil has likewise lost ground to other fuels on account of the oil price explosions in the 1970s. Oil's contribution to energy supply fell from 55 percent in 1973 to 38.5 percent in 2001. However, this still makes oil Germany's most important fuel, judging by the proportion of primary energy consumption it makes up.

Natural gas: At the end of 2000, the Federal Republic's natural gas reserves were about 342 billion cubic meters. Natural gas is imported from a number of countries, and supplies are secured well into the next decade. In 2001, natural gas accounted for around 21.5 percent of primary energy consumption.

Nuclear energy: In 2002, an act on the discontinuation of the use of nuclear energy came into power. It is guaranteed by an agreement between the federal government and the energy suppliers. It forbids the construction of new commercial nuclear power stations and limits the regular working life of existing nuclear power stations to 32 years after turnkey. The new act determines the maximum permissible amount of electricity each individual power station may produce. The electricity generation levels allocated to older nuclear power stations can, however, be transferred to more modern plants. In 2001, nuclear power accounted for around 33 percent of the electricity in the national grid.

Supply: The main aims of the federal government's energy policy are economic feasibility, the security of supplies and compatibility with the environment. Market structures are the best way to guarantee the economic supply and use of energy. In Germany, energy supply is in the hands of privately run companies. The state provides the regulatory framework. The consistent, pan-European liberalization of the electricity and gas markets is, for example, a prerequisite for competition developing in business sectors previously dominated by monopolies. Another example is the commitment to continued developments and the reduction of CO_2. Suppliers and consumers of energy must adapt to these regulations. The tax reform for ecological matters, which favors the careful use of energy, provides attractive incentives and has changed the way we consume energy.

The electricity market: Industry and private households both benefit from the increasing competition as a result of the liberalization of electricity markets. Since 1988, the price of electricity for industrial customers has dropped around 30 percent. In some cases, industrial customers have been able to achieve savings of up to 50 percent. Private households have benefited from average price cuts of 15 percent. Almost 30 percent of small customers have signed cheaper contracts with their supplier and four percent have actually switched their supplier. Since liberalization of the market in 1998, some 200 new participants have appeared in the electricity market, including many foreign companies. Electricity exchanges were established in Frankfurt/Main and Leipzig and their merger in 2002 strengthened Germany as an electricity trading market.

Being a country with little in the way of raw materials, the Federal Republic of Germany must have highly diverse sources of energy. The greater the diversity and the greater the access the country has to sources throughout the world, the more secure the supply of energy is. In addition, against the background of the discontinuation of the use of nuclear energy, the mixture of energy suppliers will change once again over the coming decades. What will be important will be an economical and rational use of energy, since a reduction in energy requirements also ensures greater security of supplies.

Information

www.bmwi.de
(Federal Ministry of Economics and Labor)
www.initiatived21.de
www.auma.de
(German Business Exhibition and
Trade Fair Committee)

Students undertaking research

Education,
science,
and research

Education

Germany is a country which highly values education and vocational training, research and the sciences. The country has produced Nobel Prize winners, high-level scientific work is undertaken here, international projects are promoted, and students from all over the world study here.

Education, science and research are structured in line with the federal nature of the Federal Republic of Germany. As a result, central government is only able to decide on and implement goals and measures in conjunction with the federal states, which are for the most part responsible for the school system and cultural matters. Central government is, by contrast, responsible for the organization of vocational training in the dual system.

Central government and the federal states work together on the "Commission of Central Government and the Federal States for Education Planning and Research Support" The federal states agree policy among themselves as part of the Standing Conference of the Ministers of Education and Cultural Affairs of the Federal States.

The constitution of the Federal Republic of Germany guarantees everyone the freedom of self-expression and freedom in their choice of profession, training, and workplace. In this context, education policy aims to provide each individual with the best possible education as well as high-quality vocational training that corresponds to their interests and abilities, thus raising young people to become mature citizens prepared to shoulder responsibility in democratic society.

Kindergarten: Since August 1, 1996, each child in Germany aged between three and six has a legal entitlement to a place in a kindergarten. The latter have a mandate to provide education and care for children from the age of three until the time they enter primary school. They are financed by the local authorities and in addition primarily by charitable organizations and churches, as well as occasionally by companies and associations. Parents are also required to make a monetary contribution towards kindergarten places, the fee as a rule being pegged to parental income levels. In addition to education, social aspects form the center point of kindergarten activities. As a rule, children attend kindergarten during the morning only.

Only some of the kindergarten, most of them in the east German states, offer day-care facilities. All the federal states have crèches providing care for babies and toddlers, although only the east German states deliver sufficient capacity to meet demand. Some states also have two other institutions which serve as a form of transition between kindergarten and junior school: pre-school classes for children mature enough, but not yet legally required to attend school, and school kindergartens for those children legally required to attend school, but not yet mature enough to do so.

Schools: In accordance with article 7 of the Basic Law, the entire school system is under the supervision of the state. The lion's share of educational legislation and administration falls within the ambit of the federal states. This is particularly the case as regards the school system.

First day at school

Children are legally required to attend school as of the end of their sixth year. State regulations stipulate that children and youngsters must attend a form of school for at least 12 years; under certain conditions, citizens who are of legal age and are doing vocational training may still be legally required to attend school. Adolescents who after attending school for nine years are no longer/not in full-time education must attend a vocational training college. As a rule attendance here is compulsory for a period of three years.

Attendance at all general public-sector schools is free of charge. Educational material is provided for pupils partly at no cost, in part on a loan basis, and some federal states levy a charge for educational material either dependent on parental income or expect full payment.

As of grade 10, pupils from low-income families attending vocational training schools and upper specialized schools as well as general education schools may under certain circumstances qualify for financial support under BAföG, the German Federal Training Assistance Act. This support takes the form of a non-repayable grant.

Primary school: As a rule, children attend primary school from the age of six, in general for a period of four years, but in Berlin and Brandenburg for six years. For the first two years the work of children in most states is not graded, and they simply receive a performance evaluation in the form of a report. In 2001, there were over 3.2 million pupils attending primary school. Since 1997, the number of pupils has been falling and this trend will continue until at least 2015.

After completing primary school, children move on to another school of general education at stage 1 of secondary education. Grades 5 and 6 entail special support, observation and orientation with regard to further education and fields of emphasis. In most of the states this orientation phase takes place in the framework of the various types of secondary schools; in some states, however, it is a separate stage, independent of school type. The decision as to which type of secondary school a child attends is based on recommendations from the primary school, the child's performance, and the parents' wishes.

Secondary general school: After completing primary school about one fifth of children attend a "Hauptschule" or secondary general school. This imparts a basic general education to its pupils, including artistic, political and physical education. Successful completion of secondary general school and receipt of the school-leaver's certificate enable admittance to a vocational training program offered in the context of the German dual system and opens doors to many occupations in the craft trades and industry for which formal training is required.

Intermediate school: The intermediate school is somewhere between secondary general schools and grammar schools (Gymnasium). In 2001, around 1.3 million children were enrolled in this type of school. It imparts a more comprehensive general education to pupils. As a rule it involves six years of schooling from grade 5-

10, and leads to an intermediate school-leaver's certificate qualifying the recipient to continue his or her education at upper-school level, such as at a "Berufsfachschule" or full-time vocational college, a vocationally oriented upper secondary school or to attend the upper stage of a grammar school.

Grammar school: As a rule this is a nine-year secondary school and in 2001 there were around 2.3 million pupils enrolled in such schools. It imparts a more in-depth general education. The upper stage of a grammar school encompasses grades 11 through 13 (in some states grades 10-12 or 11 and 12) and features a course system instead of conventional year-classes. Upper secondary education at a grammar school concludes with the "Abitur", which includes at least four and at most five examination subjects. On completion of 13 years of schooling, and having successfully sat the written and oral Abitur examinations, pupils are awarded the "certificate of general higher education entrance". An increasing number of states are now providing opportunities to sit the Abitur examination after 12 years of schooling. The certificate entitles the recipient to study any subject at a university or equivalent institution. That said, pupils holding a school-leaver's certificate from vocationally oriented upper secondary schools and technical grammar schools are likewise entitled to attend university.

Comprehensive school: Another type of school offering post-primary school education is the "Gesamtschule" or comprehensive school. In 2001, around 550,000 pupils opted for this form of education. These schools combine the three forms of stage 1 secondary schooling, usually undertaken individually, and offer secondary general school and intermediate school-leaver's certificates. Should a comprehensive school also possess an upper grammar school program, pupils are eligible to sit the Abitur. During the course of schooling, the children, parents and teachers decide together, and at specific stages, which form of education and school-leaver's certificate is best suited to the individual pupil given his or her interests, preferences and capabilities.

Special school: Children and youngsters with disabilities whose needs cannot be adequately met at general education schools receive instruction at "Sonderschulen" or special schools. There are special schools for various kinds of disabilities. Some disabled children and youngsters attend integrated classes at regular schools. The compulsory education requirement applies to the disabled as well, and without restriction. In 2001, a total of some 425,000 pupils attended special schools, whereby the majority, or almost 55 percent, received instruction in classes for the disabled.

School leavers: Since the mid-1990s the distribution of those leaving secondary education with a certificate has remained relatively stable. A quarter of school leavers graduate from full-time secondary education with a secondary general school-leaver's certificate or a certificate entitling them to higher education respectively; around 40 percent are awarded the intermediate school-leaver's certificate and around ten percent leave secondary education at stage 1 with no qualifications whatever. However, one third of the latter set of pupils later gain a school-leaver's certificate from a vocational school.

A grammar school course in Hamburg

Group work at a comprehensive school

Teachers: In the Federal Republic there are specifically trained teachers for every type and level of school. All must have completed a course of study at a higher education institution, but there are differences in the courses of study. Teachers at primary school and secondary general school level generally study for seven semesters. Longer courses of study generally lasting nine semesters are required for intermediate school, special school, grammar school and vocational school teachers. Upon completion of their studies, all teachers must pass an initial state examination. This is followed by a period of practical training (usually two years), which includes preparatory seminars and practice teaching in the various types of schools, followed by a second state examination. Teachers at public schools are generally professional state employees, in the eastern states of Germany for the most part as salaried employees.

Reforms: In order to improve the quality of teaching, the teaching environment and the individual coaching of individual pupils there are plans for additional all-day schools. For the period 2003-7 the Ministry of Education and Research has set aside the sum of € 4 billion

Basic Structure of the Educational System

further training	**Further Education** (general, vocational and scientific further education of all kinds)				

tertiary education			**degree**		
			doctoral studies degree qualifying student for a profession (ordinary degree, master's degree, state, Bachelor's degree, Master's degree)		
		vocational college	**University** **technical university** **higher technical college** **Polytechnic** **teaching training college** **academy of art** **academy of music** **technical college** **technical college for administration**		
	diploma in vocational further education	general higher education entrance diploma			
	vocational school	**evening grammar school/ course of lectures**			

Grade						Age
13	diploma as vocational qualification	general entrance qualification for Fachhochschule	subject-related general entrance requirement	general higher education entrance diploma		19

secondary education II						
12	vocational sandwich course training **in vocational school and company** (Dual system)	**full-time vocational school**	**vocationally oriented upper secondary school**	**vocational upper secondary school**	**upper secondary education** in various school types: grammar school, vocational grammar school, technical grammar school, comprehensive school	18 / 17
11	basic vocational training year – in a school or on a sandwich course					16
10						15

	middle school diploma (intermediate school diploma) after ten years, first secondary general school diploma after nine years			

secondary education I						Age
10		10th grade				16
9	special school					15
8		**secondary general school**	**intermediate school**	**compre-hensive school**	**grammar school**	14
7						13
6						12
5	orientation grade dependent on or independent of type of school					11

primary education				Age
4	special school	**primary school**		10
3				9
2				8
1				7

elementary education			Age
	special kindergarten	(voluntary) **kindergarten**	6 / 5 / 4 / 3

to be spent setting up additional all-day facilities at primary schools and secondary education stage 1. Central government and the states have agreed to introduce standards of education recognized throughout the country. These include specific skills in subjects, which schools must impart in order for centralized educational aims to be achieved. These must be able to be ascertained by examination so as to determine whether the educational system has fulfilled its duties.

Vocational training

The dual system: By far the greatest majority of youngsters in Germany – around 70 percent of school leavers every year – learn an official state-recognized trade in what is known as the dual system of vocational training. Theoretical knowledge is gained in vocational schools and practical training takes place directly at the place of work or in special training facilities. This combination of theoretical knowledge and practical expertise guarantees the internationally recognized high level of qualification of German craftsmen and skilled laborers.

The occupations for which training is provided in the dual system are determined in close cooperation between central government, the states and industry and employee associations alike. The contents are geared to the requirements of the labor market, and extensive theoretical qualifications ensure that the youngsters enjoy a high degree of mobility in their profession.

Depending on the occupation, training takes 2-3 years. The training institutions pay trainees an allowance. The dual system is financed by the companies involved (trainees' allowance) and by the state (which covers the costs for vocational schools). The dual system differs in two respects from the purely academic vocational education customary in many other countries: Learning takes place on 3-4 working days in companies, and on 1-2 working days in vocational schools.

Central government is responsible for on-the-job training, whereas classroom schooling is the responsibility of individual states.

Vocational training in firms takes place under controlled conditions and with state-of-the-art machines and facilities. Larger firms provide training in their own training workshops and at the workplace. Trainees in smaller enterprises are trained right on the job. Where firms are too highly specialized to be able to impart all the necessary knowledge, they are supported by inter-company training centers. Certain aspects of training may also be taken over by other firms.

The task of instruction at vocational schools is to support and supplement on-the-job training with special-ized theoretical training and to broaden young people's general knowledge. Two thirds of classroom instruction is focused on specialized training, and one third on general education. In 2002, there were 1.8 million young people attending schools of this kind. Those under the age of 18 who have no traineeship contract in their pocket but are legally required to attend school part-time can also attend vocational schools.

The dual system is constantly being advanced further to include new occupations and modernized train-ing for existing professions. Over the past few years, new occupations for which training is required have emerged specifically in the fields of IT and the media.

Vocational training is currently provided in approx. 350 recognized occupations by around 600,000 firms in all sectors of business, in the public sector as well as by the independent professions. In 2002, 1.7 million trainees made use of this offer in Germany. There are quite clearly delineated characteristics: more than 50 percent of all boys and more than 70 percent of all girls opt for just 20 of the 355 occupations for which training is required.

The following jobs are particularly popular with male trainees: car mechanic (every 13th trainee becomes

Training for the book trade in Frankfurt/Main

one), painter and decorator, electrician, and retail trade specialist, whereas female trainees find the following particularly attractive: commercial clerk (every 12th trainee becomes one), retail trade specialist, hairdresser and doctor's and dentist's assistant.

Training for everyone: All school leavers in Germany should receive vocational training. Qualifications in the dual system serve as one of the bases for further training to become a master craftsman and the founding of one's own firm. In as much as there is insufficient training on the part of companies the state finances programs for the creation of training places.

Academic vocational training: In addition to the dual system of training on-the-job and attending a vocational school there are various opportunities for young people leaving general secondary education to pursue a qualification in a particular occupation. They can, for example, attend a vocational school; these are run for the most part on a full-time basis. Courses lasting up to three years aim to train or prepare pupils for a specific occupation. Special schools offer training facilities for non-academic occupations such as in the healthcare sector as nurses or as care-workers.

Vocational further training: Nowadays, completion of a training course no longer spells the end of all learning. Various institutions offer opportunities for further training. More than half of all vocational further training measures are organized and financed by companies. This form of further training by companies is supplemented and supported by a wide range of inter-company and non-company organizations. The Chambers of Commerce and Industry as well as business associations and training institutions provide opportunities for further training and hold examinations for recognized qualifica-

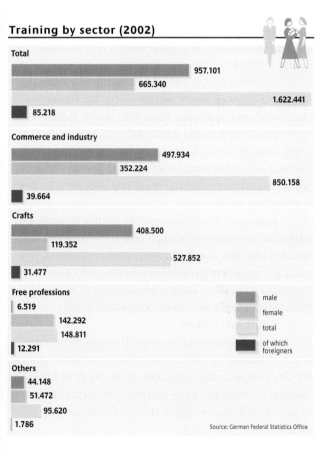

Training by sector (2002)

Total
957.101
665.340
1.622.441
85.218

Commerce and industry
497.934
352.224
850.158
39.664

Crafts
408.500
119.352
527.852
31.477

Free professions
6.519
142.292
148.811
12.291

male
female
total
of which foreigners

Others
44.148
51.472
95.620
1.786

Source: German Federal Statistics Office

Training to be a welder

tions. Attendance at a vocational school or academy provides an opportunity to acquire further qualifications following a completed training course.

In January 2002, the new Promotion Assistance Act, the "Federal Training Assistance Act for Master Craftsmen", as it is known, came into power. Skilled workers who wish to undergo additional training are entitled to the same means as students supported by the Federal Training Assistance Act (BAföG). In the years to come, central government and the states will allocate a further € 45 million to this end.

Numerous adults take part in further training and retraining programs. In 2000, a poll of 19 to 64-year olds revealed that four out of every ten men and women had taken part in a further training scheme, or 21.4 million people, of whom 14.4 million participated in further training associated with their occupation.

Adult education

Everyday working life is not the only area in which acquired knowledge becomes outdated ever more quickly. For this reason further education in the sense of life-long learning is becoming more and more important in order to understand general political and cultural developments.

Organizers: In Germany, there are numerous institutions and organizations involved in further education:

Adult education schools, of which there are around 1,000, offer extensive basic knowledge for general, political, cultural and job-related further training. As a rule they are the further education centers run by local authorities.

The most important organizers of vocational further training are companies themselves. They fulfill their tasks in their own training workshops or together with other inter-company further education establishments and providers.

Private and commercial further education institutes are particularly active in job-related retraining, the acquisition and expansion of vocational qualifications, computer training, foreign language instruction, and courses designed to enable participants to obtain qualifications later in life.

Religious adult education institutions focus on ethical questions and issues relating to everyday life, such as bringing up children, schooling, families, health and relationships.

Universities, academies, and academic bodies concentrate above all on scientific and subject-related further education.

Trade unions concentrate on enabling people to participate in political life and represent workers' interests in companies.

Charitable organizations are particularly concerned with imparting knowledge and skills pertaining to social work, health care and development assistance.

Correspondence courses offering opportunities for further education not tied to any particular time or place are offered by around 215 private distance learning institutes. These concentrate on general further education as well as vocational further training (particularly in commercial and business-related subjects). These range from classical apprenticeship work to guided, self-paced courses and nowadays ever newer forms of e-learning.

The federal and state centers for political education as well as foundations that have a close relationship with political parties also offer a wide range of further education events, focusing in particular on current political issues and basic problems of the democratic state. There is now a widespread network of opportunities for taking part in education and further education activities. Federal academies for cultural education, music and young people's art schools, socio-cultural centers and other institutions engaged in cultural education stage further education events in all areas of art and cultural fields of activity. Libraries, museums, galleries, theaters and bookshops promote and meet learning needs.

Through their radio and television programming, the public broadcasting networks help to promote the dissemination of information, education and culture. The German Institute for Adult Education (Deutsches Institut für Erwachsenenbildung) was set up by the WGL Gottfried Wilhelm Leibniz Scholarly Association and is particularly noted for the development, quality and profession-

Senior citizens working at a PC

al nature of federal-level adult education. It is funded by central government and the federal states. As a scientific institute it organizes adult education which bridges science and practice, provides the basis for practical research and conducts sound scholarly development work.

Information

www.bmbf.de
(Federal Ministry of Education and Research)
www.kmk.org
(KMK, Secretariat of the Standing Conference of the Ministers of Education and Cultural Affairs of the Federal States in the Federal Republic of Germany)
www.bibb.de
(Federal Institute of Vocational Training)
www.bpb.de
(German Central Office of Political Education)
www.dvv-vhs.de
(Association of German Adult Education Institutions)
www.die-frankfurt.de
(German Institute for Adult Education)

Researching nuclear medicine in a university teaching hospital

The World of Academia

In Germany, higher education institutions are the establishments where sciences and the arts are promoted by means of research and education.

The freedom of teaching and research in Germany is firmly anchored in the Basic Law. This gives higher education institutions a wide range of rights for self-administration, which has created a very varied, attractive university environment for students, teachers, and researchers alike. For some years now German universities have been adopting an international approach to science and research as a result of increased international competition and through cooperation and partnerships with other research groups, institutions and networks. Moreover, new courses of study, leading to international degrees such as Bachelor and Master's degrees, have given teaching a more international focus.

Structural characteristics of universities: Most German universities are public institutions, are financed entirely by the federal states, or receive substantial state funding. Private universities, such as the University of Witten-Herdecke are the exception to the rule.

Students do not pay tuition fees at state higher education institutions. Individual states charge fees for second degrees and long-term courses of study. In 2002, the German parliament passed a law stating that first degrees completed within a reasonable period of time would not be subject to tuition fees.

The German constitution stipulates that responsibility for the higher education system be divided between central government and the federal states; responsibility for the everyday operations lies almost exclusively with the federal states. Central government is, however, responsible for determining the general principles for organizing the university system, which are set out in the German "Hochschulrahmengesetz" or Higher Education Act. On the basis of this act, the 16 federal states formulate their own university acts, which regulate further details.

Central government and the states are jointly responsible for expanding existing higher education institutions and for the construction of new establishments. Following German unification this has called for tremendous effort in the east German states: a total of € 5.7 billion have been spent on refurbishing east German universities, with the result being that they have now attained international standards. That said, there is still a considerable need in east German states for renovation or conversion of existing facilities and for new construction work, as well as for an increase in Fachhochschule capacity. For this reason, since 1999 central government has increased the size of its contribution to financing the necessary investments in the modernization of tertiary education institutions, raising the sum to € 1.1 billion for 2001 and 2002.

In the spirit of Wilhelm von Humboldt, German universities adhere firmly to the ideal of the unity of research and teaching. To the greatest extent possible, students are incorporated into research projects. In many areas, universities are the most important providers of research capacity, especially in basic scientific research and the liberal arts. They are becoming increasingly important in basic application-oriented research. In applied R&D, the universities collaborate closely together with other research institutes and industrial laboratories; this promotes and accelerates the manner in which research work is put into practice. The Fachhochschule institutions play a decisive role in this application-oriented research and are important partners for small and medium-sized businesses in particular. The universities fund part of their research work with the help of grants from industry, the state and other institutions such as the German Research Council (third party funding).

As a result of reforms in the wake of the student protests of the 1960s and 1970s, the universities previously ruled imperiously by full professors have been replaced by universities administered by groups, in which all members of the university have a say in its running in accordance with the function they play in it. Thus, university teachers, (professors and junior professors), students and other employees each form a group for participation in the development of the university's objectives. With regard to research topics and the appointment of university teaching staff, the teaching group has a majority vote.

As a rule, universities are governed by a full-time rector or president, who is elected for several years.

A total of 263 institutions have united to form the Association of Rectors and Presidents and other Higher Education Institutions (HRK). This body promotes cooperation between higher education institutions, represents them publicly, formulates positions and statements on matters of scientific and higher education policy, and

New students

Students in their first semester in the winter semester 2002-3

Germany in total

299.042

of which Germans

249.958

of which foreigners

49.084

Female

150.444

Male

148.598

Law, business studies, social sciences

101.227

Languages, cultural studies and the arts

60.365

Mathematics and natural sciences

54.338

Engineering sciences

54.093

Human and dental medicine

9.103

Others

19.916

Source: German Federal Statistics Office

cultivates international relationships. Within the framework of legal parameters the student body administers its own affairs.

Types of higher education institutions:
Universities and equivalent institutions are entitled to award doctorates and, in some cases professorships. A Fachhochschule is not entitled to supervise doctoral work. There are currently 360 tertiary education institutions in Germany, including more than 90 universities entitled to award doctorates and 190 institutions at Fachhochschule level.

Universities: Most students attend a university or equivalent institution, pursuing courses of study culminating in a "Diplom", "Magister", or "Staatsprüfung" examination. Of the 1.9 million students registered at the beginning of the winter semester of 2002, almost 1.4 million were enrolled at universities or equivalent institutions. Since 1998 students have also been increasingly able to study for the degree of Bachelor or Master. After that, further qualifications up to doctoral level or a second degree is possible. Some courses of study lead only to a Magister degree or a doctorate. In order to ensure that German courses of study and degrees are more widely recognized internationally, a mandatory credit points appraisal system has been introduced.

Fachhochschule: The second mainstay of the German higher education system is the Fachhochschule, which offers practical study in the fields of engineering, IT, business administration, social studies, design and health. These courses have traditionally led to a Diplom degree; since 1998 it has also been possible to pursue a course of studies leading to a Bachelor's or Master's degree. Today almost one in four new students opts

Hamburg University

for this type of institution, where there is a shorter standard period of study and more structuring of the study course.

Open university: In 1974, the Open University of Hagen was founded as the first open university in the German-speaking world. There are currently around 58,000 students enrolled, of which some 40 percent are female. Students are supervised in regional centers, some of which are located in other German speaking countries as well as in central and eastern European countries.

In addition to the Open University of Hagen there are other private higher education institutes throughout Germany offering correspondence courses. Conventional higher education institutions are also becoming increasingly involved in correspondence study. Today, computer networking and multimedia open up numerous new options for structuring modern study courses which fit students' needs. In this respect a number of countries have established organizations offering virtual study possibilities. At the Open University of Hagen alone there are currently 27,000 students enrolled in e-study courses.

Development of higher education institutions: Education policy has opened up higher education institutions to a much broader section of the population. In the winter semester of 1952, four percent of all new students came from low-income families with no student tradition; today this figure stands at around 13 percent. Whereas in 1952 only one in five of all students were female, they now make up over 47 percent.

Since 1960 the percentage of a given age group commencing studies at higher education institutions has risen from eight percent to well over 30 percent. In 2002, 358,000 new students registered for a course of study at a higher education institution in Germany, with women (180,000) outnumbering men (178,000) for the first time. There are currently some 1.9 million students enrolled at German higher education institutions.

Admission: Despite the expansion measures undertaken, the rush on higher education institutions led to nationwide admission restrictions (numerus clausus) having to be introduced for certain subjects, as there were no longer places available for all applicants. As a rule, admission depended on the average Abitur grade achieved, and a set "waiting period". A certain amount of the study slots in those subjects are granted through the universities' selection procedure subject to the numerus clausus. In this case, in addition to the Abitur grade and waiting list, selection interviews play a significant role.

Choice of subject: The choice of subject studied is also greatly influenced by the employment market, meaning that job prospects in a particular sector impact after a time lag on the total number of students in a particular subject. Law, business studies and social sciences have been consistently popular for almost thirty years now, and today these subjects attract nearly a third of all students. Languages and the arts come next, accounting for a quarter of all students, engineering studies, mathematics and natural sciences for a sixth of applicants, followed by medicine. Female students show a preference for languages and the arts, male students for technical subjects and natural sciences, with both sexes showing a similar interest in business studies.

Length of study: Study at a higher education institution is organized in the form of study programs subject to guidelines governing curricula and procedure. These stipulate that as a rule a study program at a university or equivalent institution lasts at least four, and at a Fachhochschule at least three years (standard study time).

At present, students at universities still require an average of 12 semesters, or six years, 10 semesters at other higher education institutions, to obtain their degree. This is too long compared with other countries. The reform to the financial support provided for tertiary education as passed in 2001 and the modernization of study programs will help reduce the amount of time spent studying in the future.

Teaching staff: At the beginning of 2001, a total of 494,000 people were employed by higher education institutions in Germany. Of these, around 160,000 were full-time staff in scientific and arts faculties. Around 38,000 were professors, of which around 4,200 were female. Those in part-time employment include outside staff with a teaching mandate, assistants, and visiting professors.

Full-time staff in the scientific and arts faculties includes teachers (professors and junior professors), their staff, and teaching staff for particular subjects. Teachers at higher education institutions are themselves responsible for fulfilling their research, teaching and further education commitments. These include teaching and examining, conducting research projects, consultation and participation in study reforms, as well as the administration of the institution.

Pre-requisites for being awarded a chair are a university degree, educational skills, and a particular ability to carry out academic work. In addition, depending on the requirements of the position to be filled, candidates must have a proven record of academic or artistic excellence, or particular achievements in the professional application of academic knowledge.

For a long time, full professors played a decisive role in higher education institutions. Their name stood for both teaching and research work in a specialized subject (their chair) and, as superiors to their assistants and academic staff as well as to part-time student staff, non-academic scientific and artistic staff, they had free reign. On the one hand, they administered the public funds allocated to their chair, and, on the other, the public and private resources made available for individual research work.

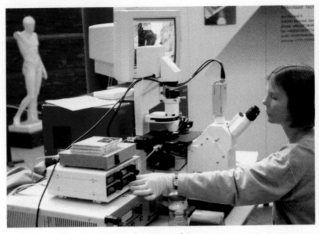

Cancer research at the University of Jena

Given this structure, up-and-coming academics were often unable to make a name for themselves and had to wait a long time to be offered a professorship. Because they saw better opportunities there, 15 percent of all young academics emigrated to the United States. To counter this trend, the prospects for such young hopefuls have now been improved. The creation of junior professorships has reformed the path to becoming a professor for life. Junior staff are given more independence and responsibility at an earlier stage and are able to qualify much more quickly. In future the proof of additional academic achievement required of prospective professors (Habilitation), which as a rule involved long and laborious research work, will no longer be a prerequisite. As is already standard international practice, the quality of the academic achievements necessary to be awarded a particular chair will be evaluated exclusively during the selection procedure. In addition to the position of junior professor, a successful career for example in business or another section of society in Germany, or even abroad, could open the doors to a professorship.

Furthermore, the salary structure for professors has been made more flexible and more geared to performance. These reforms are aimed at making German higher education and research institutions more attractive and more competitive in the international arena.

Financing courses of study: Under the German Federal Training Assistance Act (BAFöG), students have a legal right to public financial assistance if the funds they need to cover their educational and living expenses are not available from other sources, most notably from parental income. During the standard study time, half of this aid is awarded in the form of a grant and the other half as an interest-free loan that, as a rule, must be repaid in installments within five years of the end of the maximum entitlement period, i.e., the standard study time.

The vast majority of students (86 percent) receive financial aid from their parents. Almost two thirds of students cover their living costs by opting for part-time jobs, and for no less than five percent this is their sole source of income. Almost 25 percent of those students entitled to financial assistance from the state draw such grants. On the basis of outstanding achievements about 0.7 percent of students receive scholarships from one of the 11 organizations in Germany for assisting particularly gifted students.

The Training Assistance Reform Act put state-funded training assistance on a new footing, providing equal opportunities for qualified training schemes, to which somewhere in the region of an additional 90,000 youngsters are entitled. In this way, approx. € 680 million in additional funds are spent on improving assistance to those most in need and to integrating youngsters from low-income families. In April 2001, the Education Loan Program (Bildungskreditprogram), an additional government program for (part) financing of training schemes, was introduced to supplement the Federal Training Assistance Act. It has proved immensely popular.

Medicine students attending a lecture

The Offices for Training Assistance, which are part and parcel of the federal states' respective administrations, are responsible for these schemes. The student welfare offices are another body responsible for the economic, social, cultural and health care of students at higher education institutions. Local student welfare offices have together formed a national organization, the German Student Welfare Service (DSW). As a new service for prospective foreign students, the DSW now makes service packages available at more than 100 higher education institutions, offering board and lodging, as well as social and advisory services at an attractive overall price.

Foreign students: Between 1993 and 2002, the number of new foreign students at higher education institutions in Germany almost doubled, rising from 35,000 to 68,000. There were around 224,000 foreigners studying in Germany in the winter semester 2002. Today, German higher education institutions offer an increasing number of certificates and academic degrees that conform to international study structures and are recognized worldwide. Many German higher education institutions take advantage of this when devising new international courses. In total there are more than 1,800 new courses culminating in Bachelor's or Master's degrees.

Spurred on by a program initiated by central government, many higher education institutions are now offering internationally geared study programs for applicants from Germany and abroad. One foreign language (in most cases English) is used as the language of instruction.

Most foreign students interested in studying at a German higher education institution refer to the Academic Bureau for Foreigners of the respective institution. Exceptions to the rule are foreigners living in Germany who have received a German education, citizens of a member state of the European Union, or those who attended a German school abroad and whose school-leaving certificate was the Abitur and now wish to study a subject that is subject to admission restrictions. Such persons apply in the same way as German citizens to the

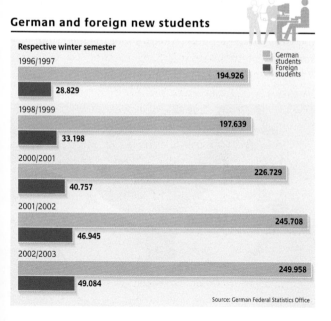

German and foreign new students

Respective winter semester

German students / Foreign students

1996/1997
194.926
28.829

1998/1999
197.639
33.198

2000/2001
226.729
40.757

2001/2002
245.708
46.945

2002/2003
249.958
49.084

Source: German Federal Statistics Office

Zentralstelle für die Vergabe von Studienplätzen, or ZVS, the central office for the allocation of study slots. Information for anyone interested in studying or undertaking research work in Germany can be found on the Internet portal www.campus-germany.de, and details for students from abroad can be obtained from the German Academic Exchange Service (Deutscher Akademischer Austauschdienst, DAAD).

Those applying for scholarships from the DAAD must do so directly to the institution itself. All other foreigners can simply apply to the Academic Bureau for Foreigners of the institution in question.

Certain subjects are so popular that there are insufficient study slots available, and a selection procedure (Numerus Clausus) has had to be introduced. However, since great importance is placed on foreign students studying in Germany, a certain percentage of places on courses subject to the Numerus Clausus is reserved specially for applicants from outside the country. The closing date for applications to the ZVS and to the Academic Bureau for Foreigners is July 15 for the following winter semester and January 15 for the following summer semester.

A flood of applications at the ZVS

Language requirements: As a rule, proficiency in the German language is a prerequisite for studying at a German higher education institute and proof of this proficiency can be obtained in one of various ways. A special language test conducted by higher education institutes in Germany, certain Goethe Institute tests and, most recently, the standardized TestdaF (a test for German as a foreign language), which can be sat worldwide, are all possible methods. Applicants who are able to prove proficiency in the language by other means, such as by having passed the Abitur at a German-speaking school, need not take a separate test. This ruling does not apply in the case of enrolment on specific international or foundation courses and regular one-semester stays, in particular in the context of academic exchange programs.

The German Academic Exchange Service (DAAD): Specifically, the DAAD (Deutscher Akademischer Austauschdienst), a joint organization founded by German higher education institutions, promotes the exchange of students, graduates and academics with institutions abroad. Its programs are open to all countries and all subjects, and are to the benefit of foreigners and Germans alike. In 2001, over 67,000 people worldwide profited from the service. The DAAD also supports the higher education institutions' international activities with a number of services, such as information and publication programs, advisory and care assistance, and plays a role in structuring German cultural foreign policy. Its regular members are (on request) the higher education institutions represented in the Standing Conference of University Rectors (HRK) and their student bodies. At the start of 2002, a total of 231 higher education institutions and 127 student bodies were members of the DAAD. It awards scholarships to foreign and German students, students involved in practical training, and to young academics and lecturers to promote continuing education and training in the field of higher education and research. Furthermore, it supports German academic teaching staff from all disciplines in long and short-term lectureships and places them with foreign universities and colleges. In addition, the DAAD provides information on opportunities for studying and researching both in Germany and abroad, undertakes international marketing for higher education institutions and maintains follow-up contacts with former DAAD scholarship holders, particularly those abroad.

Information

www.campus-germany.de
www.daad.de
www.hrk.de (The Conference of University Rectors)
www.bundesregierung.de
www.government.de

Research

In Germany, the higher education institutions adhere to Humboldt's theory of the unity of teaching and research, and are thus important centers of research work.

In addition to higher education institutions, public and private non-commercial organizations are also involved in research. Research conducted outside universities is based first and foremost on that undertaken by higher education institutions. Thus large-scale projects, especially those in the field of natural sciences, which can only be conducted in large teams involving expensive technology and large financial backing, are undertaken outside the world of academia. In such cases, research institutions financed for the most part jointly by central government and the states take center stage. These include the Max Planck Gesellschaft, the Fraunhofer Gesellschaft, the Helmholtz Gesellschaft and the Wilhelm Leibnitz Gesellschaft. Research facilities maintained by industry also play their part. In addition, central government also participates in large-scale European and international research projects in the form of research organizations, such as the European Organization for Nuclear Research, CERN, or the German Genome Project. The Arbeitsgemeinschaft Industrieller Forschungsvereinigungen, or AIF, (Working Group of Industrial Research Organizations) creates a link between research and development work conducted by industry and the basic research and impetus for joint industrial research. It also finances a program whereby small and medium-sized companies are supported in a wide variety of joint projects both at home and abroad.

Deutsche Forschungsgemeinschaft (DFG):
The German Research Council (DFG) is the central administrative body for the promotion of research at higher education institutions and state-financed research institutions in Germany. It serves all areas of science by providing financial support for envisaged research projects and is the largest donor of third party funds to higher education institutions. In addition it promotes cooperation between researchers, up-and-coming academics, interdisciplinary measures between various scientific areas as well as the setting up of research networks.

The Max Planck Society for the Advancement of Science (MPG): This society funds various research institutions, is financed for the most part from public funds furnished by central and state governments, and supports around 80 facilities for highly sophisticated research in Germany. The MPG engages in basic research which is beyond the scope of higher education institutions or requires particularly large facilities.

The Helmholtz Gesellschaft Deutscher Forschungszentren (HGF): This is another important instrument of government research policy. The Heimholtz Association of National Research Centers consists of 15 large national research centers, which together make up the largest non-university research facility. It is financed to the tune of 90 percent by the German Ministry of Education and Research, and 10 percent by the federal state in which the facility is located. Their fields of research cover nanoparticles and aerospace, cancer, environmental and climate research as well as the development of key technologies.

The Fraunhofer Gesellschaft: This is an important link between research and its practical application in industry. Its 56 institutes conduct commissioned research projects in the natural sciences for industry, service providers and the public sector.

Spending on R&D

GDP expenses in € billion

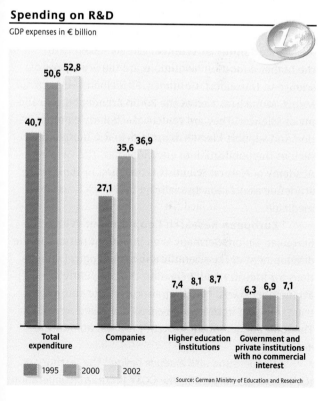

	1995	2000	2002
Total expenditure	40,7	50,6	52,8
Companies	27,1	35,6	36,9
Higher education institutions	7,4	8,1	8,7
Government and private institutions with no commercial interest	6,3	6,9	7,1

Source: German Ministry of Education and Research

Scholarship and research foundations: Other significant contributions are made by the major foundations for scholarship and research, such as the Fritz Thyssen Foundation and the Volkswagen Foundation. They and the Donors' Association for the Promotion of German Science are much in demand as sponsors of research projects, especially in collaboration with the higher education institutions. The Alexander von Humboldt Foundation, which receives financial support from central government, enables foreign scientists to do research in Germany and German scientists to work on similar projects abroad; it also pays for research trips by outstanding scientists from various foreign countries.

The Alexander von Humboldt Foundation also draws up a table of higher education institutions in Germany listing their appeal for top international researchers and posts its findings on www.humboldt-foundation.de/presse/ranking.

Academies of science: Closely linked with the higher education institutions are the academies of science in Düsseldorf, Göttingen, Heidelberg, Leipzig, Mainz, Munich, as well as the Berlin-Brandenburg Academy of Sciences. They are centers of scholarly communication and support long-term projects in the humanities, such as the publication of encyclopedias. The German Academy of Natural Scientists Leopoldina in Halle is an academic association specializing in the sciences and medicine.

European Research Cooperation: Within the European Union, Germany is an important partner in the development of the scientific and technological foundations for industry and increasing the competitiveness of EU member states. The program covers the entire spectrum, ranging from basic research to applied research. The total budget for the current program amounts to € 17.5 billion.

Cooperation also extends beyond the territory of the Union, as reflected in the COST program (cooperation with third countries on applied research), the EU's participation in the EUREKA and ESA projects, as well as the EU-EFTA cooperation under the European Economic Area agreement.

Some of this work at European level is carried out by institutions with large-scale facilities beyond the means of individual countries. They include the high-energy particle accelerator of the European Organization for Nuclear Research (CERN) in Geneva, the ultra-high flux reactor at the Max von Laue-Paul Langevin Institute (ILL) in Grenoble, the European Space Association (ESA) in Paris, the European Synchrotron Radiation Facility (ESRF) in Grenoble, the European Southern Observatory (ESO) in Garching and the European Molecular Biology Laboratory (EMBL) in Heidelberg. The German government has also proposed the establishment of two new institutions in Europe: an x-ray laser near Hamburg and an ion beam facility in Darmstadt. The aim of all these projects is to coordinate national research, hence increasing Europe's competitive edge in the international arena.

International collaboration: The promotion of international collaboration in the field of research is a major aspect of government policy. In addition to cooperation in international organizations such as the OECD and the International Energy Agency, the promotion of exchange programs and direct collaboration between German and foreign scientists, (for example, via the Alexander von Humboldt Foundation or the DAAD), there are many other forms of cooperation. Since May 2003, the Alexander von Humboldt Foundation has assumed the role of national mobility center acting as the bridgehead to other EU research projects. Germany has concluded bilateral agreements on scientific and technological cooperation with over 30 countries.

Through a concerted campaign entitled "International Marketing for Germany as a Center for Education and Research", central government, the federal states,

industry and science have had considerable worldwide success in attracting students and academics to the country (www.campus-germany.de). As a result academics from all over the world are drawn to Germany by the attractive prizes awarded by the Alexander von Humboldt Foundation; German higher education institutions cooperate with twin universities in other countries on international study programs and various scholarship schemes have been set up for foreign students.

Political consultancy: Around the world, governments are coming to rely increasingly on scientific advice, as political decisions are often related to issues which only such experts can unravel. In preparing special reports, investigations and commentaries, experts lay the groundwork for practical political decisions. Germany's own such think tanks, devised on the US model, now number about 100. Some of them are run privately, others are public enterprises.

In the European Laboratory for Particle Physics (CERN)

The best known include:

- the research institute of the German Council on Foreign Relations
- the Center for Applied Policy Research
- the German Institute for Economic Research
- the German Institute for International and Security Affairs
- the Peace Research Institute Frankfurt
- the Wuppertal Institute for Climate, Environment and Energy.

Since 1957, the Science Council has been advising central government and the state governments on matters pertaining to the substantive and structural development of science, research and higher education institutions, as well as construction of the latter. Financed equally by the federal and state governments, it is one of the most important institutes in Germany acting as advisors to policymakers. It comprises 32 male and female scientists appointed by the German President, as well as 22 representatives from the federal and state governments. The highly important contribution the Council has made on matters relating to university and research policy has played a decisive role in the restructuring of universities and research in the east German states.

In May 2001, the German government passed a resolution to set up a national Ethics Council. It is designed to serve as a forum finding answers to those questions posed by developments in biotechnology and gene technology, as well as provoking intense discussion in society about related matters.

State research funding: In 2002, despite a lack of budgeted funds, federal and state governments committed a total of almost € 4.9 billion to research projects, an increase of almost 3.4 percent on the previous year.

The German federal government specifically funds innovative research projects and ideas. The wide spectrum includes basic research in the natural sciences, long-term environment-friendly developments and new technologies. Together with new production processes, research and development in areas such as chemistry and material science, semi-conductors, laser and plasma technology form the basis for tomorrow's new technological developments. Multi-discipline developments, highly complex technology and ecological modernization are of particular importance.

Attention is focused on nano-technology, superconductors, non-linear dynamics, plasma technology and magneto-electronics, all of which are important fields that will help shape the job markets of the future. As an example, 95,000 jobs are currently dependent on electronic parts. This figure increases to 791,000 if the sector overall, i.e., software, hardware and IT services, is included. This puts it on a level pegging with the automobile industry.

With regard to nano-technology, six expertise centers are being set up, above all to advise companies that are planning to set up operations in this sector.

Pilot projects are being funded prior to the industrial application of nano-technology in practice, for example in opto-electronics, in chemical nano-technologies, in nano-biotechnology, nano-analytics and ultra-precision processing. In 2003 a total of € 78 million was spent on nano-electronics research.

Information

www.bmbf.de
(German Ministry of Education and Research)
www.aif.de
(Working Group of Industrial Research Associations)
www.dfg.de
(Deutsche Forschungsgemeinschaft)
www.mpg.de
(Max Planck Society for the Advancement of Science)
www.helmholtz.de
(Helmholtz Association of National Research Centers)
www.fraunhofer.de
(Fraunhofer Gesellschaft)
www.humboldt-foundation.de
(Alexander von Humboldt Foundation)

Opera performance in Schwerin

Society
and Culture

Out for a family walk

Society

Open-minded, modern and tolerant – these are the hall-marks of German society at the beginning of the 21st century. For the vast majority of people, the family still forms the nucleus of their lives, yet the forms people choose for living together have become far more numerous. Supported by consistent measures by the state to ensure equality, there has been a change in the interpretation of the roles men and women play. An increasing number of couples are now sharing domestic chores and the task of bringing up children, who are regarded as the parents' partners. Violence as part of bringing up children is despised, whereas peaceful co-existence with people from other countries and cultures has become part and parcel of everyday life. Around nine percent of the population is foreign. In every sixth marriage one of the partners has a foreign passport. Most Germans also go abroad on holiday, and in 2002 spent € 56 billion in the process. They do, however, also place great value on their own homes and are active as volunteers in clubs and charitable organizations.

Families: For all the changes in society, the family is still the preferred form of co-habitation. Four out of every five people in Germany (81 percent) live in a family. Almost every second person (47 percent) lives in a traditional family consisting of a married couple with children. Young people are also so comfortable with this form of existence that they, too, wish to start a family at some point.

Great importance continues to be placed on a firm relationship with a partner – in Germany 21.6 million couples live together, 89 percent of them with a traditional marriage certificate. For most couples, children make up a complete family. According to a representative poll (a mini-census) in April 2002, just 12 percent of 35 to 40-year old married women had no children. Around 2.4 million people, mostly women, lived as single parents. Of the total population in Germany, 17 percent live alone, significantly more women than men.

Even if most people still favor the traditional form of marriage, living together without being married has become more pronounced over the past few years. Since 1996, the number of unmarried couples living together in the west German states rose by 25 percent to 1.7 million, in the east German states by 24 percent to 543,000. There are no reliable comparable figures for same-sex households, but the Federal Statistics Office puts the number in the region of 53,000 to 148,000.

The Act Governing the Legal Rights of Unmarried Couples of 2002 accords partners of different or the same sex the same legal status as those applicable to members of a family.

The protection of marriage and the family is firmly anchored in the Basic Law as being the duty of the state. As such, it supports families in a number of ways. To this end in taxation matters, married couples with different incomes are given preferential treatment over unmarried couples. Families with children are given financial support in the form of children's allowances. Following the birth of a child, mothers and fathers who are in employment are entitled to what is known as "parents' time" of up to three years per child. During this period they are released from their work in full or in part, and for two years the state pays an allowance, pegged to their income, to enable them to bring up the child. The fact that the time spent bringing up children – three years for each child born after 1992 – is also taken into account in the future determination of pension levels also serves to encourage families (see p. 152).

Women: According to the Basic Law "men and women enjoy equal rights". Efforts on the part of the state to dismantle disadvantages for women have met with some success, but the process entails further challenges.

With regard to education girls and young women have gained ground. They already form the majority at intermediate schools (51 percent) and grammar schools (54 percent). In the 2002-3 academic year, the percentage of new female students (50.4 percent) was greater than

A female car electrician at work

Women in Germany

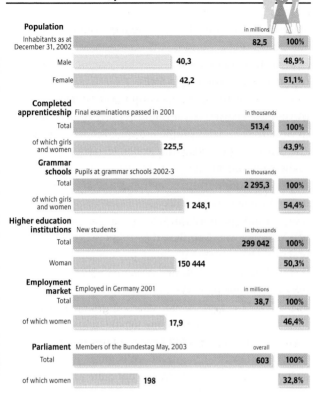

Population	Inhabitants as at December 31, 2002	in millions	
		82,5	**100%**
Male		**40,3**	**48,9%**
Female		**42,2**	**51,1%**
Completed apprenticeship	Final examinations passed in 2001	in thousands	
Total		**513,4**	**100%**
of which girls and women		**225,5**	**43,9%**
Grammar schools	Pupils at grammar schools 2002-3	in thousands	
Total		**2 295,3**	**100%**
of which girls and women		**1 248,1**	**54,4%**
Higher education institutions	New students	in thousands	
Total		**299 042**	**100%**
Woman		**150 444**	**50,3%**
Employment market	Employed in Germany 2001	in millions	
Total		**38,7**	**100%**
of which women		**17,9**	**46,4%**
Parliament	Members of the Bundestag May, 2003	overall	
Total		**603**	**100%**
of which women		**198**	**32,8%**

Source: German Federal Statistics Office

that of males for the first time. For German women, employment is an important aspect of their lives.

Just under 18 million or 46.4 percent of the total 38.7 million people in employment are women. Many of them have the dual burden of working and caring for a family. In April, 2002, 64 percent of all women aged between 15 and 65 with children below the age of 18 living at home were in employment: 63 percent of women in former West Germany, 71 percent in the east German states. The fact that women traditionally assume responsibility for the family – they work part-time more frequently and interrupt their employment to bring up children –

has an effect on their promotion prospects. In 2000, scarcely a third of those in top management in industry and public administration were female. There are scarcely any women to be found on the management boards of larger corporations, though they do account for 20 percent of the top positions in SMEs.

Since 2001, women serving in the German Armed Forces have enjoyed equal rights in every respect. If they so wish, they are now entitled to train for armed combat. The first year this option was available, over 1,500 female soldiers took advantage of it. As such all activities and career possibilities in the German Armed Forces are now open to women (see p. 212).

Although in actual working life the maxim "equal pay for equal work" applies, it is still not entirely put into practice. The average take-home pay of employed women is considerably less than that of men. In 2002, women in full-time employment in private industry earned on average € 2,517 per month, or around 30 percent less than their male colleagues. Full-time female industrial workers earned an average € 1,837 per month before tax, a good 26 percent less than their male colleagues. The discrepancy in the east German states was not quite as large, where

Female editors at work

females earned 94% of what their male colleagues earned.

Measures introduced by the state such as the "parents' time" and allowances for raising children as well as federal government funding for increasing the number of all-day schools and crèches have made it easier to combine raising a family with being employed (see p. 313). These are aimed at ensuring that males become more involved in family matters and the raising of children. The federal government has put forward a comprehensive agenda to promote equal opportunities for men and women. Furthermore, equal rights for men and women have been adapted as an integral part of all political, standardizing and administrative measures passed by federal ministries (gender mainstreaming).

A series of laws has enshrined equal rights for men and women within marriage. In 1958, when women were given the same rights as men in financial matters, the legislature still viewed women in their traditional role as housewives. This interpretation was abandoned in 1977. Since then the state leaves it up to the married couple itself to divide up the tasks in a marriage as they both see fit. At the same time, women were ensured equal rights in the case of a marriage being dissolved. Since then an agreement on equal provisions has guaranteed that divorced couples share their pension claims in old age. Equal rights for men and women were also anchored in the Act to Amend the Law Relating to Family Names, which has been in power since April 1994. Preference is no longer unilaterally given to the man's name. The federal government has made rape in a marriage just as much a criminal offence as violence in the raising of children.

In conjunction with their being awarded equal rights, a women's movement has emerged in Germany. And the efforts it has made have resulted among other things in around 440 shelters for women having been established. There, women who have been abused by their partners find protection and a roof over their heads, both for themselves and their children. The German Women's Council, the Federal Alliance of Women's Associations and Groups, also sees itself as a "women's lobby". It is made up of 52 associations with around 11 million members.

Women in Germany have had the right to vote and the right to stand for election since 1919. Just as in working life, however, for women a life in politics is more difficult if there are family duties involved. For this reason over the past few years, partly as a result of introducing quotas and partly through voluntary commitment, the political parties have considerably increased the number of women in the management committees. And it has been a success: the number of women in political committees has increased, and in Parliament from 8.4% in 1980 to 32.8% in January 2003. Since 1961 there has always been at least one woman in the federal government. Today, women head six of the 13 federal ministries, a figure that is the highest since the founding of the Federal Republic. There are around 40 female ministers in the state governments. Over the past few years, the number of women elected to positions in city and local authority administrations has also continued to rise.

Young people: Optimistic, achievement-orientated, pragmatic and communicative, but skeptical as well – this is how young people in Germany come across in polls. There are 22 million people under the age of 25, about 25% of the population belongs to this age group. Their strong social bonds are particularly striking: 76 percent have brothers and sisters, 81 percent live with their natural parents, the vast majority has a best friend, and as opposed to pop stars, their parents are most frequently cited as being role models. Family life plays a large role for them. Young people are also prepared to take part in some part of volunteer activity, but regard traditional forms of politics somewhat skeptically.

Despite the fact that risks are greater and skill requirements higher for young people now than they were 20 years ago, the young generation sees its future in a positive light. According to the latest research findings (14th Shell Youth Study 2002, "Youth in 2002 – Between Pragmatic Idealism and Robust Materialism") the ideological protest attitudes of earlier generations are a thing of the past. Their core values are now closer to those of adults. Most young people respond to the new conditions in society at the beginning of the 21st century with a positive mindset and with increased diligence. They develop their own perspectives and examine their social environment carefully with regard to risks and opportunities, whereby their aim is to make use of the opportunities and minimize the risks. They are not interested primarily in over-arching social goals. By contrast, their objective tends to be success in a society geared to achievement.

Achievement, security and influence have become more important for young people. This becomes evident in comparison with the second half of the 1980s when only 62 percent of youngsters considered "hard work and ambition" to be of any importance, that figure now stands at 76 percent.

Young people help build flood protection barriers

Youngsters: getting on instead of out

Importance for their outlook on life

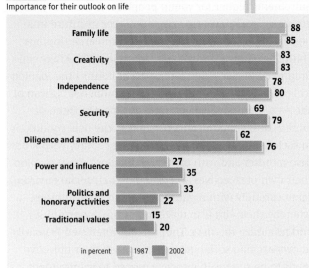

	1987	2002
Family life	88	85
Creativity	83	83
Independence	78	80
Security	69	79
Diligence and ambition	62	76
Power and influence	27	35
Politics and honorary activities	33	22
Traditional values	15	20

in percent ☐ 1987 ☐ 2002

Source: 14th Shell Youth Study

This is in line with the fact that about 50 percent of all youngsters are aiming to pass the Abitur or achieve a general entrance qualification for a university or higher education institute.

Family life enjoys a similarly high level of importance as good qualifications. 75 percent of girls and young women and 66 percent of young men say that they need a family in order "to be happy". Two thirds of young people between the ages of 16 and 25 would like children themselves later in life. For young people today, a career and a family are two central, equally important goals in their life.

The interest in politics among young people continues to dwindle. Only 34 percent of youngsters between 15 and 24 consider themselves interested in politics. In 1991, the figure stood at 57 percent. The vast majority of young people consider democracy to be a good way of running a country. There is little confidence in the political parties. State organizations that are not related to any party, such as the legal system and the police, as well as human rights and environment protection groups, are considered to be particularly trustworthy. Political extremism is rejected outright.

Despite the lack of an interest in politics, many young people play a proactive role in their immediate community. In doing so they focus on concrete, practical matters, in which they see some opportunity or use for themselves. Most important are their own interests and youth-related matters, as well as sensible ways of spending free time. Although young people are active in movements to help others, environment protection and animal rights groups, citizens' action groups, organizations such as Greenpeace and Amnesty International, parties and unions are considerably less popular than clubs, educational establishments and groups that they organize themselves. Many youngsters participate in activities on an individual basis.

Around 25 percent of youngsters are members of the 90 youth national organizations and youth associations. Many of these youth associations have united to form the German Federal Youth Association.

Youngsters: open-minded towards Europe

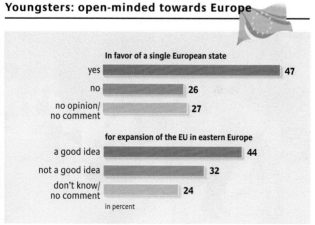

In favor of a single European state

yes	47
no	26
no opinion/ no comment	27

for expansion of the EU in eastern Europe

a good idea	44
not a good idea	32
don't know/ no comment	24

in percent

Source: 14th Shell Youth Study

Together with its 21 member organizations, five affiliated associations and 16 federal state youth rings, it constitutes a strong network. Member organizations include the Evangelical Youth Working Group, the Catholic Youth League, the youth associations of the trade unions, the federal state youth associations and the German Scouts and Guides Association. The youth organization with the most members in Germany is the German Youth Sports Association.

There are also youth organizations in the world of politics. All the major parties maintain youth organizations that identify with the party. Most of them belong to the Political Youth Ring. In addition to these it is mostly religious and trade union youth associations, adult education institutions, foundations and educational establishments as well as institutions for political education, that provide young people with an extramural knowledge of society and the state, and European and worldwide cultural affairs.

Public authorities endeavor to offer children an active exposure to art and culture at as early an age as possible. Its value in young people's development is evident in the work of music schools, youth film clubs, theaters,

Performance by a youth theater club

dance groups, libraries, youth art schools, literary working groups, museums and many other institutions.

Important subject matters such as ecology, violence and xenophobia are addressed in several cultural youth projects. Young people arrive for themselves at new insights into conditions in society today with regard to peaceful, democratic coexistence.

The Federation of Youth Cultural Associations is the umbrella association for 48 specialized nationwide associations, in whose activities more than 12 million young people participate every year. In more than 100,000 projects, competitions, workshops, encounters, seminars and conferences the specialized associations initiate, organize and supervise children's and youths' cultural work at a regional, national and international level.

An important element of state activities with regard to youth is addressing the topic of xenophobia and right-wing extremism. The federal government has called for an "Alliance for Democracy and Tolerance – against Extremism and Violence", which puts into practice and openly represents the values and guarantees of a social and democratic constitutional state.

Youth protection measures, social help and the opportunity to participate voluntarily all support the development of children and youth. To this end, a new Youth Protection Act was introduced on April 1, 2003. The federal government has resolved an agenda containing a whole raft of measures on prevention and education, legislation, the international pursuit of criminals and the protection of victims; they are all designed to protect young people from violence of a sexual nature and exploitation. The federal government will continue to focus in particular on steps geared to improving the integration of disadvantaged young people and reducing these disadvantages, especially for children and youths who descend from immigrants and those in flashpoint neighborhoods.

The federal government's central instrument for supporting its youth policy and work on behalf of children is the Federal Child and Youth Plan. In addition to helping those child-support associations and organizations operating nationwide, it also finances projects such as extramural political, sports and cultural education of youth and international youth exchanges. It likewise provides funding for social education, including the voluntary social year and the voluntary ecological year.

The federal government provides financial support for over 3,000 measures aimed at international youth cooperation, which contribute to a better understanding between peoples and stronger intercultural expertise. Furthermore around 200,000 German and French young people take part every year in projects sponsored by the German and French Youth Association, as do over 130,000 young Germans and Poles in those of the German and Polish Youth Association. Collaboration with the youth in Israel and the Czech Republic are additional regional focuses.

A club in Magdeburg

The older generation: As in the rest of the world, the number of older people in Germany is on the rise. Around 25 percent of the country's population is aged 60 or over. In 2050, this figure will be 36 percent. In 2050, those aged 60 and over will make up more than 20 percent of the population worldwide. In 1950, only every 13th person was over 60 years old.

The changes in demographic structure are leading to far-reaching changes in all walks of life and require political concepts for dealing with older people as well as a new image of old age. The federal government pursues a proactive supportive policy for senior citizens, ensuring they have access to activities and guaranteeing them long-term independence. The new approach to ageing involves making social security in old age the litmus test of future reforms to the social security system. Society must adapt to the rising number of older citizens. The federal government intends to play its part in identifying opportunities for longer life and making use of them. It is the task of politicians to create the necessary framework for an ageing process in which citizens are active and with which they can cope. Efforts must be made to ensure that the particular period in ones life referred to as "time that has been won" is a time in which there are also social responsibilities, coupled with the opportunity to develop oneself still further.

Older people are themselves interested in pursuing some form of sensible occupation in the time when they are no longer working. The trial program "Acquired Experience for Initiatives" supported by the federal government illustrates this well. It involves senior citizens performing volunteer work and finding self-expression through new responsible activities.

The Internet is an important form of support for older people. It offers those who are limited in terms of what they can physically achieve the opportunity to participate in society. As yet however older people do not use the Internet to the same extent as other sections of the population. Whereas 68 percent of 18 to 27-year olds are online, only 14 percent of 50 to 59-year olds, and just 5.7

Active senior citizens

percent of over 70-year olds have Internet access. For this reason, the federal government is financing pilot schemes to provide more opportunities for senior citizens to click onto the Web.

The senior citizen offices, which are funded by the federal government and now number 170, spread throughout the whole country, are also of great assistance. They provide a nationwide opportunity to exchange insights and organize further education events dealing with major topics of interest and current affairs. They are aimed primarily at those people no longer in full-time employment and no longer with their family at home. They are highly successful in helping older people participate in some form of volunteer work and support the establishment of older people's initiatives for all age groups.

The number of people of a very advanced age will also continue to increase. In the near future it will be the norm rather than the exception for people to live longer

than 80 years of age. Today, 60-year old men have on average a life expectancy of over 19 years, 60-year old women of even up to almost 24 years. In other words, on average, the life expectancy of 60-year olds has increased by almost five years since the early 1960s.

A ripe old age must not be considered a burden to society, nor as a threat for individuals. Advanced age does not automatically mean illness and being dependent on help and care. At all stages of their lives, in a very advanced age as well, people are proactive persons who wish to lead their lives in dignity and in the manner they themselves consider appropriate. High-quality care for the elderly is one of the most important goals of the federal government. There is widespread agreement on the fact that improvements to the care system are urgently required, especially in the case of those suffering from dementia. The "Dementia Campaign" and further development of the Alzheimer hotline provide support for sufferers and their relatives.

Information

www.bmfsfj.de
(German Ministry for Families, Senior Citizens, Women and Youth)
www.deutscher-frauenrat.de
(German Women's Council)
www.dfjw.org
(German-French Youth Association)
www.dpjw.org
(German-Polish Youth Association)
www.tandem-org.de
(Tandem)
www.dbjr.de
(German Federal Youth Association)
www.dsj.de
(German Youth Sport Association)

Germany: host to the World Cup in 2006

Sport

Sports are a favorite leisure-time activity for all age groups in Germany. The passion for sport is not just experienced passively sitting in front of a TV screen, but above all actively in more than 87,000 clubs that together form the German Sports Federation.

Today, the German Sports Federation (Deutsche Sportbund, or DSB) has a total of around 27 million members. The DSB is the umbrella organization for 16 federal sports associations and numerous specialist associations. Around 2.7 million members work in a voluntary capacity in these associations, as coaches, trainers, physiotherapists or officials.

With around 6.26 million members the German Football Association has the most members of any of the sports associations in Germany. Football is played in thousands of amateur clubs, and every week hundreds of thousands of spectators make their way to the stadiums to watch the professionals in action. In addition to dancing and riding, gymnastics is one of the few sports where female members outnumber the males in the clubs.

In 2006, the soccer World Cup will be held in Germany. The opening game will most probably be held on June 9, and the final on July 9. Entrance tickets will most probably go on sale as of spring 2005.

Where sport is concerned the vast majority of people are not interested in becoming top-notch athletes. For most, enjoying exercise and participating in some form of group activity are more important. Sport is good for the health and compensates for our sedentary lifestyles. The ever-wider ranging activities on offer in the clubs as well as the campaigns organized by the DSB, in which millions of sport enthusiasts take part every year, take this into account. Highly sought after is the DSB sports badge, which is awarded in gold, silver and bronze. Every year, around 750,000 Germans try to succeed in qualifying for one of the badges.

Owing to the constitutional responsibility of the federal government, government promotion of sports concentrates on top-level competitive sports. This funding is dependent however on sport being clean and free of all manipulative substances. To this end additional government funding has been granted for anti-doping research

The German Eight taking part in a World Cup regatta

and doping analysis. In order to increase the influence German sport exercises in international committees, the federal government supports the establishment and maintenance of international offices in the field of sport in Germany. In as much as there is nationwide interest, outstanding sports activities with widespread appeal, such as the German Gymnastics Festival, can also benefit from financial support.

Olympic training hubs and national sports centers provide top athletes with the best possible training conditions as well as extensive physiotherapy, advice on training, and medical and social care. Intensive training, all-embracing healthcare and social support as well as financial security are all fundamental prerequisites for success. The "German Sports Assistance Foundation", which was founded in 1967, and sees itself as the welfare association of the sports system, plays a prominent role in ensuring that athletes enjoy financial security.

Because of the enormous importance in society of top-level sport by the disabled, over the past few years federal government has continually increased its grants in as much as it was responsible for, and able to do so. In addition the federal government is successfully campaigning for more widespread media coverage of the outstanding competitions in which disabled top-level athletes take part.

According to the latest figures for sports facilities released by the federal states, the number of top-level and general sports facilities in Germany is high. There are around 127,000 sports complexes nationwide; of these over three quarters of the complexes offer outdoor and indoor facilities. Despite an increasing number of new-trend sports, the sports ground just around the corner remains the most widespread form of sports facility. As a result of the high number of complexes and the subsequent sound infrastructure with regard to sport, plans for new buildings can be restricted to those sports that post large growth levels. The principal challenge for the future in the field of sport will be to redevelop and modernize existing sports facilities.

By means of its "Golden Plan East" special funding program, the federal government has been supporting the building of public sports facilities in eastern Germany. In many cases existing faults in usable sports facilities have been rectified.

Information

www.dsb.de
(German Sports Federation)
www.dfb.de
www.fifaworldcup.com

Inline skaters enjoy a traffic-free day

Leisure time and vacationing

On average, adults in Germany have almost 2,500 hours
free-time. They work on average 36.7 hours per week and
have at their disposal three to four hours of leisure time
per day as well as ten hours per day at the weekend and on
public holidays. Annual leave is up to six weeks. Differences between the former West and East Germany are
gradually being eliminated. For some time now, German
households have spent between ten and 15 percent of their
disposable income on free time. In total, Germans spend
around € 225 billion every year on free time activities.

Many people spend a large part of their free time
within their own four walls: watching TV is an important
pastime. Many collect things, engage in artistic activities,
listen to music, or pursue other hobbies at home or in the
garden. Germans also like to go out, however: to the cinema, or for a trip by car, motorbike or bicycle.

There is a wide range of opportunities available for
people's leisure-time: travel, day-trips, culture, sport and
entertainment. There are swimming pools and sports com-

plexes for all disciplines, theaters, concert halls and cinemas, libraries and museums, restaurants and camping grounds. More than five million people earn their living in part or in full from free-time activities. Clubs, non-profit-making organizations and public administration also support this leisure-time infrastructure.

On average, every citizen goes to the cinema twice a year. Museums, 4,570 of them in total, are also highly popular, attracting 96 million visitors every year. Increasingly popular are "traffic-free days", on which whole stretches of roads are reserved just for bicycles for several kilometers at a time. Examples of this are along the Rhine between Bingen and Koblenz or along the "traffic-free wine route" in the Rhineland-Palatinate. At least 12 million Germans give up some of their free time to perform voluntary roles in clubs and organizations.

Clubs play an important role in free time in Germany. They number around 345,000 and have 70 million members. Activities offered by clubs and associations in the country are extraordinarily diverse. Almost one in four Germans is a member of a sports club, and over two million belong to choral societies. There are clubs for marksmen, stamp collectors, dog breeders, regional enthusiasts, gardeners, amateur radio operators and clubs specializing in carnival activities. There is much on offer specifically for women and youngsters.

Vacation: Traveling is the Germans' most popular form of leisure-time activity. And they like to travel abroad best of all. When it comes to trips abroad, the Germans are European champions, spending a total of € 56 billion on them in 2002. Seventy-five percent of all vacationers demonstrate their cosmopolitan nature and interest in other peoples by embarking on a journey that takes them beyond the German borders.

For some time now the most popular foreign countries have been Spain, Italy, and Austria, followed by Greece, France, the Netherlands and Switzerland.

Cochem Castle on the River Mosel

Around 50 percent of all Germans book a trip organized by a tour operator. Conversely, Germany is also an important destination for foreigners. In 2001, it was seventh place in the list of travelers' international destinations.

For those Germans who take their vacation at home, popular destinations are the North Sea and the Baltic Sea, with their coastlines, islands, and equable maritime climate. For hikers the Mittelgebirge and the Alps are destinations worth visiting. Numerous lakes throughout the country offer facilities for water sports. The Rhine, Main, Mosel, Neckar, Danube, Elbe and Saale valleys all offer magnificently romantic scenery.

Almost 100 tourist routes away from the main arteries, such as the "German Fairy Tale Route", the "Romanesque Route" or the "German Wine Route", run through old cultural landscapes, providing access to natural beauty spots and idyllic old towns and villages. They pass through particularly beautiful parts of the country, encouraging travelers to observe the surroundings, tarry a while and take a break in an inn. The best-known vaca-

Water sports in Vogtland

tion route is the "Romanesque Route", which particularly in places such as Rothenburg ob der Tauber, Dinkelsbühl and Nördlingen really brings the Middle Ages to life.

Innumerable regional and local festivals, some of them featuring traditional costumes, wine festivals and other public and town festivals all provide tourists with excellent opportunities for getting to know the locals.

Over the last few decades, cuisine and accommodation have reached a high standard. The spectrum ranges from inexpensive accommodation on farms and in private households, via mid-market hotels to well-equipped vacation parks and top international hotels. For gourmets there are more and more restaurants that reach international standards, such as the Michelin guide. In addition, there is a broad typical selection of regional German cooking and drinks. German wines are held in high esteem throughout the world, and it scarcely needs mentioning that the Germans still hold dear to the traditions of beer brewing. Nowadays not only German cooking is popular: in any small town there is a wide range of restaurants with international cuisine.

Whether by rail, road or on water, a well-established transportation network makes travel to and around

Germany all the easier. It is not only hikers that reach their destinations in holiday areas using well laid out short loops and longer paths. Specially laid out cycle tracks enable cyclists to experience and familiarize themselves with the German countryside. In the east German states the tourist infrastructure is being extended gradually. In those areas of Brandenburg and Mecklenburg-Western Pomerania that boast numerous lakes and rivers, several opportunities have been created for water sports enthusiasts and those who wish to explore by water.

On behalf of the federal government, the DZT German National Tourist Board acts as the national marketing organization responsible for advertising the country's tourist attractions both at home and abroad. The 27 DZT representative offices abroad and sales offices act as the truly professional partners of the tourism industry. They place trips to Germany in the catalogues of foreign tour operators, and ensure that those destinations in the country worth visiting are represented in all modern media forms. Through its Germany stand, the DZT enables SMEs to participate in important trade fairs and those open to the general public.

Information

www.deutschland-tourismus.de
(German National Tourist Board)
www.deutschertourismusverband.de
(German Tourism Association)

Living

Around 80 percent of all families dream of owning the four walls they live in. For 43 percent of west German households this dream has come true, whereas in the east German states, where when the GDR still existed there was scarcely any owner-occupied accommodation, the figure has now reached 31 percent. Those who live in rented accommodation spend around a quarter of their net disposable income on rent, excluding heating costs. On average, each individual enjoys around 40 sq. m. The apartments are well appointed: over 95 percent have a bathroom and toilet, and 83 percent have central heating.

Social housing support: The provision of accommodation for families with a large number of children, disabled and elderly citizens and citizens with low incomes is supported by the state by means of the scheme to support housing. Between 2001 and 2003, federal government funding of around € 13 billion in financial resources was made available for this cause. Over the past few years, funds have been channeled into renovating existing accommodation and helping people to acquire their own property. It is still true that there are differences between the former West Germany and the new federal states.

In the east German states there are around one million flats currently unoccupied, predominantly rented apartments in poor condition in old buildings and increasingly the GDR industrial apartments, or pre-fabricated buildings. This, given the dwindling number of citizens, and the vast amount of catching up still needed with regard to owner-occupied accommodation, there is expected to be a long-term surplus of rented accommodation. Between 2002 and 2009 a total of € 2.7 billion will be allocated to the "Conversion of Cities in the East" in order to demolish superfluous houses and at the same time enhance the status of neighborhoods, especially those in which the number of unoccupied apartments is particularly high. In addition, the agenda allocates investment incentives for the renovation and modernization of old inner-city buildings both for those investing in accommodation to be rented out as well those acquiring owner-occupied property.

A villa in Chemnitz

Housing allowances: Since housing is one of the basic necessities of humans, the state provides a grant to low-income households to cover living costs (rent or financial commitments resulting from owner-occupied accommodation).

This living allowance is designed to enable such households to afford appropriate accommodation that is suitable for families. Citizens have a legal right to a living allowance provided they fulfill the necessary requirements. At the beginning of 2001, a good 2.8 million people were receiving living allowances.

In 2001, spending on housing allowances amounted to approx. € 4.2 billion, an increase of € 0.6 billion compared with 2000. This reflects the considerable increase in benefits resulting from the reform in housing allowances, which came into force on January 1, 2001.

Rental of living accommodation is regulated by law. For this reason no tenant need fear unjustified and arbitrary rental demands. Also landlords may also evict tenants who have adhered to the terms of the contract only in the case of them being able to prove "justified interest" (for example should they require a rented apartment as their own accommodation). Rises in rent are possible only within the framework of the rents paid for comparable apartments in a given place.

Upon presentation of the requirements for financial aid, those who decide to build or buy their own home receive an "own home allowance", which is paid directly by the fiscal authorities. Depending on income, additional assistance in the form of grants and cheap loans can be applied for.

Information

www.bmvbw.de
(German Ministry of Transport,
Building and Housing)

Ecumenical Church Convention in Berlin

Churches and religious communities

In Germany, around 55 million people or almost two thirds of the population consider themselves members of a Christian faith. There are 26.6 million Roman Catholics and 26.3 million Protestants, with two million belonging to other Christian denominations. The remaining one third or so of the population belongs either to none, or to a non-Christian religious community, such as the Muslim or the Jewish community.

The Basic Law guarantees freedom of faith, conscience and religious or ideological belief, as well as the opportunity to practice one's faith unhindered. There is no established state church in Germany, i.e., no ties between state and church administration, and as such no control over churches by the state. The relationship between the state and the churches is that of a partnership; in addition to the constitution it is founded on concordats and contracts. The state participates in the financing of certain establishments run by the church such as kindergartens and schools.

The churches are entitled to levy taxes from their members; these are normally collected by the state against reimbursement of the costs incurred. Prospective theologians are for the most part educated at state universities; the churches enjoy a say in appointments to chairs of theology that is guaranteed by charter.

The social and charitable commitment of the churches is an integral part of public life. Their activities are indispensable in hospitals, senior citizens homes, care homes, in counseling and care in all situations, in schools and training establishments.

Christian churches: In Germany, the Catholic Church is divided up into seven archdioceses and 20 dioceses. The archbishops, bishops and suffragan bishops (in total, there are more than 70) consult at the annual spring and fall assemblies of the German Bishops Conference. The secretariat is located in Bonn.

The Second Vatican Council encouraged Catholic lay members ministering in the church and these ideas are being enacted by the elected representations of the lay members. Their 140 associations and institutions have united to form the Central Committee of German Catholics.

The Evangelical Church: The Evangelical Church in Germany (EKD) is a community of 24 mostly independent Lutheran, United and Reformed member churches. The main legislative body for devising canon law is the Synod, and the supreme administrative body is the Council of the EKD. The federal churches take part in decision making in the Churches Conference. The Protestant Church belongs to the Ecumenical Council of Churches (the Council of World Churches). It cooperates closely with the Roman Catholic Church.

Through their activities in state and society, the two large Christian churches made a significant contribution to the re-establishment of democratic structures after 1945. The churches, in particular the Evangelical Church, played a pivotal role in the peaceful revolution in the GDR. Numerous opposition groups found a refuge under its roof and in 1989, just like the Catholic Church, it opened many of its doors to enable peaceful protest and discussion. Numerous church representatives in the GDR were part of the opposition movement and played an important role in the various groups that made up the citizens' movement.

The Catholic Church's charitable arm is made up above all of the Deutscher Caritasverband, (German Association of Roman Catholic Charitable Organizations) and that of the Evangelical Church by the Diakonisches Werk (Association of Charitable Services). Both churches are involved in development aid. Large church welfare organizations are financed through voluntary donations from the faithful.

Following the First Vatican Council in 1870, the Catholic Diocese of Old Catholics in Germany emerged. Its establishment in 1873 represented a coming together of those believers who, as a result of their rejection of the dogmas of papal infallibility and the Pope's supremacy with regard to matters of ecclesiastical law, had been excommunicated. Today, there are around 30,000 German Old Catholics in 58 parishes. In addition there are numerous other Christian religious communities in Germany including the Orthodox, Methodists, Baptists and the Salvation Army.

Jewish communities: In 1933, there were some 530,000 Jews living in the Third Reich. Following the genocide by the National Socialists there were but a few thousand people of Jewish belief living in Germany. Today almost 100,000 people are members of a Jewish community. In addition there are, depending on the source, between 40,000 and 80,000 Jews who are not members of the community.

Over the past few years, many Jews have emigrated to Germany from the former Soviet Union. The largest

The Neue Synagoge in Berlin

Jewish community, with over 11,200 members, is in Berlin, followed by the communities in Munich with 7,200 and Frankfurt/Main with 6,600.

It is expected that the number of members will continue to rise. Following German unification, the eastern German Jewish communities with their rich traditions, such as those in Dresden and Leipzig, are once again fostering an active community life.

The umbrella organization of the Jewish communities is the Central Council of Jews in Germany, with which in 2003 the federal government signed an agreement relating to continuous and reliable cooperation. The state awards the Central Council € 3 million annually to be used to preserve and nurture the German Jewish cultural heritage, to establish a Jewish society and to support its integration and social policies.

The Central Council supports the federal government in matters relating to immigration and integration primarily thought its Central Jewish Welfare Office, which devotes itself to social, youth and senior citizens' work and which organizes its own integration programs. Moreover, the Central Council of Jews in Germany advises immigrants on the setting up of new communities. It also strives to propagate tolerance and fight racism and anti-Semitism.

The federal government also supports other organizations which promote understanding and cooperation between Christians and Jews, in particular the German Coordination Council of the Societies for Christian and Jewish Cooperation and the International Council of Christians and Jews. Because of its particular historical responsibility the state supports central establishments belonging to Jewish society in Germany and tends the cemeteries of former Jewish communities in the country.

Muslim communities: The 7.3 million foreign citizens living in Germany have caused religious communities that were previously hardly represented at all to become considerably more important. This is particularly so in the case of Islam. In Germany, there are about 3.2 million Muslims from 41 countries. Turkish Muslims form the largest group, followed by those from the former Yugoslavia, the Arab states and from South and South-East Asia.

Many Muslim organizations have now been established in Germany; these operate mosques and support

Mosque in Bremen

the religious needs of their members. On the whole, however, only a small section of the 3.2 million Muslims are
members of an organized club or association. As such,
none of the existing organizations can claim for itself to
represent Islam or the majority of Muslims. The largest
Muslim non-profit-making organization, with a number
of member associations, is DITIB, the "Turkish Islamic
Union of Establishments for Religion". According to its
own figures, in mid-1999 DITIB had 776 member associations throughout the country. Muslim organizations united to form the Islamic Council for the Federal Republic of
Germany in 1986 and the Central Council of Muslims in
Germany in 1994. Whereas the Islamic Council with more
than 30 member organizations is dominated by Milli
Görüs, an Islamic community considered extremist, the
19 members making up the Central Council represent a
wide range of nations and attitudes, though it scarcely
embraces 200 mosques. The 100 Alawite associations, a
special subgrouping of Muslims, have united under the
auspices of the AABF, Federation of Alawite Communities
in Germany.

More than 20 years ago Germany also witnessed
the development of religious dialog between Christians
and Muslims. To this end, a number of local and regional
Christian-Islamic associations were established. The beginning of 2003 saw the founding of a Coordination Council
of the Alliances for Christian-Islamic Dialog in Germany.

The Federal Government promotes dialog between
religions, supports national research establishments, takes
part in numerous forums, strives for understanding with
Islamic organizations open to dialog and includes these
in its initiatives (such as the "Alliance for Democracy and
Tolerance against Violence and Xenophobia").

Sects: In Germany, there is an opaque variety of
radical, ideological and religious groups of all colors and
persuasions. According to estimates there are around 400
such organizations. The state maintains that the limits of

what can be regarded as religious freedom are reached at the point when the basic rights of other citizens could potentially be violated. The law states that the state is within its rights to warn of the dangers, and attempt to prevent people becoming members of a sect. The two major churches are both involved in educational work with regard to sects, as are many private initiatives at regional and communal level.

Information

www.ekd.de
(EKD, Church Office of the Evangelical Church in Germany)
www.dbk.de
(Secretariat of the German Bishops Conference)
www.zentralratderjuden.de
(Central Council of Jews in Germany)
www.islam.de
(Central Council of Muslims in Germany)

Volunteers distribute food leftovers

Civil and voluntary commitment

In Germany, there is a long tradition of public welfare voluntary work that is not concerned with material profit. The work is very varied and imaginative and is to be found in all areas of social, societal and political life, and has always served to strengthen ties within society.

Around 34 percent of Germans perform honorary roles, voluntarily undertaking tasks for the community for which they receive no remuneration. In addition, outside family life and their occupations, the same number of citizens is active in associations, clubs, projects, initiatives and groups, without performing specific functions under the aegis of these organizations.

In June 2002, a German Bundestag fact-finding commission presented an up-to-date report illustrating the wide spectrum of voluntary work undertaken in Germany. It includes the work performed in clubs and associations, churches, charitable and other welfare organizations, agencies for volunteers, hospices, self-help groups, neighborhood initiatives and swap associations, citizens' initiatives, non-governmental organizations, petitions, as well as that in political parties, trade unions, foundations and non-profit-making companies. In addition there is the voluntary work performed on behalf of society by lay judges, general election helpers, parents' committees, voluntary firefighters, technical relief organizations and rescue services.

The organizations with the longest tradition of voluntary social work are the foundations. As opposed to clubs, these have a material basis, their purpose is expressed in the "founder's wish", as it is referred to, and their legal position is determined by the German Civil Code and the laws of the respective federal state. Those active in foundations donate not only their time but also in most cases money, since their prime purpose is to donate assets for the common weal. In Germany, foundations run hospitals, homes for the elderly, museums, and other establishments. They initiate and run projects, bestow prizes, award scholarships, and organize congresses. The Federal Association of German Foundations is the umbrella organization that represents the individual interests of these institutions.

Since the mid-1990s, a new type of foundation, the civil foundation, has been emerging, of which there are currently some 35. In this case a voluntary syndicate creates a foundation capital, and the voluntary work performed is normally restricted to a specific geographical area and social purpose.

Donations to charitable and welfare causes are commitments to the community. The German Donation Institute estimates that € 5 billion is donated annually, a sum which has remained steady since 1990. Around 25 percent of donations are channeled into social causes, about 15 percent awarded to religious communities, disaster relief and environmental organizations.

Public opinion and the mass media

Article 5 of the Basic Law guarantees the right to freedom of speech, freedom of the press and the right to generally accessible information. There is no form of censorship. A large number of different media struggles to attract the public's attention. In June 2002, the circulation of daily newspapers alone stood at 23.2 million copies; German households can receive on average 30 TV channels. Around 230 radio stations round out the picture.

Almost all households are equipped with one or more TVs and a radio. Germans make extensive use of the media. They listen to more than 3.5 hours radio every day, watch TV for three hours, read a daily paper for 36 minutes, and in addition peruse TV, general and special-interest magazines and glean information from weekly and monthly magazines.

According to the long-term study "Mass Communication 2000" performed by the ARD and ZDF TV stations, statistically, every German aged over 14 consumes eight hours and 22 minutes of media coverage daily. Twenty years ago the figure for the same age group stood at five hours per day.

The mass media collate their information from domestic and foreign news agencies, as well as the press offices of state institutions, private organizations, and companies, not to mention their own correspondents at home and abroad as well as their own research. The biggest German news agency, Deutsche Presse-Agentur (dpa), ranks fourth among global news agencies, following Reuters, the French agency Agence France Presse (AFP), and the US Associated Press.

In Germany, public authorities are obliged to provide journalists with information. BPA, the Press and Information Office of the federal Government, acts as intermediary between the government and the public and coordinates the Chancellery's press and PR activities. As a guest of the Federal Press Conference, an association of parliament journalists, the Speaker of the Government takes part in their press conferences and informs the press and the public about government policy. It is he who approaches the press, and not vice versa. This demonstrates how the press functions independently of the authorities. This mode of invitation also applies to press conferences, which the Chancellor and his ministers stage with the Federal Press Conference.

In Berlin, there are almost 1,200 accredited correspondents who join forces in the Government Press Conference or the Foreign Press Club.

A newspaper kiosk in Hamburg

Press

Newspapers and magazines: Newspaper reading is extremely popular in Germany. In terms of newspaper density (the number of newspapers per 1,000 inhabitants), Germany ranks seventh in Europe behind Norway, Finland, Sweden, Switzerland, Austria and England; 78 percent of Germans read a newspaper every day, on average for thirty minutes.

Local and regional daily papers predominate. The 331 local and regional subscription newspapers have the widest circulation, with 16.1 million copies, followed by the eight newspapers that can be bought on the street, with 5.4 million copies.

Of the German newspapers that can be bought on the street, "Bild" has the widest circulation, with over four million copies sold daily. The large national dailies "Frankfurter Allgemeine Zeitung" and "Die Welt" enjoy less widespread circulation but have a great influence on public opinion, as do other nationwide papers such as "Süddeutsche Zeitung", "Frankfurter Rundschau" and "Handelsblatt". Other important representatives of public opinion are the new magazines "Der Spiegel" and "Focus", as well as the weekly "Die Zeit". The range is rounded out by Sunday newspapers such as "Bild am Sonntag", "Welt am Sonntag", "Sonntag Aktuell" and "Frankfurter Allgemeine Sonntagszeitung", which have a circulation of around four million copies. Numerous foreign-language newspapers produce special German editions for foreigners living in the country.

There is also a wide spectrum of magazines available in Germany. Including the specialist journals, there are almost 10,000 in total. In terms of the number of different titles, the single largest group is specialist journals, of which there are a total of 3,450, followed by general interest magazines, with around 1,800. In addition to news magazines, these include primarily glossy magazines such as "Stern" and "Bunte", as well as women's magazines. "Special interest" magazines as they are known, which appeal to specific target groups, are attracting an increasing number of readers. In addition, there are religious publications, customer magazines (more than 2,300) and advertising papers. Publications by organizations and associations account for one third of the magazine market. At around 13 million copies the "ADAC-Motorwelt" motoring magazine, published by the Allgemeiner Deutscher Automobilclub, has the widest circulation.

The major publishing companies: Since the mid-1950s, the number of independent newspapers in Germany has steadily shrunk. Publishers with a leading edge in terms of economic and technological strength were able to force competitors out of various regional markets. Business trends in the press market have led to the formation of large publishing corporations. In the daily newspaper segment, this was above all the Axel Springer publishing house, which holds a 25 percent share of the newspaper market. There is a concentration of economic and publishing power in the following publishing groups: Westdeutsche Allgemeinen Zeitung, Süd-

Circulation of selected newspapers, general magazines and news magazines

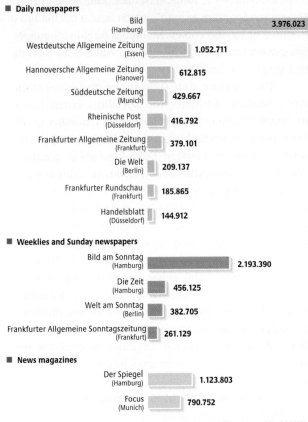

■ Daily newspapers

Newspaper	Circulation
Bild (Hamburg)	3.976.023
Westdeutsche Allgemeine Zeitung (Essen)	1.052.711
Hannoversche Allgemeine Zeitung (Hanover)	612.815
Süddeutsche Zeitung (Munich)	429.667
Rheinische Post (Düsseldorf)	416.792
Frankfurter Allgemeine Zeitung (Frankfurt)	379.101
Die Welt (Berlin)	209.137
Frankfurter Rundschau (Frankfurt)	185.865
Handelsblatt (Düsseldorf)	144.912

■ Weeklies and Sunday newspapers

Newspaper	Circulation
Bild am Sonntag (Hamburg)	2.193.390
Die Zeit (Hamburg)	456.125
Welt am Sonntag (Berlin)	382.705
Frankfurter Allgemeine Sonntagszeitung (Frankfurt)	261.129

■ News magazines

Magazine	Circulation
Der Spiegel (Hamburg)	1.123.803
Focus (Munich)	790.752

Source: Institute of Publishers, status as at March 31, 2003

deutscher Verlag, Verlag M. DuMont Schauberg, Frankfurter Allgemeine Zeitung and Holtzbrinck.

Publishers of magazines, in particular of general interest magazines, are also of importance in terms of economic power and potential journalistic reach. Here, the publishing group Bauer, Gruner + Jahr and Burda heads the list; the Axel Springer group is also active in this sector. The media company with the highest turnover in Germany is Bertelsmann AG, the third largest media company worldwide, which operates on a global basis.

The press laws of the individual federal states govern the rights of the press. They are consistent on basic issues: these include imprint obligations, the duty to uphold due diligence, and journalists' right to withhold the name of their sources, as well as the rights of those reported on to make a counterstatement.

The "German Press Council" sees itself as the controlling body of publishers and journalists; it addresses infringements of due diligence on the part of journalists and questions of ethics. In legal terms, its opinions are not binding; it does, however, make use of the sanction methods open to it, which can result in a public rebuke for the press organ in question.

Information

www.bdzv.de
(Association of German Newspaper Publishers)
www.vdz.de
(Association of German Periodical Publishers)
www.djv.de
(German Journalists Association)
www.verdi.de
(Ver.di trade union)
www.presserat.de
(German Press Council)

Radio and TV

In Germany, TV and radio are organized and financed along two fundamentally different lines. The private channels survive almost exclusively from advertising revenue. In many cases they have specialized in particular types of programs. The public broadcasting networks, by contrast, which are financed with public funds, are legally committed to a pre-defined task with regard to programs. The population should be offered a basic supply of information, education, and entertainment. This also includes highbrow cultural programs, which ideally reflect all cultural trends.

Public network channels: In Germany there are nine public broadcasting corporations which are divided up according to federal states and together form the ARD, Association of Public Broadcasting Corporations in the Federal Republic of Germany. Together they are responsible for the "Erstes Deutsches Fernsehen", the first German TV channel, but also broadcast their own TV and radio programs. The Zweites Deutsches Fernsehen (ZDF) is another public network channel that does not produce radio programs. "DeutschlandRadio" is run jointly by ARD and ZDF; it broadcasts nationwide programs focusing on information and culture. Deutsche Welle, the only federal radio station, which also comes under the ambit of ARD, is responsible for broadcasting to foreign countries. Deutsche Welle's brief is to provide foreign countries with an all-embracing picture of political, cultural and economic life in Germany as well as depicting and explaining Germany's stance on important questions.

Since 1997, ARD and ZDF together have been running "Phoenix", a channel delivering news events and documentaries, as well as the children's channel "Der Kinderkanal", the only two publicly-funded specialist channels in Germany. Both ARD and ZDF are both involved in the joint German and French cultural channel ARTE, the satellite channel 3Sat, as well as the international exchange of programs through Eurovision.

Daily news, political reporting, documentaries covering topics at home and abroad, as well as TV plays, films and entertainment account for a large proportion of the ARD and ZDF programming. As regards reporting events abroad, both ARD and ZDF maintain extensive networks of correspondents and in many countries their own studios.

The Channel Three TV programs are broadcast on a regional basis by ARD units and can be received in other parts of the country via satellite and cable. These channels are particularly important for culture and education: most ARD units regularly broadcast school TV as well as foundation courses for various forms of education.

Each ARD station produces several radio programs aimed at specific target groups. At the present time, there are more than 50 German language radio stations in the public network channels. Special programs for foreign citizens are broadcast in their respective languages.

The costs of the public network channels are covered first and foremost by the license fees paid by listeners and viewers. For TV and radio these are € 16.15 per

month. A radio alone costs € 5.32. Yet both ARD and ZDF also rely on revenue from advertising. As opposed to private radio and TV channels, advertising time on the public network channels is severely restricted.

Generally speaking, monitoring and managing of public network broadcasting corporations is the task of the Broadcasting Council, the Administrative Council and the director of the respective corporation. The council is made up of members who represent social groups and thus act in the interests of the general public. They are elected by the federal parliaments, or directly by political parties, religious communities, and business and cultural organizations. The council advises corporation directors on programming and monitors adherence to its overarching programming principles. The Administrative Council determines the budget and monitors the orderly management of the respective corporation. Its members are elected for the most part by the Radio Council. In addition, the latter elects the director, who manages the respective corporation, is responsible for its programs, and acts as its representative in the public eye. The public network cor-

Political talk show

porations are obliged to uphold a neutral political stance in their programming and ensure that the contents present a balanced view of the facts.

Private TV stations: In 1984, the public network corporations encountered competition when SAT.1, the first privately-funded TV station, began broadcasting from Mainz. That same year, RTL plus Deutschland (now RTL, based in Cologne) also went on air, since when additional private channels and pay-TV have begun broadcasting. Programs on the private channels are broadcast via cable and satellite, but can also in some cases be received on terrestrial frequencies. The privately-funded TV stations are run by consortia consisting for the most part of media companies. As opposed to the public network corporations, the private stations mainly source their financing from advertising income.

Over the past few years, the number of private radio stations has increased immensely. Whereas in 1991 there were a mere 100 private radio stations, by 2003 the figure had grown to 276 and they reach a total of at least 500,000 listeners.

The law requires that private radio stations cater for wide-ranging local tastes. The German Constitution stipulates that the private radio stations are no more permitted to have an influence on public opinion than their public network competitors. Programs must guarantee "basic standards with regard to a variety of opinions". The private radio stations are subject to a regulatory watchdog, the Federal Media Authorities, whose duties include awarding broadcasting licenses, program monitoring and ensuring that the stations show no form of political bias. In 1993, the private TV stations founded the Freiwillige Selbstkontrolle Fernsehen e.V, an organization for the voluntary self-regulation of television within the framework of legal protection for children and young people.

Information

www.ard.de
(ARD, the Association of Public Broadcasting Corporations in the Federal Republic of Germany)
www.zdf.de
(ZDF, Second German Television)
www.rtl.de
(RTL)
www.sat1.de
(SAT.1)
www.dwelle.de
(Deutsche Welle)
www.vprt.de
(Association of Private Broadcasting and Telecommunications)
www.fsk.de
(Freiwillige Selbstkontrolle Fernsehen e. V.)

Neue Pinakothek der Moderne in Munich

Culture

As a result of the country's federal structure, culture in Germany is a basic strand of the independent status of individual states; the Basic Law accords the federal government only severely limited powers. The fact that individual states are responsible for their own cultural affairs has led to the emergence of large and small cultural centers of differing standing. Germany has never had a clear cultural capital. Diverse cultural scenes have sprung up even in small towns and districts.

The fact that various cultural institutions and activities in Germany are spread throughout the regions bears witness to this variety. Deutsche Bibliothek, a federal institution, has branches in Frankfurt/Main, Leipzig and Berlin. The Federal Records Office, headquartered in Koblenz, has offices in Berlin, Potsdam, Freiburg and Bayreuth, among others. Hamburg is the city with the greatest concentration of media companies. Cologne, Düsseldorf and Kassel are three of the centers for the Modern fine arts. Berlin has the most theaters. The most important museums are in Berlin, Dresden, Hildesheim,

Frankfurt/Main, Cologne, Munich, Nuremberg and Stuttgart. The two most important literature archives are located in Marbach and Weimar.

Most cultural establishments in the Federal Republic are maintained by the states, cities and local authorities. With a few exceptions, legislation pertaining to cultural affairs is the responsibility of individual states.

For this reason there has never been a Ministry of Culture at national level. The federal government does, however, have a female official entrusted with cultural and media affairs, who serves the Chancellor at ministerial level. She coordinates the federal government's cultural activities, which had previously been distributed throughout various ministries and sees herself as a contact person and instigator with regard to the federal government's cultural policy as well as a representative for German culture on the international and in particular the European stage.

German Cultural Council: Founded in 1982 as a politically independent working group of cultural and media organizations and institutions, the German Cultural Council is an important body that operates at the national rather than state level. It is the umbrella organization of the Federal Cultural Associations, and as such a contact for politicians and government administrative bodies, the European Union as well as the federal states and local authorities in matters relating to common cultural policy. The German Cultural Council has the task of ensuring certain issues arising from all aspects of national cultural policy are included in debate at all levels. The Cultural Council is divided up into eight sections, which represent more than 190 independent associations and establishments. These sections are: the German Music Council, the Council for the Performing Arts, the Literary Working Party, the Art Council, the Architecture Council, the Design, Film and Audio-Vision sections, and the Socio-Cultural Council.

Legally independent intermediary organizations working on their own behalf are for the most part responsible for cooperation on cultural matters with foreign countries and international exchanges as part of cultural agreements. As organizations promoting cultural policy abroad they receive funding from the Federal Foreign Office budget. The most important institutions are the Goethe Institut, the German Academic Exchange Service, the Alexander von Humboldt Foundation and the Institute for Foreign Relations.

Information

www.kulturrat.de
(German Cultural Council.)
www.avh.de
(Alexander von Humboldt Foundation)
www.daad.de
(German Academic Exchange Service)
www.ifa.de
(Institute for Foreign Relations)
www.goethe.de
(Goethe Institut)

Literature

German literature in the aftermath of World War II started from a new beginning, with many authors attempting to find a way of describing the shocking, nihilistic experience of war and devastation – often taking their cue from foreign models or existentialist and traditional Christian trains of thought. Wolfgang Borchert's drama "The Outsider" (1947), short stories by Heinrich Böll ("The Train was on Time", 1949) and Arno Schmidt ("Leviathan", 1949), poetry by Paul Celan ("Poppy and Memory", 1952), Günter Eich and Peter Huchel are examples of the trend of not depicting political matters directly and realistically, but reflecting on German guilt and the German defeat through religious images and symbols for ways of looking at the world. In doing so, the authors take up the tradition of literary Modernism, which had been condemned during the Third Reich.

In the literature of the 1950s and 1960s, a current emerged whereby the manner involved in coming to terms with recent history itself became a literary topic. In many of the works that appeared in West Germany at the time, criticism of the post-War "economic miracle" is combined with efforts to work through the National Socialist past. The focus on quickly establishing new affluence was often interpreted as a method of escaping responsibility for what had happened during the Third Reich. The plays and prose of the Swiss writers Friedrich Dürrenmatt and Max Frisch illustrate this. The most important works by German authors were by Wolfgang Koeppen ("The Greenhouse", 1953), Heinrich Böll ("And Never Said a Word", 1953, "The Bread of Those Early Years", 1955, "Billards at Half-Past Nine", 1959), Siegfried Lenz ("The German Lesson", 1968) and Günter Grass ("The Tin Drum", 1959, "Cat and Mouse", 1961, "Dog Years", 1963).

The "Gruppe 47" played a pivotal role. Instigated by Hans Werner Richter in 1947, this was an informal association of German-language writers, whose annual meetings until 1967 were a literary event, and increasingly a political highlight. Many of its members, who included many well-known authors of the day, saw themselves as the champions of moral values. Their most famous representatives, Heinrich Böll and Günther Grass, received the Nobel Prize for Literature in 1972 and 1999 respectively.

In addition to these authors there was a whole host of others interested less in interpreting the realities of society as depicting it without emotion: Jürgen Becker, Rolf Dieter Brinkmann, Alexander Kluge and Dieter Wellershoff. Concrete poetry stood at loggerheads with all these currents (Max Bense, Eugen Gomringer, Helmut Heissenbüttel, Franz Mon), attempting to avoid any substantive content behind the words they used.

In the mid-1960s, the Federal Republic of Germany as well as every other western country, started to undergo a fundamental change. The student uprisings of 1968 instigated a clearly radicalized form of criticizing the "silence of our fathers" and thus the crimes perpetrated by the National Socialists. Glorifying aesthetic trends in literature were interpreted as camouflaging the social and economic reasons for an economic structure that was deemed unjust. Many authors strove to be active socially and politically – while at the same time refusing to be cornered politically. The fact that several literary figures spoke out against the war in Vietnam and in favor of the new Ostpolitik was symptomatic of this. The search for a new role and new forms for literature was also characteristic. Hans Magnus Enzensberger's theory of the "death of literature" and Peter Weiss' "aesthetics of resistance" were both radical expressions of this new train of thought.

Documentary theater also played a role in this political literature (Rolf Hochhuth: "The Representative", 1963; Heinar Kipphardt: "In the Matter of J. Robert Oppenheimer", 1964), which in terms of both content and intention was related to partisan reporting (Günter Wallraff: "Ihr da oben – wir da unten", 1973) and literature featuring the world of work.

In addition to these trends there were also individuals who nevertheless made their mark as important authors of their day: Arno Schmidt and the Austrian Thomas Bernhard are outstanding examples. The oeuvres of these two writers represents a serious and at times deeply ironic portrayal of the existence of the artist in a

Heinrich Böll   Siegfried Lenz

world full of indifference and unimaginativeness. Moreover, Peter Handke, a highly acclaimed Austrian writer at the end of the 1960s, was one of the most influential writers during the first ten years of his creative output.

If the 1960s were full of beginnings, stimuli and change, the years that followed seem to have been characterized by an exhaustion of artistic devices and potential. The novels and short stories written by those successful authors of the first decades after the war were conspicuous by their lack of originality and cutting-edge characteristic of their ideas, with very little literary output from the generation of 1968, which preferred other genres of artistic expression.

Not dissimilar to 1945, the years 1989-1990 – the end of communism, the GDR and the Soviet Union (1991) – marked a profound turning point not just in political history but also in culture. This applied in particular to those authors living in the GDR who supported a state which, despite all its shortcomings, they considered to be the better of the two states on German soil. From the very beginning, once it had been initiated into the Soviet literary idea of "socialist realism", literature in the GDR had developed in a completely different direction from that in the West.

Uwe Johnson   Christa Wolf

Those that refused to submit to this pressure left the country: Uwe Johnson, Günter Kunert, Reiner Kunze, Sarah Kirsch, Jurek Becker as well as Wolfgang Hilbig escaped the grasp of the state's intervention in the domain of literature.

As such, in the GDR of the 1950s and 1960s there emerged a form of literature that was widely conformist, advocating the idea of reconstruction and historical optimism without formal innovations and any discussion of 20th century avant-garde theories. Only the work of Christa Wolf, Irmtraud Morgner and Heiner Müller towered above this intellectual mediocrity and ideological uniformity. Even in the last throes of the GDR, the output of literary critics such as Christoph Hein, Volker Braun, Ulrich Plenzdorf, Peter Hacks, Stephan Hermlin and Stefan Heym remained infrequent and restrained.

New trends: Among the outstanding German language authors of the past 20 years are Botho Straus, whose stories and novels are an attempt to capture the present at the very moment of its outrageousness by borrowing from mystical images in language and scene sequences and the Austrian Elfriede Jelinek with her vehement attacks on all forms of authoritarian and restorative trends.

It remains to be seen whether the most recent examples of current literature, that reeks of indifference, such as the work of Judith Hermann ("Sommerhouse, later", 1998, "Nothing but Ghosts", 2003), will develop into new trends and forms.

Philosophical litereature: No less than literature, philosophy in post-War Germany was also marked by a profound rupture and continued insecurity. One of the most influential German philosophers of the 20th century was Martin Heidegger (1889-1976), who in 1927 had published "Being and Time", the fundamental work on existentialism. Due to his at times demonstrative affinity to the National Socialist regime he later became one of the most controversial post-War teachers. After the war as well, however, Heidegger's interpretation of existentialism remained the standard work for a broad-based movement in philosophy and the humanities. The theories of philosophers such as Karl Jaspers, Hans-Georg Gadamer, Karl Löwith and Jean-Paul Sartre in France all devised theories that took the philosophy of existentialism further.

Another philosophical current associated with the names Ludwig Wittgenstein, Rudolf Carnap and Karl Popper – all divergence of their thought notwithstanding – picked up the thread of positivism. It continued to develop especially in the Anglo-Saxon countries, where it profoundly influenced analytic and linguistic philosophy which became dominant there. Wolfgang Stegmüller was the most influential representative of these currents in Germany.

The influence of the "Frankfurt School" had been growing in Germany since the beginning of the 1960s. Its main representatives in the country, Theodor W. Adorno and Max Horkheimer, had fled Germany during the Third Reich as they were Jews whose philosophical stance was grounded in Marxist traditions, as had Walter Benjamin, Herbert Marcuse and Ernst Bloch. Their theories had a

Martin Heidegger

profound influence on the student movements at the end of the 1960s. The "Critical Theory" attacked both the conservative, non-political tradition that emerged from German existentialism as well as the way positivism regarded the current state of things as naturally given.

As of the 1970s, German philosophy was increasingly receptive to Anglo-Saxon traditions. The philosophy of Jürgen Habermas, who for a long time taught in the United States, is a clear manifestation of this development. It represents the attempt to combine important elements of continental, Western philosophy with those of Anglo-Saxon philosophy – an adherence to generally binding values and an alignment to facticity. Unlike Habermas, sociologist Niklas Luhmann stressed the autonomous developmental thrust of systems such as society, business and politics. Philosophical discussion in Germany today is determined in particular by questions of ethics.

Theodor W. Adorno

Book trade and libraries

In terms of book production, Germany ranks third in the
world, behind the United Kingdom and China. Every year,
around 80,000 books still appear on the market, either as
new publications or reprints. Yet the number of publishers, headquartered for the most part in Munich, Berlin,
Frankfurt/ Main, Stuttgart, Cologne and Hamburg is dwindling, the result of a gentle takeover process, whereby previously independent publishers are being gobbled up by
large publishing groups. None of these groups has a monopoly on the market yet, but under market duress the
small publishers, who have traditionally been responsible
for the rich variety of the literary scene, are being forced
to throw in the towel more frequently than in earlier
years. In 2002, total books and specialist magazines sales
amounted to approx. € 9.3 billion. The vast majority of
this turnover was produced in more than 5,223 bookshops
involved in general book retailing. Although Internet book
selling is on the increase, in 2002 it accounted for a mere
five percent of total sales – although the segment is aiming to claim a market share of 13 percent by 2006.

Along with chemists, book retailing is the only business sector in Germany in which "fixed retail prices" are permissible by law. These guarantee that almost all books are available at a uniform price, thus ensuring that the entire population has access to books as a cultural asset.

German publishers and booksellers association and book fairs: The occupational and professional organization representing the book trade is the Börsenverein des Deutschen Buchhandels in Frankfurt/Main, which was founded in Leipzig in 1825. It brings under one roof all those sections that make up the industry: publishers, intermediaries and general book retailers. In 1964, it was responsible for founding Ausstellungs- und Messe-GmbH, whose main task is organizing the Frankfurt Book Fair, which takes place every October. The fair is the outstanding annual event in the book trade calendar. It is here that a large percentage of the licensing and rights business worldwide is conducted.

The highpoint of every Frankfurt Book Fair is the award of the Peace Prize of the German Book Trade. Previous winners include Yehudi Menuhin, Teddy Kollek, Václav Havel, György Konrád, Jorge Semprún, Yasar Kemal, Martin Walser and Fritz Stern. In 2002, the prize was awarded to the Nigerian Chinua Acheba. The second important book fair is staged every spring in Leipzig and serves in particular as a bridge to east European countries.

Libraries: As opposed to other countries there is no large, centuries-old national library in Germany. It was only in 1913 that the newly founded Deutsche Bücherei (German Library) in Leipzig started acting as a copyright library for works that appeared in the German language. The division of Germany led to the founding in 1947 of the Deutsche Bibliothek in Frankfurt/Main, which assumed responsibility in the West for the tasks performed by the library in Leipzig. Just like the library in Leipzig it, too, was founded by the book trade, and since 1969 has been a federal agency.

Under the Unification Treaty of August 1990, the two libraries were merged to form a new entity under the name "Die Deutsche Bibliothek". It is the general archive for all literature written in German and the national library information center for the Federal Republic. It currently possesses around 18 million volumes, of which around 9.8 million are stored in Leipzig and 8.1 million in Frankfurt. There are 957,000 volumes in the German Music Archive (Deutscher Musikarchiv), which was founded in Berlin in 1970; this is a department of the Frankfurt section of the Deutsche Bibliothek. Frankfurt also houses the German Exile Archive (Deutsches Exilarchiv) for the period between 1933 and 1945. Specialist departments located in Leipzig include the Center for the Preservation of Books (Zentrum für Bucherhaltung) and the German Book and Script Museum (Deutsches Buch- und Schriftmuseum).

The most important scholarly libraries include the Bavarian State Library (Bayerische Staatsbibliothek) in Munich, with over six million volumes, and the "Berlin State Library – Prussian Cultural Heritage", with around four million volumes.

A library reading room

The federal, state and university libraries also house large collections. In addition to these general Scholarly libraries there are also specialist libraries, for example the Central Medical Library (Medizinische Zentralbibliothek) in Cologne. The Herzog August Bibliothek in Wolfenbüttel is a jewel among German libraries, housing over 660,000 volumes, among them 12,000 valuable volumes of Mediaeval manuscripts. In Weimar, the Herzogin Anna Amalia Bibliothek is very impressive, at one time directed by Johann W. von Goethe, it houses 800,000 volumes, including a collection of editions of "Faust" numbering more than 13,000 volumes that is unique in Europe.

There are around 14,000 public and academic libraries open to readers in the Federal Republic. Public libraries are maintained primarily by local authorities and churches. Through readings by authors, events and exhibitions, many libraries have become cultural centers. Many towns and communities have mobile libraries to give those living on the edge of towns and in villages an opportunity to borrow books.

Information

www.boersenverein.de
(German Publishers and Booksellers Association)
www.bdbibl.de/dbv
(Association of German Libraries)
www.ddb.de
(Die Deutsche Bibliothek)

"Abstract Picture" by Gerhard Richter

The fine arts

In the Western occupation zones and later in the Federal Republic, the attempt to reach new artistic shores following the isolation imposed by the Third Reich came about quickly. The young generation of painters and sculptors at the time, some of whom had served at the front, was enthusiastic about everything they had been denied by Hitler's dictatorship and the war. Wassily Kandinsky, Oskar Kokoschka, Max Beckmann, Emil Nolde, the Expressionists Erich Heckel, Karl Schmidt-Rottluff, Ernst Ludwig Kirchner, and Max Pechstein all served as role models for an art scene that was in the process or re-establishing itself.

Painters: For most young artists Pablo Picasso presented a real challenge with his multi-faceted work. Encountering Surrealism (Max Ernst, Salvador Dalí) and American Abstract Expressionism, in particular the works of Jackson Pollock, was very important. Artists such as Roberto Sebastian Matta, Jean Dubuffet, Georges Mathieu, Jean Fautrier and Wols, however, also stimulated trends in the early art scene in the Federal Republic.

Various groups played a part in the development of this scene. These included: the "Ecole de Paris", which was established around 1940; "COBRA" (founded in 1948); "junger westen" (1948); "Zen 49" (1949); and "Quadriga" (1953).

Parallel to the Tachiste movement in France, under the influence of surrealism, the "Ecole de Paris" and American "Abstraction", a style of art emerged in Germany directly after the Second World War which, far removed from figurative painting or even abstraction, preferred as its general characteristic an abstract, gesticular, semi-automatic way of painting, which is never completely out of control and follows the principal of planned coincidence. The rich variety of the German art informel is manifest in the works of artists who have long since become internationally known: Karl Otto Götz, Bernard Schultze, Fred Thieler, Gerhard Hoehme, Karl Friedrich Dahmen, Emil Schumacher, Peter Brüning, K. R. H. Sonderborg.

At the beginning of the 1950s, almost all the artists in these informal groups sought liberation from the dogmas of figurative panel painting. Thus, different currents emerged to enrich the artistic spectrum in post-War Germany. These include color field painting, i.e., painting via the concrete, dispassionate medium of color,

as Georg Karl Pfahler, Günter Fruhtrunk and Lothar Quinte focus on in their work. It also includes the Action art of the "doer" HA Schult and movements such as the happening initiated by Wolf Vostell and the Fluxus activities, which he profoundly influenced.

Joseph Beuys set completely new standards, devising a new, unusual interpretation of art, opening up art to new dimensions, new fields of signification. His often misunderstood formulae, "art is life, life is art" and "every person is an artist", his "events" with fat and felt, his ideas, rooted in Rudolf Steiner's anthroposophy, the rigorous way in which he managed to win over an ever increasing number of students at the Düsseldorf Academy: These are just some of the striking features in the life and work of Joseph Beuys. His "extended interpretation" of art provided him with an instrument which allowed him to champion "social sculpture" as the perfection of his artistic philosophy.

The Zero group also electrified the public early on with its type of happenings. Heinz Mack, Otto Piene and Günther Uecker represent a type of artist, which, following the Nazi Holocaust, was no longer interested in following ideologies but rather in designing concrete pictures.

Blocks of natural basalt by Joseph Beuys

A. R. Penck

Works by A. R. Penck, one of the major German
artists of today. He first became known for his
paintings with match-stick like human figures.
Penck relocated from the GDR to West Germany
in 1980.

Works by Georg Baselitz

Socialist realism: Whereas artists in the Federal Republic were able to pick up the thread of existing traditions and draw on all the new artistic currents in West Europe and the United States, their colleagues in the former GDR soon found their hands tied by the "Socialist Regime" proscribed for them by the regime. They were permitted to do nothing more than convey a favorable picture of socialist society and its image of man. New trends in this type of painting came largely from the Leipzig Academy of Art, and were evident in the works of Werner Tübke, Bernhard Heisig, Wolfgang Mattheuer, Walter Libuda, Volker Stelzmann, Hartwig Ebersbach, Wolfgang Peuker, Gerhard Altenbourg as well as by the sculptors Wieland Förster and Fritz Cremer.

The German art scene: Several of the painters and sculptors who have risen to prominence both in the Federal Republic and beyond have their roots in the GDR. These include A. R. Penck with his idols reminiscent of the Stone Age, Georg Baselitz with his paintings and sculptures heralding violence, Sigmar Polke with his playful, ironic pictures, and Gerhard Richter, who treads the fine line between figurative and abstract art, who skillfully shifts at will from representations reminiscent of the Old Masters to the most extreme forms of abstraction. They are important names in the German art scene, as are the sculptors Ulrich Rückriem and Jochen Gerz, performance artist Rebecca Horn, painters Jörg Immendorff, Anselm Kiefer, Markus Lüpertz and Hans Haacke, who with his installations and montage questions the world as it appears.

Art promotion: Today, very few painters and sculptors can live from the sale of their work alone. They receive government aid, grants, and assistance from private companies with a keen appreciation of the arts. Kunstfonds e. V., founded in 1980, helps recognized artists finance ambitious projects. The cultural section of the Federation of German Industries also awards prizes to painters and sculptors.

The Church of St. Matthew in Düsseldorf, designed by Gottfried Böhm

Architecture

German architecture set trends in the first 30 years of the 20th century. The strongest influences came from Weimar and Dessau, where the Bauhaus school was founded in the 1920s, and the style that bears its name evolved. Under the leadership of Walter Gropius and Ludwig Mies van der Rohe, the style spread to the far corners of the earth. Today, masterpieces of its synthesis of architecture, technology and functionality can be found all over the world.

Germany's contemporary architecture suffered for some time from the country's difficult situation after 1945. Destroyed cities had to be rebuilt quickly. Millions of people needed a roof over their heads. Architectural quality often took a back seat to a primarily economically-oriented functionalism in building and construction, which paid little heed to shaping a livable residential and working environment, the consequences of which are still visible in many places today.

In the western part of divided Germany, bitter complaints were increasingly heard as early as the 1960s about the monotonous architecture of satellite towns, the faceless industrial and business districts on the peripheries of towns as well as the ill-considered construction marring the inner cities. There was talk of what Alexander Mitscherlich termed the "inhospitable nature" of the inner cities before a town-planning concept focusing on preservation of a city's architecture and character was accorded political and social priority in the mid-1970s.

Architectural and town-planning sins of at least equal magnitude were also committed at this time in the former GDR. Valuable old buildings, which were still standing, most of them in the inner cities, were left to dilapidate or were demolished. The scarce resources earmarked for residential construction were channeled into massive uniform edge-of-town housing estates. With few exceptions, architects had too few opportunities to implement a style of architecture in keeping with the times.

Today, Germany boasts an increasing number of examples of modern experimental architecture which is nevertheless in tune with human needs. Many a superb

The Photonics Center in the Adlershof district of Berlin

building still owes its origination to the style and philosophy of Bauhaus. More recent trends in architecture have, however, also resulted in the construction of remarkable buildings, such as high-tech buildings in which important functional elements such as elevators, escalators, and supply lines have been moved to the outside of the structure, where (often painted in different colors) they concurrently serve as decoration.

Today, other forms of ornamentation such as capitals, cornices, and ornaments in the Art Deco style are being used in a greater variety of ways as eye-catchers in the sense of architecture as art, breaking away from the postulate of architecture as mere fulfillment of function. Germany's top echelon of architects includes:

- Gottfried Böhm, who in 1986 became the first German to be awarded the Pritzker Architecture Prize.
- Günter Behnisch, who designed not only the buildings and grounds for the 1972 Olympic Games in Munich but also the new plenary chamber of the German Bundestag in Bonn in 1993.
- Frei Otto, who made a name for himself in the fields of flexible suspended roof structures and ecologically-oriented buildings.
- Oswald Mathias Ungers, whose buildings exhibit a stringent geometric design.
- Josef Paul Kleihues and Hardt-Waltherr Hämer, who as planning directors of the International Building Exhibition in Berlin have profoundly influenced both debates on new architecture and the treatment of residential accommodation in old buildings.
- Volker Staab, who set important trends in museum construction with Munich's Pinakothek der Moderne and the Georg Schäfer Museum in Schweinfurt.
- Axel Schultes, who won the 1993 Berlin "Internationaler städtebaulicher Ideenwettbewerb Spreebogen" and (together with Charlotte Frank) masterminded the new Federal Chancellery Building.

Outstanding structures: The Federal Republic has some fine representative buildings. Public clients in particular usually hold architectural competitions before they decide on the execution of a specific design. These ideas and project competitions are key instruments for promoting architectural quality in Germany, as manifested not least by the impressive number and quality of the parliament and government buildings in Berlin. Norman Foster's conversion of the Reichstag building is one of the highlights, and is likewise open to the public.

The numerous museums built over the past 50 years as a result of public competitions are particularly noteworthy. These include Hans Döllgast's reconstruction of Alte Pinakothek in Munich in 1957, the "museum mile" along the River Main in Frankfurt/Main – Deutsches Architektur Museum (Oswald Mathias Ungers, 1984), the German Film Museum (Helge Bofinger, 1984), the Museum of Applied Arts (Richard Meier, 1984), the Museum of Prehistory and Early History (Josef Paul Kleihues, 1989), the Jewish Museum (Ante Josip von Kostelac, 1986), the German Postal Museum (Behnisch und Partner, 1990), through to the three museums in Bonn – the Art Center of the Federal Republic of Germany (Gustav Peichl, 1993),

The Hackesche Höfe in Berlin

the Art Museum (Axel Schultes, 1993), the Museum of Contemporary German History (Ingeborg and Hartmut Rüdiger, 1994), as well as the unique Jewish Museum in Berlin (Daniel Libeskind, 2000), which has rapidly developed into a crowd puller in a city where there is no shortage of museums.

Contemporary architecture manifests itself in elegant, spacious constructions that are filled with light. This applies not just to the new buildings on the Potsdamer Platz in Berlin (the Daimler-Chrysler Building, where the architectural team was led by by Renzo Piano, or the Sony Center, designed by Helmut Jahn), but also to many recent functional buildings, for example the Photonics Center in the Adlershof district of Berlin (Sauerbruch/Hutton), the "Stadttor" in Düsseldorf (Petzinka, Pink and Partners), the Kunsthalle in Halle (Braun/Köhler/Schlockermann), the swimming pools in the Grünau district of Leipzig (Behnisch und Partner), the RWE high-rise in Essen (Ingenhoven) and the Federal Labor Court in Erfurt (Weinmiller/Grossmann). The Hackesche Höfe (Faust/Weiß) in Berlin are a particularly good example of old buildings which have been successfully renovated.

Information

www.bda.baunetz.de

(Association of German Architects)

Design

Design has a long tradition in Germany. At the beginning of the 20th century, Peter Behrens designed products, posters and buildings for AEG, the electrical goods firm. In 1907 the Deutscher Werkbund was founded with the purpose of promoting the "refinement of working life through the combined influence of art, industry and the craft trades". The Bauhaus, founded by Walter Gropius in 1919 and which existed until 1933, became world famous. The same is true of the Ulm College of Design, which was founded in 1953 by Inge Aicher-Scholl, Otl Aicher and Max Bill. While it initially followed in the footsteps of the Bauhaus, it soon pursued concepts of its own and set internationally acknowledged standards for design during the 15 years of its existence and strongly influenced many prominent designers.

For many years, the name Braun was closely linked, especially abroad, with the concept of German design, which combines functionality with complexity and technology. Braun design was largely defined by Dieter Rams. Other German firms set and indeed still set styles with their products: Wilkhahn in Bad Münder and

Vitra in Weil am Rhein for furniture, Lamy for writing implements and Erco for luminaires.

In the information age, the importance of design in creating new media is assuming an ever greater role. Apart from the aesthetic dimension while deciphering complex information, design plays an important intermediary role between IT advances and the cultural and social developments.

The German Design Council advises and supplies information in matters of design to trade and industry, cultural institutions as well as the public. One of the focuses of its activities is presenting German design outside Germany. On behalf of the Federal Minister of Economics and Labor it awards the "Federal Prize for Product Design" and on alternate years the "Federal Prize for Design Promotion".

In addition to the German Design Council there are a range of other design institutions in Germany. Among the most important are the International Design Center (IDZ) in Berlin, the "designcenter" in Stuttgart, and the Essen-based Design Zentrum Nordrhein-Westfalen.

The interests of designers vis-à-vis the political sector and the public are represented by the German Designer Forum, which among other things constitutes the Design section of the German Arts Council, the umbrella organization of the federal arts associations.

Information

www.designertag.de
(German Design Forum)
www.german-design-council.de
(German Design Council)

Neue Staatsgalerie in Stuttgart

Museums, collections and exhibitions

There are around 6,000 museums in Germany: state, municipal, society and private museums, as well as treasure vaults, diocesan museums, cathedral treasures, and museums attached to royal residences, castles, and palaces, not to mention open-air museums. They have emerged over the centuries out of royal, church, and later civic collections.

The royal collections were not, however, intended for the erudition and entertainment of the general public. Instead, they served to prominently display the sovereigns' wealth of treasures and precious objects. In this respect Munich, for example, was an international art center as early as the 16th century. The Bavarian dukes collected not only works of art but also technical equipment of the day, craftsmen's tools, musical instruments, minerals and exotic items. In the 17th century, the Green Vault of the Saxon rulers in Dresden was probably the largest treasure house in Europe. Its collections eventually grew to fill an art gallery, a salon of mathematics and physics, as well as a mineralogy museum and a coin museum.

Deutsches Museum in Munich

In keeping with the fashion of the day, many wealthy burghers also amassed collections of their own. As a result of this passion for collecting, there has come to be a museum in Germany for nearly every field of art and nearly all types of activity. Today, the large museums in particular strive to exhibit as broad a range of their objects as possible. Due to a lack of sufficient space, however, nearly all museums are forced to place many objects in storage; these can only be put on public display during special exhibitions.

The variety of exhibitions appears limitless: from Rembrandt and Picasso to tapestries (Kassel), from wine-making equipment (Koblenz) to meteorites (Marburg), from mummies from the moors (Schleswig) to optical instruments (Oberkochen) or the oldest boat in the world re-constructed from original parts (Bremerhaven).

Nowadays, Germany's museums, both traditional and modern, try to appeal to all segments of the population, regardless of their level of education. Germans now visit museums as eagerly as they used to go to the cinema; long lines form in front of the museum ticket counters when individual exhibits of the great classical Modernist painters are featured. Year in, year out, millions of people visit museums, which in many large cities have come to form large ensembles. Along the banks of the River Main in Frankfurt, for example, along the "Museum Mile" in Bonn or in Berlin, where the Prussian Cultural Heritage Foundation, founded in 1951, fills several museums with its collections.

As in the past, wealthy private patrons of the arts have been partly responsible for the current museum boom. Peter Ludwig, who died in 1994, was one of the best known. He donated many modern works of art to predominantly newly-built museums. The "Ludwig Forum", housed in a former umbrella factory in Aachen, focuses among other things on art from the former GDR; Ludwig's collection of contemporary French art is on display in the former House of the Teutonic Order in Koblenz.

In Bonn, Kunst- und Ausstellungshalle der Bundesrepublik Deutschland and the Museum of Contemporary German History attract thousands of visitors. In Berlin, the Museum of German History presents German history in its entirety, right through to the present time.

Because of the wide spectrum of their exhibits, museums of cultural history and ethnology play a special role.

The Deutsches Museum in Munich, unparalleled worldwide, has original items and models depicting, among other things, the global development of technology

The Jewish Museum in Berlin

and science. The Museum for Communications in Berlin has an extensive collection of German postal and phone exhibits from over the centuries, while the Germanisches Nationalmuseum in Nuremberg houses the largest collection on the history of German art and culture from pre-history to the 20th century. The large number of ethnological museums is also worth mentioning. These are attributable to the fact that Germany has brought forth many explorers and scholars who were keenly interested in foreign cultures. In addition to permanent exhibitions, more and more extensive, high-quality special exhibitions have contributed to the increased attractiveness of museums throughout Germany.

The broad regional distribution of Germany's museums makes them accessible to large sections of the population. There is no central government "museum policy", but museums cooperate with one another in a number of fields – such as restoration and museum security, central documentation and research. These joint activities are coordinated by the Federation of German Museums, established in 1917, to which all Germany's museums belong.

Museum architecture is likewise very diverse, ranging from the 19th century art temples to the new buildings of the present time, which are often architectural highlights, for example the Neues Museum in Nuremberg, the Pinakothek der Moderne in Munich, or Daniel Libeskind's two buildings, the Felix Nussbaum House in Osnabrück and the Jewish Museum in Berlin.

The Wagner festival in Bayreuth

Theater and Music

Germany's theatrical landscape is defined above all by the country's approximately 180 public theaters. These state and municipal theaters, orchestras and regional theaters are complemented by around 190 private theaters and more than 30 festival theaters. There are also countless independent groups and amateur theaters. This variety is characteristic of the German theater world. Instead of a single "theater capital", which attracts almost all the talent and attention – as does Paris in France, for example – the Federal Republic has a wealth of theaters which are frequently in no way inferior to one another in terms of quality. This great diversity is traditional: In the 17th and 18th centuries, nearly every regional sovereign took great pride in his own court theater, and generally spared no expense to ensure that it was well equipped. In the 19th century, under the increasing influence of a prosperous middle class, many towns and cities made the theater a public institution.

Theater: The multi-purpose theater offers a wide range of dramatic arts, dance and music theater (operas, operettas, musicals) under a single roof.

A performance by the Berliner Ensemble

These theaters perform a repertoire of 20 to 30 works in a given season. Each year, approximately ten newly-staged productions enter the repertoire. People thus have an opportunity to become acquainted with many works of drama and music theater in their own cities. In addition there are puppet theaters, as well as children's and youth theater, which can be either another branch of the multi-purpose theater or an independent operation altogether.

The musical theaters, by contrast, perform one and the same piece month after month and year after year in what is termed en suite operations. Much the same is true especially of the smaller private theaters, which usually perform one piece en suite for several weeks and then go on to present a new production.

The artistic profile of a given theater is defined largely by its ensemble. Building up and maintaining this ensemble is consequently of particular importance to the theater. Especially the municipal and state theaters have a permanent staff of actors and actresses, singers and dancers.

The German theater makes its contribution to international cultural exchange and to European integration, above all in the form of festivals. A further feature are the exchanges of individual productions with theaters in other countries and collaboration with foreign actors and actresses, singers, dancers, theater managers, conductors, directors, craftsmen and other members of staff.

Directors: Apart from the established directors such as Jürgen Flimm, Peter Zadek, Claus Peymann and Peter Stein, who caused a stir in the 1970s and 1980s, in the 1990s in particular Frank Castorf, Einar Schleef, Andrea Breth and Christoph Marthaler have been setting new and important standards in theater as have Pina Bausch and Hans Kresnik in the world of dance. They are joined by a younger generation of directors with fresh ideas and trailblazing productions: Martin Kušej, Sasha Waltz, Thomas Ostermeier and Thirza Bruncken.

Festivals: The festival calendar for theater lovers includes: the Berlin Theater Encounter in May presenting the best German-language productions; the Ruhrfestspiele in Recklinghausen, also held in May, which showcases classical and modern works for a broad public, and the Euroscene in Leipzig. There are also numerous festival venues whose historical forts, castles and churches offer stunning backdrops for the performance of works by mainly classical authors: Bad Hersfeld, Ludwigsburg, Schwäbisch Hall, Jagsthausen, the Haidplatz in Regensburg, the Wartburg near Eisenach, and many others besides. The Kissinger summer, the Calderón Festival in Bamberg, and the "Hornberger Schiessen" are also very popular. The oldest festival in Germany is the Oberammergau Passion Play, which takes place every ten years in fulfillment of a pledge made in the year of the plague in 1634. The most recent performance was in 2000.

Music: There are more than 100 festivals devoted to music. Every three years in September, Bonn celebrates its international Beethoven Festival, in August and Sep-

Anne-Sophie Mutter

tember Augsburg is home to the Mozart Summer, at which concerts are performed in a Rococo ambience.

The festival in Eutin celebrates the opera composer Carl Maria von Weber, who was born there. In Halle and Göttingen, Georg Friedrich Handel is honored, as is Richard Strauss in Munich and Garmisch-Partenkirchen. The Richard Wagner Festival in Bayreuth has been held since 1876. The Bach Festival in Leipzig honors the work of Johann Sebastian Bach.

Almost every large city participates in the round of festivals. Munich hosts an opera festival, Frankfurt/Main the Frankfurt Festival, Stuttgart the European Music Festival, and Berlin the Jazz Festival in November. In addition there are numerous regional and local festivals.

Germany has a total of 141 professional orchestras, some of which have a long tradition. The country's leading orchestras are the Berlin and the Munich Philharmonic Orchestras, while the Bamberg Symphony Orchestra, the Gewandhaus Orchestra in Leipzig, the Dresden Staatskapelle and a number of the radio symphony orchestras enjoy an international reputation. German conductors such as Kurt Masur and Christoph von Dohnányi, soloists such as outstanding violinist Anne-Sophie Mutter, viola player Tabea Zimmermann, trumpeter Ludwig Güttler, singers such as Hildegard Behrens, Waltraud Meier, Gabriele Schnaut, Kurt Moll, Peter Hofmann and René Kollo are among the best in their fields in the international scene.

Today, composers try to win public support for music outside the realm of familiar harmony with great music theater and the most unusual of effects: Hans Werner Henze, Aribert Reimann, Karlheinz Stockhausen, Mauricio Kagel (an Argentine living in Cologne) and Wolfgang Rihm. "Chamber operas" with small casts are enjoying increasing popularity.

Thanks to the radio networks, which feature works by modern composers and commission new compositions, today anyone can participate in the discussion of contemporary music. The radio stations also organize workshop-like encounters, the most well-known of which are the "Donaueschinger Musiktage" and the "International Holiday Course for New Music" in Darmstadt. The German Music Council promotes the performance of contemporary works through its "Concert of The German Music Council".

Each year around 40 million people of all age groups attend theater productions and concerts, attesting to the uninterrupted interest in theater and music. A subscription system makes it possible to book ahead a series of performances for a particular season. Many people, when planning a trip, consider a visit to a theater performance one of the most important considerations; numerous travel agents offer special trips and package deals (especially for musicals).

Popular music: Over the last ten years or so, the German Pop music scene has enjoyed a tremendous surge in popularity. Before that English and American singers and bands had dominated the charts. German Pop songs, which at one time had been wildly successful, had come

Die Fantastischen Vier live in Munich

to appeal to only a very limited audience; home-grown Pop stars such as Udo Lindenberg were the exception.

Although they never hit the big time, however, bands such as "Tangerine Dream", "Can" and "Kraftwerk" were pioneers in the field of electronic music and the hard rock of the "Scorpions" even made the charts in the United States. Trombonist Albert Mangelsdorff, organist Barbara Dennerlein and Klaus Doldinger's band "Passport" put the German jazz scene on the international map.

At the beginning of the 1980s, the "New German Wave" showed that German musicians could indeed achieve success with songs in their native language. Marius Müller-Westernhagen, Peter Maffay, Herbert Grönemeyer and Cologne band "BAP" established themselves as the country's leading rock musicians. To this day their fans – like those of the punk rock groups "Die toten Hosen" and "Die Ärzte" – continue to pack stadiums and concert halls.

Since the beginning of the 1990s, the German Pop scene has become increasingly diversified. Every international music trend is represented here: "Selig" picks up on grunge, "H-Blockx" plays with a crossover between rock and hip-hop, and "Jazzkantine" fuses traditional jazz with German rap. "Fury in the Slaughterhouse" and "M. Walking on the Water" take up the thread of English-language folk rock, while "Die Fantastischen Vier", Sabrina Setlur, Xavier Naidoo and "Fettes Brot" have been successful with German-language hip-hop. The spectrum ranges from cheery Pop music by "Pur", "Die Prinzen" and Stefan Raab, to more thought-provoking texts by "Sterne" and "Element of Crime".

More than 300,000 people earn their living as composers, performing artists, music teachers, and as specialists in academic and government institutions, the media and the music industry. They are trained at specialized institutes: academies of music, universities, conservatories and specialized academies, schools and universities, specialized training colleges and further training academies. There are a variety of competitions to promote talented young musicians. The best-known is the Young Musicians Competition.

The work performed by public music schools, private music teachers, around 40,000 choirs, 25,000 amateur and semi-professional orchestras and other ensembles must not be underestimated. Music is a compulsory subject at general-education schools, where participation in ensembles is encouraged.

Instrument making is a crafts trade with a long tradition in Germany: musical instruments from Vogtland and especially violins from Mittenwald are world famous. Around 25 percent of young Germans play a musical instrument or sing in a choir, the most popular instruments at music schools being the piano, flute and guitar.

Information

www.buehnenverein.de
(Association of German Stages)
www.deutscher-musikrat.de
(German Music Council)

Run Lola Run

Cinema

After World War II, both East and West German cinema
dealt with the national disaster ("The Murderers are
among us", 1946, by Wolfgang Staudte, "Marriage in the
Shadows", 1947, by Kurt Maetzig, "Between Yesterday and
Tomorrow", 1947, by Harald Braun). Very soon, however,
in line with the contrasting political developments in the
two halves of Germany, the two went their separate ways.

Predominantly conventional films deprived of
political impact ("Heimat" films as they were known) but
with occasional cabaret-style references to it ("Wir Wun-
derkinder", 1958, by Kurt Hoffmann) were affiliated with
the period of successful economic reconstruction in western Germany. It was not until the 1960s and 1970s that
cinema in the Federal Republic began to blossom artistically. In the mid-1960s, for the first time "new German
cinema" emerged, in which young filmmakers, taking
their cue from the "Oberhausen Manifesto" and assuming
that "conventional German cinema has collapsed", put
forward a new art form in 1962. It was untrammeled by
convention and commercial pressures. This new style of

film embodied a change of generation and a new aesthetic approach. Experimental attitudes, formal ambitions and a critical stance towards society characterized the "auteur films" by Alexander Kluge, Jean-Marie Straub, Volker Schlöndorff, Werner Herzog, Reinhard Hauff, Rudolf Thome, Hans Jürgen Syberberg, Theodor Kotulla, Peter Fleischmann and Christian Ziewer.

The most creative and productive of these filmmakers was Rainer Werner Fassbinder (died 1982), who focused on the oppressed individual and the innate contradictions of German history, expressing these in a diversity of forms and stories. Borrowing from melodrama, Fassbinder took the cinema limelight with major narrative films such as "The Marriage of Maria Braun", 1978, "Berlin Alexanderplatz", 1980, "Lola", 1981. Fassbinder won the "Golden Bear" at the 1982 Berlin Film Festival for his film "Veronika Voss".

In the 1980s, the filmmakers of the New German Cinema increasingly enjoyed commercial and international success. In 1979, Volker Schlöndorff won the "Palm d'Or" in Cannes for his film version of Günter Grass's novel "The Tin Drum" for which he also won an Oscar in Hollywood in 1980. In 1984, Wim Wenders was awarded

Wim Wenders

the "Palm d'Or" in Cannes for "Paris, Texas", and in 1987 he surprised the film world with his fantastic "Wings of Desire".

The prize for Best Director in Cannes in 1982 went to Werner Herzog for his sensational film "Fitzcarraldo", which used an exotic setting to depict the drama of a manic individual. Margarethe von Trotta, commenting critically on the situation in the Federal Republic, made a name for herself with her impressive portrayal of women in films such as "Leaden Times" (1981) and "Rosa Luxemburg" (1986).

In spite of such successes however, New German Cinema did not continue to flourish. With the waning of the social criticism of the 1968 student-revolt movement, the discursive film lost its political background and in general "auteur films" did not establish a stable economic base for themselves which could withstand the onslaught of commercial American films.

Films in the GDR were produced by the monopolist company DEFA. The latter was financed and controlled by the state and subject to the political goals of the Party. It produced propaganda films of all genres. On the other hand, artists attempted to avoid party dogmas.

"The Legend of Paul and Paula"

This constant fluctuation between departures for something new and being defeated can be witnessed in the films produced by DEFA. They offer a panorama of the time, full of contradictions, yet they give rise to concrete images of life, artistic subjectivity and outstanding film quality.

Initially these ups and downs were experienced by the Babelsberg film studios, which in their early days were artistically moved forward by Wolfgang Staudte. In 1951, he filmed "Man of Straw", a famous satire based on the novel by Heinrich Mann, before turning his back on east German cinema as a result of his problems with delivering duly socialist realist celluloid. At the end of the 1950s, the Communist Party forbade close depictions of everyday life, such as the "Berlin films" by Gerhard Klein and Wolfgang Kohlhaase. In 1965, almost all productions which criticized the reality of communism were either banned or stopped. The following year the government banned Frank Beyer's film "Traces of Stone", which grappled furiously with the realities of the day, shortly after its premiere.

The "anti-fascist" DEFA films which took German guilt as their theme were also a way to dodge the image which filmmakers were told to paint of the day. Impressive films emerged, such as "I was nineteen" (1967), by Konrad Wolf. In the 1970s, a number of unpolished experimental films emerged, such as Egon Günther's "The Keys", 1974, with Heiner Carow's "The Legend of Paul and Paula" (1973), enjoying particular success.

In 1980, Konrad Wolf, the most prominent DEFA film director, who died in 1982, presented in his film "Solo Sunny" a picture of the GDR free of illusions. Various other critical films of great artistic merit followed, ("Explorations in the March", 1982, by Roland Gräf), but soon the film studio was virtually brought to a halt by the Party. By contrast, documentary films managed to find a realistic and poetic niche for themselves, examples being

"Shuntyard" 1984, by Jürgen Böttcher, "Life in Wittstock", 1984, by Volker Koepp, "Goodbye to Winter", 1988, by Helke Misselwitz.

After unification in 1990, DEFA ceased production. Its studios in Babelsberg near Berlin with their long-standing tradition (which previously belonged to Ufa) have nevertheless managed the quantum leap into the future: They are presently establishing themselves as one of Europe's leading locations for media companies and have attracted numerous firms and institutes into the area.

Current trends: On the one hand, the 1990s were determined by the difficulties of integrating east German cinema; this was mostly achieved by young artists and producers, particularly in the area of television. On the other hand the general situation was increasingly dominated by Hollywood films, which jeopardized not only German but also European cinema as a whole.

Only a few German films managed to make a name for themselves, like the films of Joseph Vilsmaier ("Brothers of Sleep", 1995, "Comedian Harmonists", 1997) or those by Helmut Dietl, who with his social satire "Schtonk" (1991) parodied the ostensible discovery of

"Nowhere in Africa"

Hitler's diaries by the magazine "Stern", and in "Rossini" (1996) exposed the vanities of the Munich film community's "high society".

In recent years, German filmmakers have increasingly dared to try their hand at comedy and satire, with great success on the local scene ("Nobody loves me", 1995, by Doris Dörrie, "Man, Moved", 1994, by Sönke Wortmann). With their idiosyncratic sense of humor however they were unable to amuse wider international audiences, though they did kindle a surge in the popularity of German cinema. Some of the new works did, however, arouse international attention, such as Romuald Karmaker's debut film "The Death-Maker", 1995, in which Götz George played a mass murderer.

Hopeful signs of the last few years were Tom Tykwer's "Run Lola Run", an existential drama which also enjoyed widespread international success, and "Sonnenallee", the debut by east German theater director Leander Haussmann in which he recalled his youth in the GDR in a rather grotesque way. And some of the "old masters" reappeared: Volker Schlöndorff with "Silence after the Shot", Wim Wenders with his fascinating documentary "Buena Vista Social Club", which portrayed a group of old musicians from Havana, and Werner Herzog, who paid tribute to the most important actor in his films, Klaus Kinski, in "My Dearest Enemy". The Oscar for Best Foreign Film, which Caroline Link's "Nowhere in Africa" won in March 2003, gave a boost to New German Cinema.

The fresh spark evident in German cinema today is reflected in the fact that German film companies are going public, and that more films are being internationally co-produced as well as major productions being funded. German contributions to the international film market are much in evidence with producers like Bernd Eichinger as with directors Wolfgang Petersen and Roland Emmerich, who have managed to get themselves established in Hollywood.

Cinemas: Over the past ten years, companies have been investing in German cinemas like never before. The construction of Multiplex theaters, in which international corporations and media groups have been investing since the beginning of the 1990s, is changing the very face of the cinema landscape. In many cities, these modern multi-entertainment centers, popular especially with the young, are replacing traditional cinemas. There are, however, increasing signs of a reversal in the trend: There is excess seating capacity in multiplex cinemas, and some of them have already closed down.

Festivals: The numerous well-organized and highly effective film festivals are particularly important for the cultural image of cinema in Germany and its reputation abroad. The most important forum for film is the Berlin International Film Festival (the "Berlinale"), which was established in 1951, and which together with those of Cannes and Venice is one of the major film festivals in Europe. Consequently it is one of the most prominent meeting places for people in the film industry. The film festivals in Mannheim, Oberhausen and Leipzig also enjoy

The Berlin International Film Festival

international status. Specialized festivals and film festivals in Hof, Munich, Lübeck, Hamburg and other cities place local films in an international context while contributing to the further development of film art and its economic stability.

In spite of the success that German cinema has notched up, cinema schedules continue to be dominated by the elaborately produced and marketed Hollywood films, Germany being their major European market. In addition, cinema has to put up with ever-stiffer competition from TV and other media, in particular with the continuously growing variety of entertainment provided by private television as well as cable and satellite TV, pay-TV and video. That said, cinema films are frequently being co-produced with television networks.

Film grants: This necessitates that a fair balance be struck with the film industry. One of the prerequisites for promoting domestic films is to strengthen the rights of independent film producers, something to which the federal government is committed within the framework of its modern culture and economic policy. In 1999, the federal government created its "Alliance for Film" in order to improve the legal, structural and financial situation of German cinema for all parties involved. Strengthening it and its international image also entails strengthening its European scope and indeed strengthening European cinema in general, which is what the Franco-German Film Academy, founded in 2000, also endeavors to do.

Public funds from the federal and state governments as well as from the German Federal Film Board (FFA) are used to defend the cultural asset of cinema against overly powerful competition, as well as to actively promote its development. The FFA, established under the German Federal Film Promotion Act, obtains its funds from a levy paid by all cinemas, TV networks and the video industry. These funds are used not only to promote the production, distribution and marketing of films but also cinemas.

At the core of government funding of film culture is the German Film Prize, which since 1951 has been awarded in honor of top-notch German film production. It showcases individual performances and awards large sums of prize money to outstanding films, whereby the monies are intended for the production of new films.

Information

www.spio.de

(Umbrella Organization of the German Film Industry)

www.berlinale.de

(Berlin International Film Festival)

Index

Figures set in italics refer to the illustrations.

Photos and illustrations

Front cover:
Artevent, Wien (Siegfried Layda)

Photos:
Auswärtiges Amt: 232
Bundesbildstelle: 81, 85, 87, 89, 96/97, 98/99, 105, 110, 112/113 (16), 117, 123 (6), 157, 181, 189, 198, 216, 218, 221, 251
dpa/picture alliance: 9, 10/11, 12, 13, 14, 15, 16, 18, 19, 24, 28, 30/31, 32, 34, 36, 38, 40, 42, 44, 46, 48, 50, 52, 54, 56, 58/59, 60 (3), 61, 62 (2), 63, 64, 66, 69, 70/71, 73, 74, 75, 77, 79, 82, 84, 91, 93, 95, 100, 104, 115, 118, 119, 121, 124, 126, 128, 129, 130, 133, 134, 135, 136, 137, 138, 140, 142, 144, 146, 149, 152, 154, 155, 156, 160, 163, 164, 166, 171, 172, 175, 176/177, 178, 179, 180, 185, 186/187, 188, 191, 193, 194/195, 196, 200, 202, 203, 205, 208, 209, 210/211, 212, 213, 215, 217, 223, 224/225, 227, 231, 233, 234, 237, 240/241, 243, 244, 246, 247, 248, 250, 253, 254, 256, 260, 263, 264, 265, 267, 270, 272, 277, 279, 282, 283, 286, 290/291, 292, 297, 298, 299, 300, 303, 304, 306, 307, 311, 312, 314, 317, 318, 322, 324, 326, 328, 332, 336, 338, 340, 343, 348/349, 353, 356, 358, 351, 364, 366/367, 368/369, 371, 372/373, 375, 377, 378, 380, 381, 383, 386, 387, 390, 392, 394, 398, 400/401, 403, 406, 408/409 (4), 411, 412, 413, 415, 417, 418/419, 420/421, 422, 424, 425, 427, 429, 431, 432, 435, 436, 438, 440, 442, 443, 444, 446
Fremdenverkehrsamt München: 26
Goethe-Institut: 229
mauritius: 7, 354
Partner für Berlin/FTB-Werbefotografie: 103
Presse- und Informationsamt des Landes Berlin/G. Schneider: 127, 433, 448/449

Maps:
Westermann: 8, 22

Charts:
Deutscher Bundestag/Media Consulta: 114
Karl-Heinz Döring: 11, 17, 116, 151, 165, 167, 169, 183, 207, 236, 238, 239, 245, 261, 273, 274, 287, 296, 319, 323, 331, 339, 345, 357, 362, 363, 396